HOW POETS SEE THE WORLD

WILLARD SPIEGELMAN

# How Poets See the World

## the World

The Art of

Description in

Contemporary

Poetry

OXFORD
UNIVERSITY PRESS

2005

# OXFORD
UNIVERSITY PRESS

Oxford University Press, Inc., publishes works that further
Oxford University's objective of excellence
in research, scholarship, and education.

Oxford   New York
Auckland   Cape Town   Dar es Salaam   Hong Kong   Karachi
Kuala Lumpur   Madrid   Melbourne   Mexico City   Nairobi
New Delhi   Shanghai   Taipei   Toronto

With offices in
Argentina   Austria   Brazil   Chile   Czech Republic   France   Greece
Guatemala   Hungary   Italy   Japan   Poland   Portugal   Singapore
South Korea   Switzerland   Thailand   Turkey   Ukraine   Vietnam

Copyright © 2005 by Oxford University Press, Inc.

Published by Oxford University Press, Inc.
198 Madison Avenue, New York, New York 10016

www.oup.com

Oxford is a registered trademark of Oxford University Press

Library of Congress Cataloging-in-Publication Data
Spiegelman, Willard.
How poets see the world : the art of description in contemporary poetry / Willard Spiegelman.
   p. cm.
Includes bibliographical references and index.
ISBN-13 978-0-19-517491-5
ISBN 0-19-517491-7
1. American poetry—20th century—History and criticism. 2. Vision in literature.
3. Art and literature—United States. 4. Visual perception in literature. 5. Landscape in literature.
6. Description (Rhetoric) 7. Nature in literature. 8. Art in literature. 9. Ekphrasis. I. Title.
PS310.V57S67 2005
811.009'22—dc22      2004012519

9 8 7 6 5 4 3 2 1

Printed in the United States of America
on acid-free paper

# CREDITS ✐

# ACKNOWLEDGMENTS ✐

Although this book has had a long gestation, I hope that its appearance still qualifies as timely. I began to collect my thoughts about description in poetry—and about the relationship of ornament to "meaning" or essence—about ten years ago, when the culture wars raged more fiercely than they do today, when aesthetics and aestheticism did not find a comfortable home within the academy. Many aspects of the literary culture have changed since the early and mid-nineties and, as many critics have observed, a fin du siècle has ushered in a revival of interest in purely aesthetic matters.

My major debts are to institutions and to individuals, and in some cases to individuals as parts of institutions. I wish to thank James F. Jones, Jr., and Jasper Neel, the past and present deans of Dedman College at Southern Methodist University, for their encouragement and for the generous gift of time in the form of research leaves. The John Simon Guggenheim Foundation offered me a fellowship in 1994–1995, allowing some of the chapters in this book to come into focus. In the spring of 1995, I lived in London, courtesy of Donald and Doris Bowman, where I met and interviewed Charles Tomlinson (an interview that subsequently appeared in *The Paris Review*), whose poetry I had long admired. He and his wife Brenda entertained me splendidly at their Gloucestershire cottage on a day I still remember for its beauty, fellowship, and good talk. The Bogliasco Foundation invited me to spend a month at its Liguria Study Center in September 1999, at which I hammered more chapters into shape; on a subsequent visit in September 2003, I made the necessary final touches to my manuscript and was delighted to receive the book's official acceptance from Oxford University Press on my last day in residence. The golden light of the Mediterranean, the comfort of the surroundings, and the consummately professional, not to say pampering, attentions of the staff at the Center (notably those of its director and associate directors, Anna Maria Quaiat, Ivanna Folle, and Alan Rowlin) made the Villa dei Pini into the ideal scholar's retreat. The presence of other companionable artists and writers in residence helped turn work into pleasure. I happily acknowledge the stimulation and good cheer provided by the two sets of fellows during my extended stays and single out especially, as a part for the whole, the friendship and intellectual companionship of Fernando Cervantes, Gabriella de Ferrari, and Helen and the late Anthony Hecht.

I owe other personal, practical, and scholarly debts to the following individuals, some of whom may have already forgotten what they did for me (in the form of advice, criticism, direction, invitations to lecture, last minute bibliographical aid, and general literary wisdom): Geoffrey Atherton, Rick Bogel, Robert Boyers, Alan Bradford, Paul Christensen, Bonnie Costello, Terrence Diggory, William Flesch, Paul Fry, Thomas Gardner, Roger Gilbert, Dana Gioia, Warren Goldfarb, Debora Greger, Rachel Hadas, Nick Halpern, Langdon Hammer, John Hollander, William Logan, James Longenbach, David Lynn, Charles Mahoney, J. D. McClatchy, Leslie Mealer, Steven Monte, James Olney, Donald Pease, Jahan Ramazani, Helen Vendler, Rosanna Warren, and Steven Weisenburger. I am also grateful to the two readers of my manuscript for Oxford, who made compelling and persuasive recommendations, many of which I accepted. At Oxford University Press Elissa Morris, Eve Bachrach, and Jessica Ryan have craftily steered my manuscript into its berth, finding (to change the metaphor) a home for my pages between the hard covers of this book.

Of the poets I discuss in these pages, I have already acknowledged my debt to Charles Tomlinson. Like him, Charles Wright gave generously of his time and learning (and also provided substance for an interview, this one for *Literary Imagination*). Listening to Jorie Graham recite her work at Southern Methodist University in 1997 allowed me to hear, and therefore to begin to understand, the essence of one of our most "difficult" poets. The late Amy Clampitt, whom I knew slightly when she was alive, but have come to know much better as a result of editing her letters for publication by Columbia University Press, was a model of eager engagement, intellectual enthusiasm, and political fervor.

Sections from this book appeared earlier, in slightly different form, in the following journals, to whose editors, especially the redoubtable Herbert

Leibowitz who wields the red pen every writer for *Parnassus* dreads to see yet finally welcomes, I am indebted not only for publishing me but also for helping me refine my thoughts and my prose: *Kenyon Review*, *Parnassus*, *Salmagundi*, *Southern Review*, and *Verse*. I appreciated the chance to have rehearsed my ideas before audiences at the Modern Language Association, the Association of Literary Scholars and Critics, the American Literature Association, and the Amon Carter Museum; and before faculty and students at Brandeis University, Connecticut College, Dartmouth, Lousiana State, Texas A&M, the University of Connecticut, and the University of North Texas.

I have dedicated this book to my best teacher of more than three decades and to my students, who have heard me talk about contemporary poetry and other (often extraneous) things, and responded with that heady combination of eagerness, bemusement, skepticism, disagreement, and (on one's best days) appreciation that any teacher comes to cherish. I shall let a baker's dozen, in chronological rather than alphabetical order, stand in for their fellows: Cathy Wilson, Shelley Shaver, Sally Spurgin, Jeanne Haflinger, David Stocks, Tim Allis, John Sare, Stephen James, Katie Kent, Mark Canuel, John Utz, Brad Williston, and Ashley Aull.

# CONTENTS

HOW POETS SEE THE WORLD

# ONE

## "THE WAY THINGS LOOK EACH DAY"

### Poetry, Description, Nature

You really don't believe all that stuff. You're just like me. Neither of us
has any philosophy. It's all description, no philosophy.
—Elizabeth Bishop to Richard Wilbur on the subject of organized
religion.

The 1954 Fall Term had begun. Again the marble neck of a homely Venus
in the vestibule of Humanities Hall received the vermilion imprint, in
applied lipstick, of a mimicked kiss. Again the *Waindell Recorder* discussed the Parking Problem. Again in the margins of library books earnest freshmen inscribed such helpful glosses as "Description of nature,"
or "Irony"; and in a pretty edition of Mallarmé's poems an especially
able scholiast had already underlined in violet ink the difficult word
*oiseaux* and scrawled above it "birds." Again autumn gales plastered dead
leaves against one side of the latticed gallery leading from Humanities to
Frieze Hall. Again, on serene afternoons, huge, amber-brown Monarch
butterflies flapped over asphalt and lawn as they lazily drifted south,
their incompletely retracted black legs hanging rather low beneath their
polka-dotted bodies.
—Vladimir Nabokov, *Pnin* (1957)

It is time to reconsider description. It struck Elizabeth Bishop as the
antithesis to philosophy, religion, indeed, to thought itself. And it may
strike impatient general readers, especially of prose fiction, as a superfluous or extraneous interruption of the dialogue and narrative action that, by

3

one way of reckoning, constitute the more important parts of literary adventure. But from another perspective it might be considered the very essence of poetry. Even Nabokov, in the wicked passage above, subtly duplicates the very terms he is mocking—"description of nature" and "irony"—by the deft offhand humor in his condescension to the Waindell students and then, even more excitingly, by his own seemingly careless remarks about the gorgeous departures of the butterflies, flying south over asphalt and lawn. The observing eye cannot be still: we cannot bid it be so, as Wordsworth announced at the very start of *Lyrical Ballads*. And, in the case of a writer, neither eye nor tongue nor pen can remain still, as the human observer assays to "get something right in language" (Howard Nemerov's phrase),[1] not only remaining faithful to the contingencies of the human heart but also adhering to the strict reality of the *things* of the world, which one wishes to honor by duplicating them. All writing in part recreates some prior event or feeling; the act of describing, especially in poetry, both reproduces (in words) a visible external provocation and adds a new item to the totality of available reality.

This book tackles a different subject from that of an earlier book of mine, *The Didactic Muse*, which dealt with poets for the most part in the Horatian tradition of W. H. Auden: discursive, colloquial, meditative, sometimes philosophical.[2] Even the very un-Horatian Allen Ginsberg and Adrienne Rich staked out claims that Auden would have found congenial: social engagement, gay sexuality, and an overtly political agenda. In this book I examine poets less "didactic," an epithet that I applied earlier to the discriminations of Nemerov as well as the pseudo-scientific chatter of James Merrill's prophetic books. Not even a generous definition of "instruction" will accommodate the poets in these pages under a georgic mantle. (Gary Snyder, however, whom I treat later in this chapter, often seems incapable of separating a description of nature from a description of his work within it.) Instead, they look carefully at the world, either natural or artistic, and they commend themselves to us by their own attention to external circumstances. Some of them have minimally audible or visible personae: Jorie Graham, John Ashbery, and Irving Feldman are hardly autobiographical in any conventional sense. Rather, they construct rhetorical schemes that invite us to see the world through their eyes. Amy Clampitt is often anecdotal, though seldom confessional. Her friends and relatives make appearances as subjects but usually in the service of larger moral, ethical, or aesthetic observations. Even Charles Wright, a first-person describer, imposes little of his adult life or that of his family on his work. Instead, landscape and artifact are all. The scope of his vision extends to the numinous. All of these poets (Ashbery, Clampitt, Feldman, Graham, Snyder, Charles Tomlinson, Theodore Weiss, and Wright) have written on a range of subjects and in a variety of tones.

Although each has worked to develop a "style" or several styles apposite to the matters at hand, my main focus throughout these pages is on their methods of observation and the ways each of them approaches and uses description itself. In other words, I am concerned equally with styles of describing and description itself as style.

My argument extends as well from another earlier work, *Majestic Indolence: English Romantic Poetry and the Work of Art,* in which I argued for a Kantian realm of the "aesthetic" as an antidote to those trends in contemporary literary criticism that examine art through one of several political, sociological, or ideological lenses. Description, although never innocent of motive and never "pure," or lacking meaning and feeling, might prove the hardest measure of art's seriousness, as we often confuse it simplistically with scientific objectivity or "mere" ornament, as though objectivity and ornament themselves were things to be despised or avoided.[3]

How does description contain or convey meaning? What do we do when we describe something? Reproduce, account for, picture, portray, trace, parcel out? How does one take the measure of the external world? How neutral or objective a form can such an effort take? Does the "I" always interfere with, interrupt, or color the seeing "eye"? Can language hope for a scientific rendering? In a 1925 anthology, *The Art of Description,* Marjorie Hope Nicolson reminded an older audience (for whom such reminder was less necessary than it might be today) that "description is not that artificial thing—a 'form of discourse'; it is the use of several moods or attitudes of mind through which a writer or speaker, who has found his world interesting, beautiful, ugly, or effective, endeavors to transfer to others his pleasure or his interest in that world."[4] Words like "beautiful" and "pleasure" need to be brought back into discussions of literature.[5]

For every impulse to describe, we can find a countertendency to resist description. We can cite those famous sympathetic epigrams of Wittgenstein: "We now demonstrate a method, by example," or "We must do away with all explanation, and description alone must take its place." Or the judgment of Maurice Merleau-Ponty: "It is a matter of describing, not of explaining or analyzing."[6] But to these we may oppose the premise of Roland Barthes, who, playing and punning with the notion of "still life" (*nature morte*), found description deadly: "Adjectives are the tools of [a] delusion [making things *seem* alive]; whatever else they may be saying, their very descriptive quality makes them funereal."[7] Hoping to point toward transcendent meanings and spiritual correspondences, description is bound up instead with self-portrayal. Michael Riffaterre expresses similar impatience or disapproval: "The primary function of literary description is not to make the reader see something. Its aim is not to present an external reality. Description, like all literary discourse, is a verbal detour so contrived that the reader understands something else than the object ostensibly represented. . . . Its primary purpose is not to offer a representation, but to dictate an interpretation."[8] Description is never neutral, therefore; it always carries the freight of an unannounced purpose.

Barthes has revised the prejudice of Paul Valéry ("Degas, Danse, Dessin"):

> The invasion of Literature by *description* was parallel to that of painting by *landscape*. A *description* is composed of sentences whose order one can generally *reverse*: I can describe this room by a series of clauses whose order is not important. A gaze roams as it wishes. Nothing more natural, nothing more *true*, than this vagrancy; for . . . *truth is chance*. . . . This mode of creating, legitimate in principle, and to which we owe so many beautiful things, leads, like the abuse of landscape, *to the diminution of the intellectual part of art*.[9]

Such condescending opposition to description traditionally locates the objects of its disapproval largely in prose; in poetry, there may well be little "thought" to be diminished or interrupted. And, as I demonstrate below with regard to the seemingly artless lyrics of Gary Snyder, juxtaposition, ordering, and sequence are, especially in poetry, not merely arbitrary and reversible but themselves constituents of poetic effect, and therefore of poetic meaning. Even Lessing, whose *Laocoön* we might take as the first modern articulation of skepticism toward description, takes his primary examples from prose or narrative poetry. Calling description a haven for the second-rate, he argues that whereas painting is seen in space, literature is experienced temporally; that painting uses iconic, representational, and nonsymbolic images, whereas poetry uses noniconic and arbitrary ones; and that any attempt by one art to replicate the other results in something of a generic mismatch.[10]

We can detect distrust of description as mere or frivolous ornamentation still earlier in history. In *Medieval Rhetoric and Poetic*, C. S. Baldwin reminds us that ekphrasis (which he takes as a synecdoche for *all* description) is a form of interruption or (at best) amplification, rather than progression. For medieval rhetoricians, it stood for everything extraneous, detachable, and literally *in*consequential: "Ecphrasis is . . . a form of Alexandrianism . . . [which] perverts description because it frustrates narrative movement."[11] It is not too far a leap from such sentiments to the condemnation of description in general as indulgence, adornment, diffusion, even the temptation of a siren's song. Horace impatiently dismisses poetasters who "can do nothing else" but describe. And Pope famously followed Horace and denigrated description. According to Warburton: "He uses PURE equivocally, to signify either chaste or empty; and has given in this line what he esteemed the

*[margin note: argument against ekphrasis]*

true character of descriptive Poetry, as it is called. A composition, in his opinion, as absurd as a feast made up of sauces."[12] Once description seems to have lost a specific purpose, it disrupts some imagined unity. One might extend distaste to fear: W. J. T. Mitchell has suggested that such divagation or disruption has often had specific connotations of gender. Directness, pointedness, and truth telling (often gendered as male in medieval textbooks of rhetoric) are the opposites of wandering, dilation, and description, the province of the feminine.[13] Although another critic might wish to follow the path of a gender-oriented criticism, I intend in this book to deal with poetic and rhetorical schemes without reference to gender. Suffice it to say that in the United States, at least, there has always inhered a partial ideological impatience with circumferences instead of centers and an analogous distrust of periphrasis instead of straight-talking, inventive recreation instead of laconic directness. Even A. R. Ammons, our premier poetic explorer of peripheries, makes poems big and small by veering between central orders and blurry, entropic peripheries. His own poetic exuberance wittily unfolds loops of observations:

> poetry is itself like an installation at Marine
>
> Shale: it reaches down into the dead pit
> and cool oil of stale recognition and words and
>
> brings up hauls of stringy gook which it arrays
> with light and strings with shiny syllables.[14]

But for every expansive reach into the depths of garbage and compost, there is an equivalent crystalline epigram, pure and simple.

Imagining his own epigraph, "Nature I loved," says Walter Savage Landor, "and next to Nature, Art." Poets, especially as I present them in this and the fifth chapters, usually describe either an external scene or an imagined representation, either nature or art. Contemporary poets have in some ways ignored or gone beyond the reaction of their modernist precursors, themselves rebelling against the affirmations of people like Landor. Most famous is Yeats's late proclamation, in his 1936 preface to *The Oxford Book of Modern Verse*: "The revolt against Victorianism meant to the young poet a revolt against irrelevant descriptions of nature, the scientific and moral discursiveness of *In Memoriam* . . . the political eloquence of Swinburne, the psychological curiosity of Browning, and the poetic diction of everybody."[15] The appeal of nature as a relevant subject for description is easy to understand, especially in this country: American culture has been permeated by the notion of landscape since the beginning, as I briefly show below. The recent popularity of ekphrastic poems, descriptions of visual works of art (verbal representations of visual ones), may have something to do with the relative skepticism that has crept into our individual and collective dealings with all forms of knowing (as well as with the kinds of exercises routinely expected of novice poets). We disbelieve in eternal truths, in permanent values, in scales of judgment. Radical skepticism has rendered problematic the knowledge of external objects. (This is the burden of Romanticism that Kant and his contemporaries inherited from Hume and Hartley.)[16] Even more radical have been post-Nietzschean assaults on the integrity of persons or subjects. With a painting or sculpture we have an external, unchanging field to which we can return for verification. Because most paintings now reside in public spaces—museums, churches—a poet can observe them, retreat for contemplation, and then reimagine or recreate them. Readers may respond in kind. The spatial permanence of painting, when compared to the temporality of music, makes for an anchor, if not exactly a safe harbor, when we are at sea in a changing world.

There are relatively few descriptions of music. Howard Nemerov wrote about Bach cello suites, although his poem is more a meditation inspired by listening to the music than an actual attempt to describe the various forms of the counterpoint. Charles Tomlinson has several poems that start with an allusion to specific pieces of real or imagined music, but none of them follows a descriptive path. Instead, the poems personify instruments ("Consolations for a Double Bass," "Da Capo," *The Way In and Other Poems*) or figure music in terms of landscape ("Ode to Arnold Schoenberg," "Chaconnne for Unaccompanied Violin," *A Peopled Landscape*). Pater's famous adage notwithstanding ("All art continually aspires to the condition of music"), the fact that music is nonrepresentational may encourage aspiration or envy, but because most poets lack the proper technical vocabulary to describe it accurately they seldom describe it in any interesting way. And although it would involve the eye, descriptions of architecture are less prominent in poetry than descriptions of painting, because buildings are by and large unrepresentational and hence unrepresentable or at least poetically unuseful. Ekphrastic poets are drawn to portraiture, landscape, pictures of people in a landscape, and still lifes, and somewhat less to sculpture. (In Chapter 5 I discuss some relatively unusual recent ekphrastic experiments.)

Nature and its description are another, more complicated, story. For one thing, all "descriptions of nature" must strike us as to some degree imagined and reconstructed. Poetic self-consciousness can never be eliminated. Thus, Dave Smith asks a simple question:

A man comes to love the ground where he lives, yet
How does this begin, in what sun-varnished split
Of time, what yellow leaf-fall, what graying scrape
Rain drags along the dirt road?[17]

"Varnished," "scrape," and a humanized "rain" render the landscape an
artifact here; time and space come together. When Elizabeth Bishop,
inspired by Sir Kenneth Clark, presents "Brazil, January 1, 1502," she
understands nature itself mostly as tapestry. Thomas Bolt says succinctly:
"The Pontiac / Is a natural object" (see Stevens: "A poem is like a natural
object"),[18] especially if it is rusting in a field, overgrown with vines and
having outlived its functionality. Like Bishop and Smith, as well as (still
earlier) Frost and Stevens, Bolt handily breaks down the too easy binaries of nature/art and nature/culture. Besides, nature always triumphs,
patiently eroding all human artifacts: "The earth is conservative. The car
sits still." To describe nature means to place oneself within the history of
the tropes of nature description. As Robert Pinsky argued persuasively
almost thirty years ago, "Poetically, the question is what tone or status we
will find appropriate for the act of description. Description is the great
rhetorical burden."[19]

But for another and more specific reason, an ecological piety has accompanied us in the United States since our first important literary forays into
the wilderness in the nineteenth century. I mean not only that a politics of
conservation has balanced a politics of exploitation, or that nostalgic primitivism keeps pace with manifest destiny. Rather, the American observer is
often timid, anxious, nervous. Not only do we look at the landscape but
we also frequently have the uncanny sense that the landscape is looking
back at us. Wallace Stevens's congenial phrase "the way things look each
day" can be understood in complementary ways, as I show below. Fastidi-
ous uncertainty, occasionally verging on paranoia, informs such diverse (but
intrinsically similar) poets as Emerson, Whitman, Stevens, Ashbery, and
Graham. It is easy to locate our central tradition in the idea that the things
of the world invite us to describe them, in an act of celebration, as though
"observation" were compounded of equal parts of watching and participating. (John Haines has said, "I think there is a spirit of place, / a presence asking to be expressed.")[20] The titles of two of Richard Wilbur's most famous
early poems, "The Beautiful Changes" and "Love Calls Us to the Things
of This World," summarize an entire ethos of aesthetic wonder. But those
same things also look at us, so it requires an active and daring, almost heroic
imagination to "brave the landscape's looks," whether as painter, poet, or
mere onlooker. Here is Emerson:

See thou bring not to field or stone
The fancies found in books;
Leave authors' eyes, and fetch your own,
To brave the landscape's looks.
("Waldeinsamkeit")

An early Emersonian rearticulation comes in Dickinson's poem #627 ("The Tint I cannot take—is best—"), especially in the fourth stanza that lists what she would, but cannot, take away with her:

The eager look—on Landscapes—
As if they just repressed
Some secret—that was pushing
Like Chariots—in the Vest—

Harold Bloom reminds us of the older meaning of "repress" as a voluntary concealment rather than an involuntary, Freudian one.[21] The humanized landscape has an appearance (an intransitive "look") as well as a stare outward at us (a transitive one). Dickinson's "Gazing Fields of Grain" in "Because I could not stop for Death" is yet another troping of the way things out there look back to us.[22] If the landscape is looking at us, we might legitimately wonder which gaze is originary, which responsive. Like Wordsworth's Boy of Winander, who makes "mimic hootings" to the silent owls (who have already cried out to him), or like the unnamed man in Frost's "The Most of It," who asks for "counter love, original response" (as though a response could ever be anything but secondary, not original), we are from the start inextricably engaged in patterns, not sequences.

For a poet like Jorie Graham (Chapter 7), looking out from a standpoint of relative security and invisibility has always been the preferred condition. She wishes to see, or to frame a view, without either imposing herself on nature or allowing herself to be seen by others (see Ruskin: "My entire delight was in observing without being myself noticed,—if I could have been invisible, all the better"). Thus, in her early poem "Self-Portrait," she says hopefully:

After fresh snow I'll go up to the attic and look out.
My looking is a set of tracks—the first—
a description of the view
that cannot mar it.

The Emersonian "transparent eyeball" has come indoors for greater safety. In a later poem she is more attentive to the response of the external world than to her own wish to capture-by-looking, without doing harm:

Then just the look on things of being looked-at.
Then just the look on things of being seen.[23]

The world is filled almost animistically with people and other life forms, all of which solicit our attention, virtually demanding to be seen and described. For our part, we prefer to stay hidden, gazing from behind the window, or through a frame, and generally taking cover.

From the start, Americans have been phenomenologists, sensitive to the interrelations between external reality and subjective being. Henry Bugbee brings a Wordsworthian note to twentieth-century philosophy: "In our experiences of things as presences, reality conveys itself and permeates us as a closed electrical circuit in which we are involved with things. . . . The subject-object distinction converts the genuine mutual independence of self and other *in the closed circuit* into the separateness of closed paths. . . . To think experientially is to partake in thought of the closed circuit of reality, in which we live and move and have our being."[24] As Nemerov says succinctly, "There is a knowledge in the look of things."[25] The natural world and our view of it come to stand, in an increasingly secularized world, for objects of religious contemplation. Thus, Anthony Hecht's speaker in "The Venetian Vespers" observes hopefully: "I look and look, / As though I could be saved simply by looking." In a published interview, Hecht himself quotes from Simone Weil's *Waiting for God*: "One of the principal truths of Christianity, a truth that goes almost unrecognized today, is that looking is what saves us."[26]

Looking saves, but it also seduces. When Emerson in England during 1847–48 was quizzed on the American landscape, he answered: "There, in that great slovenly continent, in high Allegheny pastures, in the sea-wide sky-skirted prairie, still sleeps and murmurs and hides the great mother, long since driven away from the trim hedge rows and over-cultivated gardens of England."[27] In the twentieth century, Auden proposed the American landscape as compensation for a culture devoid of history: "Many poets in the Old World have become disgusted with human civilization but what the earth would be like if the race became extinct they cannot imagine; an American like Robinson Jeffers can quite easily, for he has seen with his own eyes country as yet untouched by history."[28] This emptiness, far from being a calamity, is both a challenge and a blessing. But what tropes of description can we use to reproduce the landscape's looks? And was ever a European as conscious of being looked at by the landscape as Americans are? Our self-consciousness humbles, frightens, and stimulates us into fearful piety as well as acts of aggression that a European might not attempt.[29]

Certainly, such consciousness conditions Emerson's complex responses. In "Nature" he says, "I am not alone and unacknowledged. They [the fields and woods] nod to me, and I to them." The interchange is reciprocal: "The power to produce this delight, does not reside in nature, but in man, or in a harmony of both." This is what Wordsworth labeled "action from without and from within."[30] Emerson begins his "Divinity School Address" with a poetic landscape description of the luxuries of summer, the happy display of nature's mystery, and an invitation to "enjoy and subdue it." If the first verb suggests the passive pleasures of aesthetic response, the second certainly allows for the possibilities of conquest. The pairing extends from Wordsworth's comparable depiction of his younger self in "Nutting" as an aesthetic ravager in a hazel bower, first relishing a site and then attempting to destroy it. But, Emerson continues, when one thinks harder, the world seems "a mere illustration and fable" of the human mind; it has a personality and a will of its own.

He proposes a grimmer formulation in "Experience": "Nature does not like to be observed, and likes that we should be her fools and playmates. . . . Our relations to each other are oblique and casual." And in "Nature" (*Essays*, 1st series): "There is nothing so wonderful in any particular landscape, as the necessity of being beautiful under which every landscape lies. Nature cannot be surprised in undress. Beauty breaks in everywhere." By this formulation, "beauty" (nature's own dress, or our projected or responsive appreciation of it) clothes and protects the landscape, and it also takes it—or us—by surprise or storm. Naked, that is, ugly nature is a logical and experiential impossibility. Further: "To the intelligent, nature converts itself into a vast promise, and will not be rashly explained. Her secret is untold."[31] And to the unobservant and unresponsive? To them clearly nature offers neither promise nor temptation nor ultimate disappointment. But to the poets, philosophers, and other would-be describers, Nature, as mother or as Sibyl, promises all and delivers . . . nothing. F. Scott Fitzgerald records a later sense of our disturbed, nervous response to nature in *The Great Gatsby*: "For a transitory moment man must have held his breath in the presence of this continent, compelled into an aesthetic contemplation he neither understood nor desired, face to face for the last time in history with something commensurate to his capacity for wonder."[32] "Neither understood nor desired": Do we shun the aesthetic and remain unaffected by it? Do American Puritanism and fear counter our sensuous appetites?[33] In the rest of this chapter I try to answer these questions with reference to the sometimes playful, sometimes frustrating poetic theorizing of Wallace Stevens and the material affirmations of Gary Snyder, poets who in most ways could not be more dissimilar.

Central to an American approach to landscape is the collective and complex effort to reply to its invitations or temptations by honoring, with or without subduing, it. To the literary as well as the scientific eye, accurate description is the logical starting point for any act of understanding and appreciation. But it is often a first step only. "Description is revelation," announces Wallace Stevens in "Description Without Place" (*Transport to Summer*), a poem that oscillates between abstraction and anecdote in seven sections of sometimes frustratingly reductive or redundant couplets.[34] It describes, in fact, relatively little. Stevens begins by distinguishing "the way things look each day," what he calls "actual seemings" (like sun, moon, night, and sleep) from "potential" (i.e., imagined, constructed, or metaphorical) ones, through which we reach a point "where / Dazzle yields to clarity and we observe, / And observing is completing." In the poem's central section, Stevens offers as examples of human contemplation of place the figures of Nietzsche and Lenin, both "reflecting" beside reflecting bodies of water: Nietzsche's "revery was the deepness of the pool," whereas Lenin "was not the man for swans," somehow out of place in a park with his own apocalyptic political dreams.

From "observe" to "describe" to "complete" to "reveal" is a logical progression, although Stevens, in spite of his formulas and facile equations, never makes things quite so easy for his readers. He imposes a conundrum at the beginning:

It is possible that to seem—it is to be,
As the sun is something seeming and it is.

The sun is an example. What it seems
It is and in such seeming all things are.

Is "seeming" identical to "being" or opposed to it? The poet does not say. Furthermore, his poem never distinguishes between the act of *describing* and the finished, composed product, a "description." In the last three sections, Stevens labels both the past and the future "description without place"; they exist only in our making or recording of them. But act and action come together rhetorically, as in Stevens's final couplet: "And because what we say of the future must portend, / Be alive with its own meanings, seeming to be / Like rubies reddened by rubies reddening." Only in the act of describing is a thing described, only by making itself does it seem to be. (This is how Stevens might know a dancer from a dance.) The strategies, or stratagems, of describing weigh heavily with the duplicities of gerunds and participles, and with the dangling uncertainty of a single transitive verb ("portend") used intransitively.[35]

I take Stevens's own method in this poem as a general model for coming to grips with landscape and the processes of describing it. The playfulness of his epigrams, formulas, and nursery rhymes gives way to expanded and repeated forms, longer sentences, larger articulations of central ideas. At the start, a mythical summer deity presides over the poem's landscape. Then abstract nouns define abstract nouns: "Description is revelation. It is not / The thing described, nor false facsimile. / It is an artificial thing that exists, / In its own seeming, plainly visible." Despite the faux-naïf pseudo-logic of Stevens's iterations, "plain" is not one of the likely adjectives a reader would apply to them. The poem's hypnotic opacities might encourage us to think of it as a "description of description." It defines or muses on description with little reference to a specific place or thing, with the exception of the exemplary figures of Nietzsche and Lenin at the center and of the sun at the beginning. Just as past and future come together in the artifice of (a) description without place, so even place itself is hard to capture. Stevens uses adjectives—the observer's linguistic friends—parsimoniously.

Instead, throughout, he defines by means of predicate nouns and copulative verbs: "To seem is to be"; "Seeming is description without place"; "Description is revelation." At the end, echoing the logos of the Gospel of John, Stevens says that "the theory of description matters most," especially to those "for whom the word is the making of the world." His conundrums do not admit of reduction, summary, or fulfillment. Here, as throughout his greater poetry, he implicitly forces us to consider the relation between sentence structures and sentence sounds, and the limits of reality, the things represented. Always "mak[ing] the visible a little hard // to see" ("The Creations of Sound," CP, 311), he does not trouble himself to describe a scene: How can he? This is a "description without place," a description of nothing at all. We may, he seems to say, describe description, but we can never know it, just as we perhaps can neither know nor possess the objects of our gaze and of our description. All attempts at surrounding or capturing are doomed to at least partial failure. We seem to exist at one remove from the world, always disenfranchised even when we attempt to perceive it accurately, as Stevens remarks in a letter: "We live in the description of a place and not in the place itself."[36] This same uncertainty might explain why, for every resonantly simple formula about perception, imagination, and consciousness in Stevens (e.g., "to see was to be"; "Chocorua to Its Neighbor," CP, 297), one finds another one with a more desperate undertone:

... But to impose is not
To discover. To discover an order as of
A season, to discover summer and know it,
To discover winter and know it well, to find,
Not to impose, not to have reasoned at all,
Out of nothing to have come on major weather,

It is possible, possible, possible. It must
Be possible.
("Notes Toward a Supreme Fiction," *CP*, 403–404)

The suggestive though frustrating interplay in this poem among the constituents of a world—seeming, being, revealing, saying—sets the stage for the equivalent efforts of those contemporary poets who are Stevens's legitimate heirs. Vision penetrates aggressively; to see *through* something is to dig beneath the surface to its essence. We speak of a cutting glance. But vision also, to turn the phrase, sees us through, by accompanying us and providing something that adequately maintains balance, sanity, presence in—and in the face of—the world. Irving Feldman writes aphoristically, "Looking at is seeing through."[37] Such an elegant formulation deliberately evades the dangers that Wordsworth warned against when he called the bodily eye "the most despotic of our senses."[38]

The poets I deal with in this book can be characterized as paradoxically selfless and individuated, because although they often tend to do without much personal revelation, their distinctive poetic styles create their poetic identities. These are not self-confessing poets, nor do they cannibalize their friends and family. Although they invariably deal with their own histories, their own life experiences, they often do so at a remove. Ashbery, Graham, and Wright especially have expanded the bounds of lyric poetry, and not simply with regard to length; their long poems often combine facets of a cri du coeur, a narrative, and an extended meditation. In all cases, the self is apprehended, apprehensible, and available through that which surrounds it. It is often located in a landscape, and the poets define themselves by virtue of their surround. They do not preach, they do not teach; instead, they create themselves in their dealings with something beyond them. The self is what they construct or is constructed after the surround has been noticed. And in all of these cases, such notice takes the form of describing the world, of expanding the available means for descriptive assaults on the landscape.

In terms of the vexed relationships between the external world and what we can label either a seeing eye, a lyric consciousness, a poetic "speaker," or a constructed "subject," we might begin with the often selfless Gary Snyder, whose poetry connects descriptions of nature to his individual and our collective place in it. In many rhetorical ways he is, of course, Stevens's polar opposite: a poet of single, specific, and immediate observations, sensitive to ecological holiness. Although Helen Vendler exaggerates when she claims for Snyder an egoless identity that transforms the ego-centeredness of traditional lyric and moves it away from the confessional and prophetic modes of his contemporaries, she correctly ascribes to him the (at least occasional or partial) goal of stripping away the self.[39] Snyder is, however, a presence in many of his poems, especially the later ones that attempt social commentary or daily diaries. Because of his political and ideological commitments and also because the English language will simply not tolerate efforts to render it Japanese, Snyder can never completely disappear. His primitivism is often too easy, and, as Bonnie Costello has observed, Snyder "seems altogether embarrassed by active consciousness, including metaphor, asking us to settle instead for a combination of presentational and didactic modes."[40] In addition, like Ammons he risks the flaws of chattiness and banality. His best writing remains the early poetry from *Riprap* and *The Back Country*. Here his Miltonic sense of man, first in Eden and afterward dispossessed of it, underlies his treatments of nature and of his own work in nature. And his legacy from Ezra Pound—direct treatment of "the thing," going in fear of abstractions, attempting to capture natural scenes—stands in stark contrast to that of Charles Tomlinson (Chapter 2) and Charles Wright (Chapter 4), both equally indebted to Pound but able to move beyond his imagism as well as the epic pretensions of *The Cantos*.

The frequently phrasal quality of Snyder's poems suggests an attempted release from time. What he tries to do without in poetry—conventional punctuation, verbs, definite articles, people—is in part the inheritance from Pound and the Imagists that he shares with Wright, in many ways his diametrical opposite. Given his genuine knowledge of Japanese culture, art, and religion (as opposed to Pound's ersatz and borrowed Orientalism), Snyder struggles to fashion a genuine alternative to the tradition inspired by English Romanticism that takes the self as complementary to its surroundings.[41] The very title of his selected poetry, *No Nature*, deliberately matches a Zen-like detachment from the world to a simultaneous attachment to it:

> Nature also means the physical universe, including the urban, industrial, and toxic. But we do not easily *know* nature, or even know ourselves. Whatever it actually is, it will not fulfill our conceptions or assumptions. It will dodge our expectations and theoretical models. There is no single or set "nature" either as "the natural world" or "the

nature of things." The greatest respect we can pay to nature is not to trap it, but to acknowledge that it eludes us and that our own nature is also fluid, open, and conditional.[42]

Such a pronouncement sounds like Emerson redivivus (Nature "will not be rashly explained. Her secret is untold"). It also reflects the essential qualities of haiku and renga, which do not merely describe but attempt to perceive and render. According to Basho, one must concentrate on an object until the distance between self and object disappears: "The secret of poetry lies in treading the middle path between the reality and the vacuity of the world."[43]

For Snyder, a "description of nature" often literally brackets the perceiving self, as in the early, much anthologized "Mid-August at Sourdough Mountain Lookout" (4):

> Down valley a smoke haze
> Three days heat, after five days rain
> Pitch glows on the fir-cones
> Across rocks and meadows
> Swarms of new flies.
>
> I cannot remember things I once read
> A few friends, but they are in cities.
> Drinking cold snow-water from a tin cup
> Looking down for miles
> Through high still air.

One stanza of "objective" observation precedes an anecdotal detail that is paradoxically a statement of lack and absence, forgetfulness and distant friends. The final three-line fragment continues, on the one hand, a description of a "personal" activity, but, on the other, by virtue of its temporal vagueness, it removes the speaker from selfhood into a realm of pure physical sensation. No pronoun, therefore no subject; no verb, no time. Adjectival participles pretend to objectify action; in fact, they require that a reader insert them in a temporal grid. Such a procedure becomes something of a stylistic habit through all periods of Snyder's poetry. Another example, "Late October Camping in the Sawtooths" (320), opens with four lines of scene setting, followed by five of personal activity (building a fire, drinking tea, putting on a sweater, having a smoke) before subsiding into further natural detail:

> a leaf
> beyond fire
> Sparkles with nightfall frost.

An I-less, eye-full poetry looks impossible. The self is literally central, in both landscape and poem. In "Three Deer One Coyote Running in the Snow" (293), Snyder might be Wordsworth-in-the-Sierras: "I stand dumb . . . I walk through," he says, inserting his own response to the animals between lines describing their actions. Even if the poet absents himself from a scene, human life is often unavoidable, as in the lovely "Kyoto: March" (which I treat below).

Snyder frequently sharpens his perception by reducing observation to acts of list making. The opening stanzas of a much later poem show what he wishes to do without in his efforts to observe nature:

> salt seas, mountains, deserts—
> cell mandala holding water
> nerve network linking toes and eyes
> fins   legs   wings—
> teeth, all-purpose little early mammal molars.
> primate flat-foot
> front fore-mounted eyes—
>
> watching at the forest-grassland (interface
> richness) edge.
> scavenge, gather, rise up on rear legs.
> running—grasping—hand and eye;
> hunting.
> calling others to the stalk, the drive.
> ("Toward Climax," 254)

Such pure sensuousness—with little metaphor—does without metaphysical or even psychological support or corroboration. Lists of nouns and participial phrases and the withholding of verbs not only suspend time within the poem, they also impel the Western reader forward, in anticipation of some grammatical and thematic closure. Like the equally suspenseful but deeply subordinated syntax of Amy Clampitt (Chapter 3), Snyder's paratactic orderings arrange his world. Dicta like Marianne Moore's "the power of the visible / is the invisible" ("He 'Digesteth Harde Yron'") or Stevens's "the poet is the priest of the invisible" (*OP*, 195), both of which are American versions of Rilke's hieratic statement, "we are the bees of the invisible," occupy the other end of a spectrum from Snyder's often stripped-down observations. He forswears transcendental correspondences, but his apparent simplicity has its own pretensions.

Although Snyder often cannot resist political discursiveness, ecological judgments, or the occasional satiric jibe, his major distinctiveness in American poetry emerges from his deference to the things of the world regardless of the extent of his own involvement with them. Unfortunately, that involvement is inescapable, and many of his poems, by ending on a pointedly satiric note, undermine the unstated initial wish to present "nature" (whether still or in motion) with as little human presence, let alone interference, as possible. What intrudes is either Snyder himself as participant (as in "Mid-Summer at Sourdough Mountain Lookout") or Snyder the easy moralizer. "Marin-An" (89) begins with two five-line stanzas of natural description and ends with a third that takes notice of "thousands of cars / driving men to work." The juxtaposition is too simple. "By Frazier Creek Falls" (234) offers—as redemptive sermonizing after natural description—the unconvincing (because untrue) exclamation: "We could live on this Earth / without clothes or tools!" The industrial-military complex is never far from Snyder's thoughts; "pure" description is increasingly not a poetic option, just as a simple life in a purifying wilderness is not a human one.

Because he is so often at work in nature, it is better to call Snyder (like Wendell Berry on his Kentucky farm) a georgic poet rather than a pastoral one. Like Frost, he is too sophisticated not to imply literary tropes when he places at the center of a poem ("The Spring," 91) the image of an almost pastoral *locus amoenus*, to which his workers make a retreat from the heat, and from which they return, to get "back on the job" after refreshment. He demands mental and physical discipline of his students: his list of "What You Should Know to Be a Poet" (184) begins with specific details: "all you can about animals as persons. / the names of trees and flowers and weeds," before rising to greater, more dangerous ecstasies and "real danger. gambles. and the edge of death." Description is accompanied by human action more frequently than it stands alone as mere still life or Poundian Imagism. "Above Pate Valley" (9) describes trail blasting and the pleasures of a noonday meal in language of intensely sensuous, Hemingway-like simplicity. But simplicity never comes without evidence of history: Snyder discovers arrowheads on the trail, marks of now destroyed civilizations; and the poem ends with another kind of destruction:

> . . . Picked up the cold-drill,
> Pick, singlejack, and sack
> Of dynamite.
> Ten thousand years.

In the twinkling of an eye much vanishes.

Snyder also uses his physical work as the basis of an ars poetica. "Riprap" (21) takes as its central conceit the relation between the laying of rocks along a mountain path and the laying down of thoughts into words. One might infer that Snyder includes man merely as one element in nature rather than its consummation, were it not for the fact that so many of the poems place humanity, or the poet himself and his work, in a terminal position, thus granting them the authority of conclusiveness. "Work to Do Toward Town" (113) goes even farther in this direction: eleven lines of scenery, then two lines about farm women, and then the end: "I pack my bike with books—all roads descend toward town." The self and the city are Snyder's inevitable destinations.

When even a mildly conventional simile appears, it has a startling effect, especially coming from a poet who prefers metonymy to metaphor almost all of the time:

> A few light flakes of snow
> Fall in the feeble sun;
> Birds sing in the cold,
> A warbler by the wall. The plum
> Buds tight and chill soon bloom.
> The moon begins first
> Fourth, a faint slice west
> At nightfall. Jupiter half-way
> High at the end of night-
> Meditation. The dove cry
> Twangs like a bow.
> ("Kyoto: March," 17)[44]

What aims at pure reportage disguises its own artfulness: one is struck by the reluctance to embellish; the constant pressure exerted by monosyllables to slow down the rhythm; and the implied human presence in "night-meditation." When we reach the poem's midpoint ("The dove cry / Twangs like a bow"), Snyder has made us tacitly aware of his own imaginative presence, and he also prepares us—as he often does in poems that begin as "pure" description—for the human element with which he ends. Fifteen lines of morning description lead him to imagine the human lives within houses, to witness the awakening of lovers, parents, and grandparents embarking on the daily round.

Although he wants to make us think that nature is not necessarily preparing the way for human details, as is so often the case in poems grounded more solidly in Western aesthetics, and although he tries to alight on the human element not as a climax but as simply another aspect of a harmonious, decorative composition, the fact that Snyder's poems so often end with human details and observations proves the unavoidable presence of humanity and of civilization itself. One may not be entirely convinced by the poet's effort to situate himself and his work as components of a larger scene rather than the climax of it. Tim Dean, one of Snyder's sympathetic and often astute critics, has remarked (of "Mid-August at Sourdough Mountain Lookout"), "The 'I' does not order or dominate the landscape in any way . . . but neither does the landscape dominate the subject as an occasion for a sublime experience."[45] The absence of some final revelation or significant vision does not, however, mean that Snyder has successfully avoided the self-centeredness of the Romantic poets or of his more extravagant, self-dramatizing contemporaries. Neither transcendence nor moralizing is a desired end: the poet merely waits and watches. It is as though he has heeded the Wordsworthian formula "I gazed and gazed," often stopping himself before a subsequent realization is able to break through. For him there is no equivalent to Wordsworth's "but little thought / What wealth to me the show had brought." Looking is not subsumed by any other function. The self, by one way of figuring it (the way Snyder and Dean would have us follow), abjures consciousness and self-realization.[46] The evidence of the poetry, in terms of both explicit theme and the workings of syntax, often suggests otherwise. Taking him at his own word, Snyder's sympathetic critics want to find in him the purity of egoless observation, but he does not always comply.

As I have suggested, the very fact of work, whether physical or mental, referred to or enacted, prevents Snyder from being labeled a pastoral poet, in spite of his often longed-for retreat from modern life. There are, nevertheless, poems in which description, with minimal figurativeness and without meditation and the self-involvement of a first-person speaker, comes as close as possible to "pure" imagism. Even these, however, cannot subdue the human element. Here, for example, is a descriptive lyric:

Firewood under the eaves
    ends trimm'd even

Scaly silver lichen
    on the plum
        bark
Ragged, rough, twisted,
    parts half-rotted

A few blossoms open:
    rich pink tiny petals
        soft and flutter;
Other fat buds.

Fat buds, green twigs,
    flaky gray bark;

pigeons must all
Flap up together
("Aged Tamba Temple Plum Tree Song," 185)

Humanity appears only implicitly (someone has built the temple with its eaves; someone has trimmed the firewood). Otherwise, nature predominates. For seven lines all action is also implicit, having passed into adjectival participles ("trimm'd," "twisted," "half-rotted"). Time cannot be stopped: we are asked to look back. The third stanza presents complex possibilities for action and observation. "Open" may be verb or adjective; "flutter" is clearly a verb, but its place makes it *work* more like an adjective: "Petals / soft and flutter." Its location between a genuine independent clause and a subsequent short verbless phrase heightens the ambiguity of its meaning: Could "soft," on the other hand, be a verb? Even at the end, where animal life complements the vegetation, action is implicit rather than certain: the necessity of "must all / Flap up" suggests futurity as well as the present moment. The pigeons' ambiguous undulations are probably yet to come; we must imagine them occurring only *after* the poem's song ends.

When language attempts to imitate or reproduce still life and to use description with no suggestion of action or its possibility, it is doomed to failure. For one thing, inescapable temporality means that things happen—or are described—sequentially. Verbal sequence, like any form of artistic juxtaposition, confers meaning. For another, the attempt to remove verbs invariably demands their reentry in the form of participles, past or present, active or passive. Time does not disappear; it is merely reconfigured. And finally, for a poet like Snyder, although keeping the self out of the poem is one goal among many, it is often more honored in the breach than in the observing. The thinking subject overwhelms the passive seeing eye.

Even his instruction to would-be poets to learn the names of animals and plants places Snyder squarely in the camp of a Western, Romantic tradition, one of whose most articulate spokesmen was Howard Nemerov:

Poems, far from resting in nature as their end, use nature as a point from which they extrapolate darkly the nature of all things not visible or mediately knowable by reason—the soul, society, the gods or god, the mind—to which visible nature is equivocally the reflection and the mask. Such poetry is magical, then, because it treats the world as a signature, in which all things intimate to us by their sensible properties what and in what way we are. Poetry is an art of naming, and this naming is done by story-telling and by metaphorical approximations and refinements.[47]

Knowledge proceeds only by means of signs, dark mediations, and approximations. Description per se looks into and through the natural world but always serves the greater needs of its more aggressive, literally or figuratively "grasping" partners, apprehension and comprehension. The riprap that Snyder proposes as his primary metaphor for poetry, "a cobble of stone laid on steep slick rock to make a trail for horses in the mountains" (3), is also his version of T. S. Eliot's famous "indirection" ("Tradition and the Individual Talent"), because the rocks can never be laid straight. They tack, like sailboats; they scuttle back and forth up the terrain. The ascent to the summit can never be made directly, and in poetry the shortest distance between two points is never a straight line.

It is no coincidence, therefore, that the most famous twentieth-century "imagist" poem in English reveals the pretensions and inevitable failures, as well as the successes, of any Western desire to respond to an external scene by describing it, and to make observation and recreation appear instantaneous and equivalent. Coming from the man who urged poets (among other things), "Don't be descriptive," Pound's "In a Station of the Metro" is all verbless, atemporal detail, devoid of both action and a lyric speaker:

> The apparition of these faces in the crowd;
> Petals on a wet, black bough.

The poem's easy binary makes a twinned pairing, in a pseudo-couplet, of humanity and nature and of city and country. Just as a contemporary popular lyricist heard a nightingale singing in Berkeley Square, Pound saw flowers in the subway stop. But the breakdown or the mergings of oppositions continue. "Apparition," in addition to its ghostly mythological overtones (the crowd in the Underground is Virgil's or Dante's shades in the Underworld) is a verbal noun: the faces must have appeared from somewhere. And no verb could be clearer than the absent "is" or "is like" or "resembles" that separates the two lines. Mere identity vigorously asserts itself. Finally, there is no "thing itself" that can be directly treated; the poem can observe only indirectly through metaphor. Even its odd punctuation moves us away from atemporality, inaction, and objectivity. We might expect a colon at the end of the first line, which would signify a pseudo-mathematical equivalency between X and Y, faces and petals. Instead, the semicolon implies clauses rather than phrases, action rather than still life, time rather than eternity, and also a human observer rather than an instant photo or an English haiku. The punctuation suggests (if not means) something like: "First I see the apparition of these faces in the crowd; then they remind me of petals on a wet black bough." *Post hoc*, in poetry, bears the strong implication of *propter hoc*.

Figuration in its many forms (metaphor and metonymy as chief rivals for the poet's favor) invariably intrudes. The father of Imagism has left to his descendants an example and a proof of the hypothesis that nothing exists of or by itself. Again, the very un-Poundian Nemerov makes the provocative but virtually unarguable point: "If you really want to see something, look at something else. If you want to say what something is, inspect something it isn't . . . if you want to see the invisible world, look at the visible one."[48] Words carry and rehabilitate absence, and the human observer participates in his scene as well as in the act of his seeing. Mark Strand's most anthologized poem illustrates such participation: "In a field / I am the absence / of field" ("Keeping Things Whole"). Merely to "look" is a first step toward vision; vision may lead to things invisible to mortal sight, but even if such things are implicit, metaphorical, transient, or secular, rather than transcendent and permanent, they test the poet's capacity to move from looking to seeing to rendering. Description "completes" and "reveals" (I return to Stevens's terms) only through figuration. What Robert Frost "found" in his famous discovery of "Design" in nature was not just the deadly *nature morte* trio of spider-moth-flower but "assorted characters of death and blight," "a flower *like* froth," and "dead wings carried *like* a paper kite" (my emphasis). Such discovery involves the patience of a Zen master or Gerard Manly Hopkins, of Wordsworth, Bishop, and Hecht, who "gazed and gazed" or "looked and looked" and "look[s] and look[s]."[49]

Such patience is what Charles Tomlinson, to whom I turn next, calls the "labour of observation." In the following chapters I am concerned with poets' artistic strategies, ranging from grammatical and syntactic constructions to verse forms and prosody and tropes and figures. Description, like truth in Oscar Wilde's witticism, is never pure and rarely simple. Nor can it be naked. Rather, it is necessarily controlled, amplified, and ultimately produced by poetic utterance. In the figure of Professor Eucalyptus (named for the plant meaning "well-hidden," which suggests all of his creator's poetic efforts to uncover and to reveal), Wallace Stevens gives us his version of a man involved in such strategies:

> . . . He seeks
>
> God in the object itself, without much choice.
> It is a choice of the commodious adjective
> For what he sees, it comes in the end to that:
>
> The description that makes it divinity . . .
> ("An Ordinary Evening in New Haven," *CP*, 475)

The commodiousness of adjectives, which Amy Clampitt turned into a stylistic signature, allows us to move from the essential barrenness of nature or a "first idea" into a fuller, thicker version of reality: thicker because more densely perceived and described. The difference between trimmed, essential identity and more gloriously multifaceted, but still essential, identity, is Stevens's subject in section xxix of the same poem. His northern mariners come upon Goethe's "Land wo die Citrönen Blühen" to discover that the land of the lemon trees, for all its exotic splendor, is very much like home: "'We are back once more in the land of the elm-trees, // But folded over, turned around'":

> . . . It was the same
> Except for the adjectives, an alteration
> Of words that was a change of nature . . .
> (*CP*, 487)

Description *makes* difference; consequently, in poetry, it also makes meaning. What might seem extraneous, and either literally or figuratively *in*consequential, demands our critical attention. We must match the poet's laborious observation with our own.

TWO

# "JUST LOOKING"

*Charles Tomlinson and the "Labour of Observation"*

To include in a book dealing primarily with American poetry a chapter on an Englishman may seem illogical or counterintuitive, but Charles Tomlinson makes an important connection between the age of high modernism and the contemporary scene and between the two sides of the Atlantic Ocean. As a technician he has remained conservatively, solidly at home, with few extraterritorial excursions in style or subject. To some readers his poetic landscape might seem spectral or monochromatic. But is consistency a flaw? Must the poet constantly reinvent himself? We can pose the question analogously with reference to painters: Matisse and Picasso offer one paradigm, the more exciting one, for the modern artist; Mondrian, Morandi, and Rothko another, perhaps more exacting one. Having found their terrain, they exploited it for all that it was worth.

Tomlinson fits comfortably in the second category: he has looked steadily at his subject for more than five decades, and having found a congenial style and method early on, he has stuck with them. Not for him a continual, heroic quest for new techniques or changes of heart. Reading his books seriatim, one experiences small surprises that only in retrospect look predictable. One lands in a terrain wherein, "though all things differ, all agree." Pope's assured epigram from "Windsor Forest" has special resonance for Tomlinson's work, which examines the minutest fluctuations and nuances in the natural world, where difference and agreement go happily hand in hand. Constancy, in nature or in art, has a great deal to recommend it, especially in a poet who, responding to a question of Gerard Manly Hopkins ("What by your measure is the heaven of desire?") replies: "This inconstant constancy—earth, water, fire."[1]

Tomlinson's subject matter—the "inconstant constancy" he observes all around him—may explain his relative obscurity. It lacks frisson in an age that wants to be shocked. Ask any American reader of poetry to name the most important contemporary British or Irish poets, and the first choices would surely be Seamus Heaney, Geoffrey Hill, Ted Hughes, and Philip Larkin. In the slightly older postwar generation, John Betjeman, Basil Bunting, Donald Davie, David Jones, C. Day Lewis, and Dylan Thomas would spring to mind, and in the slightly younger one, James Fenton and Craig Raine have the widest readership in the States. W. H. Auden and Thom Gunn qualify as semi-Americans. Tomlinson might not make the list, an omission that says more about the uncertainties of poetic fame and the process of reputation building than it does about literary value. But Tomlinson is certainly the most interesting poet of the generation that came of age in the waning of high modernism and survived through postmodernism and the end of the millennium.

Born in 1927, he began publishing in the fifties; his influences have included Americans (first Stevens, then Moore and Williams), in addition to the more predictable English topographers of landscape like Wordsworth, Hopkins, and Edward Thomas, and, from the start, those two English eccentrics Blake and Lawrence. He has dedicated poems in a single volume (the 1963 *A Peopled Landscape*) to James Dickey *and* Marianne Moore. A former resident in the States and a fan of the American southwest, he has been hard to pin down even though he is a poet of place, because his places have ranged from Mexico (old and New), to upstate New York, Provence, and northern Italy, in addition to his native Stoke-on-Trent and the Gloucestershire countryside where he has lived for most of his adult life.[2]

Tomlinson has had his partisans, fit but few, for decades. Marianne Moore and William Carlos Williams gave encouragement at the start, and critics Hugh Kenner and Donald Davie (his former Cambridge tutor) "saw and believed," as Tomlinson gratefully acknowledged in the dedication to his third volume, *Seeing Is Believing* (1958), wherein he discovered his true voice. His poetry combines an imaginative perception of natural abundance with linguistic exactness; what some readers might find chilly—Tomlinson's discipline, toughness, and austerity (which Calvin Bedient sums up as the poet's insistence on making "of beholding an *ascesis*")[3]—in fact is central to his special achievement. He is a poet at once prosaic and refined, less self-involved than Williams, clearer than Stevens. Though his eye is alert to the whole world, he seems willing to wait for revelations. All persistence, he never importunes the natural world for vision, but rather witnesses its performance, attends diligently to its harmonies, and cares for his own place in it. The result is a poetry that impresses its own intelligence on the reader without vulgarly proclaiming it.

Tomlinson's originality and poetic voice must be heard beneath, above, or despite his own protests of impersonality. In the preface to *Collected Poems*, explaining the omission of some early work, he claims that he came to discover that he wanted to create poetry "where space represented possibility and where self would have to embrace that possibility somewhat self-forgetfully, putting aside the more possessive and violent claims of personality" (vii). "Self-forgetfully" sounds, of course, the note that we on this side of the Atlantic have come to associate with Elizabeth Bishop, that other poet whose modest, self-denigrating demur ("it's just description . . . they're all just description") forces us to ask a series of related, significant questions: What *is* description? What are we doing (or what *else* are we doing) when we do it? How does a poet create a language that will represent both the observed, external world and the interior life of the discovering and inventive eye? How does he or she translate outer space into representations of inner space? Like Stevens observing "the way things look each day" and Emerson "brav[ing] the landscape's looks," Tomlinson relies on description to represent what he calls "The Insistence of Things" (the title of a transcription of journal paragraphs reprinted in *The Way In and Other Poems*):

> At the edge of conversations, uncompleting all acts of thoughts, looms the insistence of things which, waiting on our recognition, face us with our own death, for they are so completely what we are not. And thus we go on trying to read them, as if they were signs, or the embodied message of oracles. (260)

*As if they were signs*: but for Tomlinson, more often than not, they are not signs or symbols of anything we can readily identify. Instead, "things," whether living or dead (parts of nature or of still life, *nature morte*), confront us as we confront them, a deliberate reminder of our final "completion" as well as a constant provoking (or "uncompleting") of all our thoughts.

Both Bishop and Tomlinson make complementary gestures, unmilitant but strong-willed, of escaping from the ego obsessions of many other twentieth-century poets. They are, of course, not alone in this effort. David Jones's late, Poundian *Anathemata* (1962) swerves away from psychological or even personal poetry, but Tomlinson has managed a comparable escape without suffering any of the insidious effects of Pound's pretensions or, still worse, his ideas.[4] To write concretely and humbly generates a new kind of individuality, which locates itself in the world and in regard to our commerce *with* the world ("the world of all of us, the place [as Wordsworth put it] wherein / We find our happiness or not at all"). For all the constancy, Tomlinson makes each poem different from the others: in some, description serves its own end; in others it provokes questions about transcendence. Even when examining "stone certitude" (as in "The Peak," *The Return*, 22), Tomlinson never sounds as impoverished as some American poets (W. S. Merwin, for example) when they look at the same bare objects. Rock, stone, and water are for him elemental but never naked, always embellished by language, by light, by one another. George Oppen, whom Tomlinson quotes, once suggested, "let's take out all the adjectives" ("In Memory of George Oppen," *The Return*, 25). But this has never been Tomlinson's strategy. His dignified diction doesn't shy away from ornate description, nor does it seek out ornateness for its own sake. Eliot's prescription from "Little Gidding" comes to mind: "The common word exact without vulgarity, / The formal word precise but not pedantic."

Within his language, unvulgar and unpedantic, Tomlinson's stylistic changes are subtle and slow in coming. In the first volumes one finds very few first-person experiences or even pronouns; the confessional, self-explorative, or (to use Auden's word in "The Horatians") *foudroyant* mode always made Tomlinson uncomfortable. Over the years, one comes to piece together the external data of the poet's life: his wife, daughters, and grandchild, his love of music, his travels to Italy and the States, his friendships with Donald Davie, Octavio Paz, and the Italian poets Attilio Bertolucci and Paolo Bertolani. And in *Jubilation* the easy flow of pentameter couplets celebrating birthdays and retirements (his own among them) sounds a tone of release after years of scrutinizing practically everything but himself.

When Tomlinson met Marianne Moore they discussed their mutual, intense admiration of Ruskin (*Some Americans*, 32–36). All three are ardent observers, sharing a patient willingness to look hard at the world. "Description is revelation," Wallace Stevens's terse epigram ("Description Without Place"), might stand on the title page of each of Tomlinson's volumes. Some readers might be untouched by this formula. To those who want their poetry full of passion, politics, and the parade of the ego, one can only answer that Tomlinson's investigations of the external world are strangely rich and austere at the same time. The precision and abundance of his language are even more impressive when one considers all those things his poetry does without: notably, self-analysis, deep or dream images, heavy-handed symbolism ("visions are not my style," he admits in "To a Yorkshireman in Devon," a birthday poem to Davie in *Jubilation*, 43), exclamations or frequent apostrophes (and, by and large, questions), sexual passion, and most other forms of excessive outburst. Tomlinson has absorbed and then gone beyond the lessons of Pound and Williams concerning what to include in and exclude from poetry.

It is not to Imagism, however, but to the nineteenth-century Romantic-Realist tradition of seeing and depicting, exemplified by Constable, Ruskin, and even the highly idiosyncratic and melodramatic Hopkins that Tomlinson owes a greater allegiance than to the Americans I have already cited. For sheer visual precision, Ruskin and Hopkins are Tomlinson's only peers. We might take as a lengthier epigraph to his poetry Ruskin's remarks in "Of Truth of Space" from *Modern Painters*: "Nature is never distinct and never vacant, she is always mysterious but always abundant; you always see something, but you never see all . . . hence in art, every space or touch in which we can see everything, or in which we can see nothing, is false. Nothing can be true which is either complete or vacant; every touch is false which does not suggest more than it represents, and every space is false which represents nothing."[5] Tomlinson has termed his pervasive, Ruskinian theme "the fineness of relationships," a phrase from which we may infer two kindred concerns: the contact between the artistic eye and its objects, and the relationship of the reader to the words of the poem. The patient poetic observer uncovers the world's mysterious vitality, which rewards him with opulent detail; the complexities of poetic syntax and sound duplicate that show before the reading eye. In Tomlinson, as in Stevens, we can watch poetry happening. That is, we become aware of our own responses to language as we work our way through entangled phrases, oblique diction, unexpected or irregular rhymes, disclosures that what we thought was a verb is really a noun, what a direct object really a subject, and so on. We are conscious of ourselves reading and listening as well as of the text before us. The poem illuminates not only its nominal subject—herons, houses, oxen, or swimming—but us as well.

Over the years, Tomlinson has become both sterner and (in his recent small volumes) gentler. The rituals of perception in which he engages have deepened. Yet mere refinement has never been enough. Even as early as *The Necklace* (1955), when the touch of Moore-ishness and preciosity was most pronounced, Tomlinson knew that decor could not confer value, that shimmering facets of light (a major fascination throughout his career, as one might expect from a painter-poet) come from rhinestones as well as diamonds:

> . . . Proportions

> Matter. It is difficult to get them right.
> There must be nothing
> Superfluous, nothing which is not elegant

And nothing which is if it is merely that.
("The Art of Poetry," 11)

The last sentence reminds us of Tomlinson's debt to Stevens: no Snowman he, but a less puritanical version of the blackbird's eye or Emerson's transparent eyeball. With Ruskin (and with Jorie Graham, who in every other way is his diametrical opposite), he might very well say, however, "My entire delight was in observing without being myself noticed,—if I could have been invisible, all the better" ("The Col de la Faucille," *Praeterita*, in *Genius of Ruskin*, 514). Delight is at the heart of Tomlinson's responses. With the coolness of a collector, he constantly seeks out new Edens in nature and verse. He captures the singularity of objects but never destroys their freedom, as he grips them in polite scrutiny.

A real believer in limits, caution, and the difficult necessity of proportion, Tomlinson also acknowledges and turns away from the "instructive fury" of an artist like Van Gogh, or from any apocalyptic fervor that denies the expected round of natural fulfillment: "The world does not end tonight / And the fruit that we shall pick tomorrow / Await us, weighing the unstripped bough" ("Farewell to Van Gogh," *Seeing Is Believing*, 36). In *The Shaft*, a series about Charlotte Corday and Danton, and "Assassin" (on the murder of Trotsky), pick up Tomlinson's concern, in the earlier "Prometheus" (*The Way of a World*, 156) and the Van Gogh poem, with extremism in its historical and artistic forms. "The time is in love with endings," he observes in "Against Extremity" (*The Way of a World*, 163), but he prefers for himself spanning and sustaining, bridges and nets. His antiself takes center stage during one surreal moment, in "A Dream" (*The Way of a World*, 157), when he imagines himself at a reading with Yevtushenko and Voznesensky: "I lack their verve / (I know) their red reserve / Of Scythian corpuscles, to ride in triumph through / Indianapolis." But then something wonderful happens: his voice opens stentorianly as he reads his "bits of ivory" and the crowd is swayed: it's October 1917, or 1789, once more. The gentle Englishman, Tamburlaine for a moment, is "laurelled in vatic lather" and then, we assume, wakes up.

Although his inquisitive sensibility is rooted in the English values of contemplation and reticence and in characteristic British landscapes, Tomlinson seems equally at home elsewhere in the world. He combines British politeness with a flare for the foreign; his excellent translations from Italian prove that he has inherited the benign international leanings of Poundian modernism. Likewise, his poetic technique favors a small number of fairly conventional poetic forms but a vocabulary richly loaded with polysyllabic, Latinate, and, above all, descriptively accurate terminology. The best analogy for Tomlinson's method is the tension, which he has noticed, between the supposed objectivity of nineteenth-century science, which separates the observer from the observed, and the methods of Cézanne and post-Impressionist painting, "an outward gaze that would draw the sensuous world closer to the inner man and that would narrow the gap between abstraction and sensation, between intellect and things."[6] Objectivity may be the best way of achieving depth of feeling. Another way of putting this is to say that only through acknowledging the strange otherness of a scene, a place, or a meteorological phenomenon can one negotiate an understanding of that scene and consequently of oneself. As Hopkins famously observes in a journal entry: "What you look hard at seems to look hard at you, hence the true and false instress of nature."[7] One comes to self-understanding by examining the surround. Although he seldom deals overtly with philosophical, especially metaphysical, questions, Tomlinson qualifies as an important phenomenological poet; his language and form force his readers to confront a verbal reproduction of his own confrontation with an external scene. (The syntax of Amy Clampitt, another deeply observant poet, does the same thing, as I demonstrate in the following chapter.) Like Williams, Moore, and Ruskin, Tomlinson usually begins with *fact*, which then opens him up to the possibility of plenitude and of artistic creation. He has obeyed Emerson's famous command in his 1872 "Poetry and Imagination": "Ask the fact for the form."

Description may be neither an end in itself nor a logical earnest of something to come. Still, each descriptive effort constitutes both itself and something else, although that something else exists at different levels. "Apples Painted" (*Annunciations*, 44) may allude to Cézanne, but the unnamed subject becomes the emblem for Everyman-as-Artist, whether master or Sunday dabbler, and for the poet as well, because by and large all otherwise unspecified pronouns in Tomlinson are versions of himself:

> He presses the brush-tip. What he wants
>    Is weight such as the blind might feel
> Cupping these roundnesses. The ooze
>    Takes a shapely turn as thought
> Steadies it into touch—touch
>    That is the mind moving, enlightened carnality.
> He must find them out anew, the shapes
>    And the spaces in between them—all that dropped from view
> As the bitten apple staled on unseen.
>    All this he must do with a brush? All this
> With a brush, a touch, a thought—

Till the time-filled forms are ripening in their places,
And he sees the painted fruit still loading the tree,
 And the gate stands open in complicity at his return
To a garden beneath the apple boughs' tremulous sway.[8]

Tomlinson's pseudo-elegiac unrhymed couplets (a favorite form) depict depiction. The poem is not technically ekphrastic but rather descriptive of a process that brings the apples into focus only at the end, when we have moved backward from result (the apples *painted*) to source. The apples are now "seen" for the first time, but at a double remove: not *in* the painting but in the garden. (For a different response to the same painter, more concerned with the result than the actual process of painting, see my discussion of Charles Wright's "Homage to Paul Cézanne" in Chapter 4.) "Enlightened carnality," the fleshly pleasures that appeal to touch and soul simultaneously, provokes the painter to duplicate his delight within his picture and then within his audience. And the entire poem returns us, at its end, to the first garden from which we were all, long ago, cast out. Any artistic enterprise implicitly attempts to regain Eden.

Tomlinson self-disparagingly referred to his "bits of ivory" in the poem imagining his reading with Yevtushenko and Vosnesensky ("A Dream"). A more generous evaluation would include his remark "It is the mind sees" ("Skullshapes," *The Way of a World*, 191), because every creation of a bit of ivory demands an act of total, self-forgetful concentration, whether on works of art by Braque, Constable, Eakins, Soutine, and Vermeer; physical scenes ("What is a place?" he asks characteristically in the title poem of *The Return*, 8); changes in the weather; or even history and politics, which make infrequent but important appearances in his collected work. I would be tempted to appropriate at face value Walter Savage Landor's self-evaluation ("Nature I loved, and, next to Nature, Art"), except that in Tomlinson nature and art form two sides of a triangle, the third side of which is the human world: he once accurately described himself as "poised between paradise and history."

Like Hardy, Housman, and Edward Thomas, Tomlinson has the English countryside in his very bones; like any sensible rain-soaked Englishman, he has also come to value the sunny landscapes of Italy and Mexico. As a poet of place(s), he understands implictly that place is an event in time as well as space, that even when "the place has changed, the image still remains," as he announces to his friend Paolo Bertolani in a retrospective poem (the title poem of *The Return*, 8) that does for Serra and La Rochetta what Wordsworth once did for Yarrow: "For place is always an embodiment / And incarnation beyond argument, / Centre and source" (9). Tomlinson can delicately modulate between such abstract, polysyllabic phrasing and concrete or monosyllabic language, as in an earlier section of this multipart poem:

... And now
The summit gives us all that lies below,
Shows us the islands slide into their places
Beyond the shore and, when the lights come on,
How all the other roads declare themselves
Garlanding their gradients to the sea,
How the road that brought us here has dropped away
A half-lost contour on a chart of lights
The waters ripple and spread across the bay.
("The Return," 7)

With a painter's eye he appreciates and then renders the effects of light on stone and water, especially in his hilly native terrain or the Italian Appenines and Ligurian coast.

The real proof of Tomlinson's eye and ear comes in poems (for example, "In Oklahoma," *The Return*, 26) depicting bizarre, unpromising, or unconventional landscapes. Prairie flatness challenges the poet to discover the appropriate beauty of an unexpected or unlikely place. The landscape also provokes a recollection of historical urgency: near this spot the Tonkawa Hills massacre occurred in 1864. Where landscape seems "to have nothing to hide" Tomlinson must look even harder to distinguish genuine presence:

... Only the red
Declared itself among the leeched-out shades,
Rose into the buttes, seeped through the plain,
And left, in standing pools, one wine-dark stain.
The trees, with their survivors' look, the grasses
Yellowing into March refused their space
Those colours that would quicken to the ring
Of the horizon each declivity
And flood all in the sap and flare of spring.
The wideness waited. Sun kept clouded back.
An armadillo, crushed beside the road,
Dried out to a plaque of faded blood.
Here, fundamentalists have pitched their spires
Lower than that arbiter of wrath to come—
The tower of the tornado siren
Latticed in iron against a doubtful sky.

The poem's largely but not rigidly iambic pentameter, its casual rhymes (plain/stain, ring/spring), consonantal or half-rhymes (grasses/space, road/blood), and alliterations (flood/flare, wideness/waited) suit its subject. Just as we hear random, almost lazy sounds approaching but never achieving regularity, so we can bear witness to the historical past and contemporary society in a seemingly barren landscape. Every possible historical, meteorological, and theological disaster inevitably threatens us in this Limbo, but Tomlinson's congenital reticence forbids him any moralizing tone or judgment. Still, the omnipresent humanizing details—another legacy from Ruskin and his "pathetic fallacy"—turn even this desert scene into an arena for human adventures.

Wallace Stevens said that the poem "must resist the intelligence / Almost successfully." For Tomlinson it is Nature that offers resistance, but Nature and Art often become one. Comminglings in nature recall "the ways a poem flows" ("Nature Poem," *The Shaft*, 295); in fact, all the flowings in Tomlinson's work are tropes for poetry. The shades, depths, and recesses in an autumn scene are characters of a shifting text, which "no single reading renders up complete":

> ... a poem, too, in this,
> They bring the mind half way to its defeat,
> Eluding and exceeding the place it guesses,
> Among these overlappings, half-lights, depths,
> The currents of this air, these hiddenesses.

What he calls "the civility of nature" is the obverse of his occasional sense of something less than civil in natural disorder and tumult. As a connoisseur of chaos, he is often a match for Ted Hughes or Geoffrey Hill, in his fascination with skulls, for example, "helmeted cavities" that invite contemplation as well as shadows to fill their recesses ("Skullshapes," 191). Or in images that offer a shock just when we think we have been settled into comfort, as in a poem about a heavy-packed bloom of chrysanthemums that ends: "But the eye / of Courbet is glutted with petals / as solid as meat that press back the sky" ("Composition," *The Way of a World*, 187).

Skirting danger or flirting with disaster infuses Tomlinson's poetry with a sense of chillingly elegant mystery and at the same time demonstrates exactly why he looks so hard to rhyme, vision, or elaborate schemes of formal organization as energies to combat confusion. Without them we would be mastered by the terrible gusts that so often lie at the heart of his landscapes. The assured opening lines of "Northern Spring" (*Seeing Is Believing*, 28) are an eerie invitation to the assaults and mufflings of the elements:

Nor is this the setting for extravagance. Trees
   Fight with the wind, the wind eludes them,
Streaking its cross-lanes over the uneasy water
   Whose bronze whitens.

The first sentence catches us off-guard and provokes us to ask: What else is not a setting for extravagance? Or, of what else is *this* not the setting? After two stanzas of painterly description, the speaker construes a house to be placed in the midst of the scene to "define / In pure white from its verdant ground / The variegated excess which threatens it." Only at the end, having imaginatively domesticated the landscape in which the elements combat one another, does he offer some balance to the opening "nor":

Spring lours. Neither will the summer achieve
   That Roman season of an equable province
Where the sun is its own witness and the shadow
   Measures its ardor with the impartiality
Of the just. Evening, debauching this sky, asks
   To be appraised and to be withstood.

Neither "extravagant" nor "equable," the English seasons are a system of checks and balances, requiring the fortitude of withstanding and the clear-sighted judgment of appraisal.

The demands of the season, like the demands of art, can be answered only by human awareness of their rich inscrutability. Those readers of Tomlinson who admire the precision of his eye and the elegance of his sustaining details must be taken aback to find him aligning himself with the dynamic and unfinished instead of the perfect and limited ("Against Portraits," *Written on Water*, 230):

if there must be
an art of portraiture,
let it show us ourselves as we
break from the image of what we are.

Throughout his poetry, science and factuality work with and against imagination and fancy. Objectivity may be merely a myth, tempting and frustrating us in equal measure.

It is for these reasons, among others, that Eakins and Constable are two of Tomlinson's model painters. He admires the former for the accuracy of his experiments with anatomy, reflection, and perspective, and for the human depth that always manages to undermine human vanity in his portraits. This is what he means in his quasi-Stevenesian aphorism: "The figures of perception / as against / the figures of elocution" ("A Garland for Thomas Eakins," *American Scenes and Other Poems*, 141). When he asks, "What does the man / who sees / trust to / if not the eye? He trusts / to knowledge / to right appearances" (140), he leaves us wondering about the possible disjunctions between that eye and those appearances. At the very beginning of his work, Tomlinson said quite simply, "Facts have no eyes. One must / Surprise them, as one surprises a tree" ("Observation of Facts," *The Necklace*, 11). Although Emerson claimed that "Nature cannot be surprised in undress," Tomlinson's eye is composed of equal parts passive responsiveness and aggressive excursiveness.

Eakins's portraiture gauges human proportions and the human abyss; it looks within human beings for scientific principles. The human figure is a created fiction as well as a factual given. For Tomlinson, Constable, who humanizes the landscape, works the other way around. In addition, he invites us to judge, and thereby to finish, the imitation he has begun in paint: "The end is our approval / Freely accorded, the illusion persuading us / That it exists as a human image." It is an illusion that "must persuade / And with a constancy, not to be swept back, / To reveal what it half-conceals. Art is itself / Once we accept it" ("A Meditation on John Constable," *Seeing Is Believing*, 34). In another poem in the same volume ("Cézanne at Aix," 37), Tomlinson remarks conclusively of Mont St.-Victoire that it is "a presence / Which does not present itself." Human politesse underlies artistic renderings: for Tomlinson; it is as though Cézanne were making a personal introduction: "May I present to you . . ." Looking at landscape or at landscape painting is invariably a social activity.

It is Constable who exemplifies the "labour of observation" that Tomlinson most admires in any artist, visual or literary. The Coleridgean paradox—revelation through concealment—suggests a variation on Tomlinson's glowing reciprocities: in art, as in nature, it is the perceiving eye that confers, not merely discovers, meaning, and so the viewer of Constable can close the work that Constable himself began. What we perceive, and half create, Tomlinson might say, testifies to our place in the world's reticulations: "Art / Is complete when it is human." And it is human only when the pigments of paint, the shafts of light and shadow in a landscape, "Convince, as the index of a possible passion, / As the adequate gauge, both of the passion / And its object" (34–35). Science has its own limitations. In a Constable landscape we see a landscape, Constable, and finally ourselves.

But what exactly are we seeing? Tomlinson, who watches the skies and tracks the weather with quickness and depth of perception, opens his poem with a description. Poet and painter are united in their mutual "labour of observation / In face of meteorological fact" (33). Both of them record a process of variable change:

. . . Clouds
Followed by others, temper the sun in passing
   Over and off it. Massed darks
Blotting it back, scattered and mellowed shafts
   Break damply out of them, until the source
Unmasks, floods its retreating bank
   With raw fire. One perceives (though scarcely)
The remnant clouds trailing across it
   In rags, and thinned to a gauze.
But the next will dam it. They loom past
   And narrow its blaze. It shrinks to a crescent
Crushed out, a still lengthening ooze
   As the mass thickens, though cannot exclude
Its silvered-yellow. The eclipse is sudden,
   Seen first on the darkening grass, then complete
In a covered sky.
(33–34)

This might refer to a scene the poet witnesses, but it might just as easily describe one of those vast Constable canvasses in which the heavy impasto calls as much attention to itself as to the clouds that it depicts in different parts of the same sky. The poet's own thickness of description replicates the density of detail, the colors, light and shade, and the depth of landscape that Constable has forever made us see when we think "Rural England."

Like Constable, Tomlinson admires accidents because they are governed by laws, however difficult to fathom (just as his poetry careens between seeming laxness and the occasional inevitability of rhyme and meter); he most values the peculiar combination of revelation and concealment brought about by changes of light in a landscape. The pleasure of seeing and then rendering, whether in paint or in language, the unstable, flickering effects in an external scene "discovers" (his word) one's true identity, allowing the artist to become himself only during the moments when he is actively engaged in reproducing his passive observations. What we see uncovers what we are; what we are defines what we discover. By using as an epigraph to his poem Constable's own inquiry into the relation between science and painting ("May not landscape painting be considered as a branch of natural philosophy, of which pictures are but the experiments?"), Tomlinson implicitly asks whether landscape poems might not constitute equivalent experiments. Such experiments, whether descriptions of nature or of painted landscapes, necessarily involve the encounters between the eye and its object.

Such encounters, Tomlinson's major theme and strategy, sometimes involve union, sometimes struggle. Opposites merge, or fail to, and at his most luminous moments, he perceives the dearest freshness which his forebear Hopkins also discovered, "deep down things." Angularities change at the command of light; there is "calmness within the wind, the warmth in cold"; oxen are "a white darkness" ("Winter Encounters," "Oxen: Ploughing at Fiesole," both in *Seeing Is Believing*, 18, 19). But then there are moments in which Tomlinson encounters absence itself, and in the face of this, even silence is insufficient as response. Of his poetic travel encounters, "On the Hall at Stowey" (*Seeing Is Believing*, 40–42) is the most moving, because sadness, emptiness, and waste seem to be at the heart of activity, abundance, and harvest. (For a shorter version of the same principle, see "The View" in *The Way of a World*, 167.) Human negligence is the fruit of human artistic energy, as Tomlinson the traveler notices when he visits a manor house tastelessly transformed in accordance with modern standards; nature's bounty turns ironically into its "battery," which "completes by persistence / All that our negligence fails in."

The poem reads as though the Philip Larkin of "Church-Going" were walking the countryside with the Wordsworth of "The Ruined Cottage," but Tomlinson refuses to preach or to stretch toward symbolism. (In fact, a subsequent poem in this volume, "The Castle," begins forthrightly: "It is a real one—no more symbolic / Than you or I.") What he sees on his excursion is a hall ruined by updating and supposed improvements and then undone by abandonment, neglect, and the persistence of natural decay. Tomlinson pictures an "unweeded yard, where earth and house / Debated the terrain," but where, although the house is neglected, the land is still farmed. The "latest tenant," unlike Wordsworth's Margaret, suffers from the blight of bad taste:

> Each hearth refitted
> For a suburban whim, each room
> Denied what it was, diminished thus
> To a barbarous mean.

In a rare moment, for Tomlinson is not a poet given to sarcasm or hostility, he is "saddened, / Yet angered beyond sadness" at the human and aesthetic disease from which owner and hall suffer. This is a rare statement of clarified emotion. Art, not nature, has felt the sting of human inadequacy; the present, barbarous mean is a gross parody of the "sturdier compromise" that an earlier mingling of styles, aiming at a "civil elegance," hit during five centuries of building and design. The "eager excrescence" (a reminder of the

word's origin in Latin *crescens*, growing) of comfortable, organic additions
has turned upon itself to effect gross ugliness.

Tomlinson's interest in architecture, his enthusiasm for building as the
primary human art, recalls him from a distant position of witnessing to a
central place in our shared humanity. When a landscape lacks a house (as in
"Northern Spring"), he often feels obliged to imagine one; when one exists
and is ill-tended, he feels sadness tempered with anger. Stone symbolizes
patience itself, a constancy that

> resists
> > the slow corrosives
> > > and the flight
> of time
> > and yet it takes
> > > the play, the fluency
> from light.
> ("The Picture of J. T. in a Prospect of Stone,"
> *A Peopled Landscape*, 74)

Even Eden is more of a proto-city than a garden, more a spirit than a place:
"It is a light of place / As much as the place itself." (See Stevens's poignant
reminder: "We live in a description of a place and not in the place itself.") It
gives promise of urbanity:

> . . . And the same
> Wind stirs in the thicket of the lines
> In Eden's wood, the radial avenues
> Of light there, copious enough
> To draft a city from.
> ("Eden," *The Way of a World*, 159)

If the Fall was happy for Tomlinson, it was so because it allowed man and
nature to achieve their civic unity. In the solidity of stone, enduring yet
always changing in new light, we can see the human life of cities and nature.
We are reminded once more of Tomlinson's debt to the first and greatest
English writer about stones and architecture. Tomlinson would agree with
Ruskin that "to see clearly is poetry, prophecy and religion,—all in one" ("Of
Modern Landscape," *Genius of Ruskin*, 91). His poetry often gives the sensa-
tion of returning to Adam on the first day.

His reimaginings of Eden—and accompanying exercises in description,
nostalgia, and landscape painting, let alone any more complicated Emp-
sonian pastoral schemes—are only a part of Tomlinson's arsenal or of his
temperament. Tomlinson, man and poet, was a traveler if not a bona fide

adventurer before it became easy to move transcontinentally. It's a nice irony that *Jubilation* contains one poem entitled "Against Travel" ("These days are best when one goes nowhere," it begins [16]), and then two entire sequences about journeys to Portugal and Japan. The urge to move everywhere challenges the need to stay put. At an earlier stage, he is surprised to discover that New Zealand shearsmen have turned up in his Gloucestershire valley as migrant workers, only to realize that "Shearsmen and poets travel far these days," and, more important, that even the world is on the move:

> The field now is empty of sheep, the migrants gone.
> Homebound, they must circle the world again,
> Itself a traveller through space and season,
> Trailing the wool wisp vapour of their jetplane.
> ("From Gloucestershire," *The Door in the Wall*, 39)

The turns of verse, here in quatrains, match the returns and revolutions to which Tomlinson everywhere gives notice. Such notice is generously bestowed in "Hartland Cliff" in the same volume (46), another quatrain poem (in which the stanzas contain differently rhymed units) that makes an equation between poetry and natural movements of the sort I have already mentioned:

> only the turns of verse
> could contain and then let go
> the accumulation of that flow
> to the shift of light
>
> late afternoon brings
> —to the reshaping of the waters
> by a moon unseen,
> to the sheen and spread of wings.

Like the eye patiently witnessing and absorbing a landscape, the mind that composes a poem takes in and lets go external stimuli through the reshapings of verse itself.

Because change and stasis provide a pair of antithetical poles around which he organizes much of his work, we might think of Tomlinson as a poet drawn equally to rendering scenes as still lifes and to depicting action itself. The moment of violent action, of any action, in fact, is like frozen lightning or the crest of a moment's wave when it seems the wave will never again recede. But because Tomlinson sees an almost Lucretian fluidity of motion in the visible world, he always prefers those actions that, when done, are not done, but withdraw, repeat, continue, and amplify themselves. As

I suggested in Chapter 1, there can be no genuine Imagist poem, because action always comes in—if only through the back door—in the form of temporality. Likewise, as I claimed above with reference to the description of clouds in "A Meditation for John Constable," the stasis of painting encourages the recreation of movement in any attempted poetic description of the painting. "Movements" (*Written on Water*, 236) illustrates a universe "where everything / Seemed to be at pause, yet nothing was." Thus we also have the pairings throughout the poetry of rock and water, which prove their resemblances above or beneath their obvious differences:

> "Written on water," one might say
> Of each day's flux and lapse,
>     But to speak of water is to entertain the image
> Of its seamless momentum once again.
> (237)

"To entertain" is both to consider and to host: in Tomlinson, thought is kindly and hospitable. Beneath "the wide promiscuity of acquaintanceship" he finds the music of constancy; water's ways permeate the rock of time itself. Is "the constancy of stone" (in "The Picture of J. T. in a Prospect of Stone," *A Peopled Landscape*, 74) merely hardness, or is its stillness, which takes and plays with the fluency of light, an element of perdurable grace? In "Autumn Piece" (*Written on Water*, 218), an exquisite picture tempered by Shelleyan skepticism, Tomlinson wonders whether the leaves are struggling to be free or the wind is stripping them from the trees. The turbulent "choreography of the season" is as graceful as a dance, twisting and "dragging all certainties out of course." Even in menace is artifice: the poet misreads a "Danger" road sign as "Dancer."

Tomlinson can suggest hostility so tactfully that we never know exactly how grim a profusion of possible threats he notices around him. He makes us see infinity in single scenes. Blakean vision? Certainly, but modified by a common, public language, objective sighting, and without myth making. He elicits tension, but without extravagance; he infers more tumult from the slightest ripples on a stream than Shelley from the wave-cleaving Atlantic. And he discriminates between healthy and neurotic responses to such extravagant confusion: emulating it impoverishes the resources of folly, but "to taste it is medicinal" ("Northern Spring," *Seeing Is Believeing*, 28). Tomlinson never immerses himself in the destructive element; he just gets his feet wet, and that's danger enough.

Here, for example, is one of his auguries of innocence that figure a world in a tremulous flash:

> Having mislaid it, and then
>     Found again in a changed mind
> The image of a gull the autumn gust
>     Had pulled upwards and past
> The window I watched from, I recovered too
>     The ash-key, borne-by whirling
> On the same surge of air, like an animate thing.
> ("The Way of a World," 165)

The visual phenomenon is duplicated by the suspenseful syntax, which settles us only gradually into a main clause and is filled with ambiguous phrases. "In a changed mind" suggests logically the place where the object, whose identity is also withheld, was found; "borne-by whirling" could have been "borne by whirling," meaning something different but related. The insistent but not overpowering alliterative effects and the enjambments sustain the scene's delicacy. The counterpoise of this spectacle, framed doubly by both a window and a memory, is like that of Wordsworth's recollected daffodils, flashing suddenly and reduplicating themselves ex post facto. One appreciates the wealth only after the event, which comes

> With its worth and, like those tree-tips,
> Fine as dishevelling hair, but steadied
>     And masted as they are, that worth
> Outlasted its lost time, when
>     The cross-currents had carried it under.
> In all these evanescences of daily air,
>     It is the shape of change, and not the bare
> Glancing vibrations, that vein and branch
>     Through the moving textures: we grasp
> The way of a world in the seed, the gull
>     Swayed toiling against the two
> Gravities that root and uproot the trees.
> (166)

Losing and remembering are cross-currents in the human world, veins through the brain's texture; the gull "swayed toiling" combines in its two participles the action and passivity necessary for balance. And the final image presents a static product of causal forces that pull in opposite directions. Gravity's counterforce is more than a mere breeze: it is the "weightless anarchy of air" mentioned earlier in the poem, itself the dark mirror or the dangerous twin of the rooting instinct.

Tomlinson's exciting, dramatic syntax owes a great deal to what he learned from Williams's triads and Moore's enjambed stanzas. A short poem like "At Sant' Antimo" (*Written on Water*, 210) depicts, in fifteen almost pauseless lines, the "continual breathing" and wavering of a cypress by a stone tower and compares foliage floating upward to an underwater motion as the lines move gracefully downward. Another example is the lovely "Sconset" (*Seeing Is Believing*, 1960 edition, 47):

> I have never been
> To Sconset, but the gleam
> Of painted houses
> Adding a snow-tone
> To the sea-tone in the mind's
> Folder of the principal views
> With the courthouse
> Seen from the harbour, the harbour
> Obscured by the whiteness
> Of the church, crouched
> Behind a dark shrub
> Whose serrated leaves
> Hang mounted (as it were)
> On the spine of a feather—
> These have invaded
> All I shall ever hear
> To the contrary.

Subordination is the game here: the whole world described in the poem is a system of dependencies, in which grammar and syntax demonstrate interconnectedness. Tomlinson deploys his participial phrases and clauses like flickers of light. The move from the present perfect tense in line 1, repeated in line 15, to the single present tense verb ("hang," line 13), to the future (line 16), parallels the use of repeated words and sounds and gives the illusion of continuity.

Like "At Sant' Antimo" and "Sconset," most of Tomlinson's titles are thoroughly neutral, often suggesting still lifes or landscape paintings: "The Snow Fences," "The Butterflies," "September Swamp," "The Mediterranean," "Object in a Setting," "The Mausoleum," "The Gorge," "The Crane," "The Ruin," "The Beech," "The Hawthorn in Trent Vale," "The Jam Trap." The list is virtually endless: no other poet has such predictable and passionless titles. They connote the poet's strong homing instinct, but the turbulent activity in the poems themselves often upsets any yearning for stasis. Both the descriptions of actions and the enactment of them through sentence structure—snaking its way from line to line down the page, with what often look like desperate caesuras or enjambments—seem to confuse or blur the poems' subjects. Nevertheless, Tomlinson's style holds us off initially, the better to bring us, ultimately, in.

The middle path between action (which corresponds to the violence of force in the poems about extremism) and stillness (which stands for Tomlinson's "aesthetic" patience) is clearest in a poem like "The Atlantic" (*Seeing Is Believing*, 17), in which a rendering of movement begins when the title seems to thrust itself forward as the subject of an opening sentence:

> Launched into an opposing wind, hangs
>   Grappled beneath the onrush
> And there, lifts, curling in spume,
>   Unlocks, drops from that hold
> Over and shoreward.

What we took as a main verb ("Launched") turns out to be a past participle. The contrast between past and present participles, between active and passive constructions, and especially between verbs and nouns that we must take, on closer inspection, as entirely *verbal* nouns (e.g., "onrush" and "hold"; later in the poem we have "ripple" and "motion") synthesizes transience and permanence, a gesture of which Tomlinson is master. After a description of the momentum and collapse of the wave, its legacy of a sun-glaze on the beach, Tomlinson pauses, entertains an image of equivalent displacement in his own mind, and then articulates the human application or analogue of the scene with an equal, strongly verbal, force:

> . . . That which we were,
> Confronted by all that we are not,
>   Grasps in subservience its replenishment.

The "its" of the final line refers both to our own recent past that sustains us and the otherness of the wave, which, by repeating itself through retreat and reformation, also replenishes our view of it.

Tomlinson's fascination with what Octavio Paz calls "the continuous generation and degeneration of things"—those moments of becoming when things change—accounts for the way his poems hypostasize action and animate stillness.[9] Such fascination also creates the tension in some of his earlier graphic art between event and item, action and thing. Process and product are equally vital. By combining the chance designs of a piece of paper pressed against another smeared with paint (decalcomania) and the willed arrangement of these shapes, cut up in a new context, Tomlinson arrived at a visual equivalent of poetic rhyme: "The chances of rhyme are like the

chances of meeting— / In the finding fortuitous, but once found, binding"
("The Chances of Rhyme," *The Way of a World*, 194). One can have formality without rigidity, and openness without entropy. Finding and binding are two words for discovery and capture; Tomlinson is a poet in whose work, as Paz has remarked, the distinction between subject and object becomes "a zone of interpenetration."[10] Rhyme may be either discovery or creation, depending on whether it arrives mysteriously and suddenly or striven for and plotted (and who can ever tell?). Consequently, it is a synecdoche for all poetic learning, proving, as Tomlinson goes on to confirm in "The Chances of Rhyme," that art and life are themselves the major zone of interpenetration, joined in a shadowy area where boundaries blur:

> . . . Yet why should we speak
> Of art, of life, as if the one were all form
>     And the other all Sturm-und-Drang? And I think
> Too, we should confine to Crewe or to Mow
>     Cop, all those who confuse the fortuitousness
> Of art with something to be met with only
>     At extremity's brink, reducing thus
> Rhyme to a kind of rope's end, a glimpsed grass
>     To be snatched at as we plunge past it—
> Nostalgic, after all, for a hope deferred.

Found or invented, rhymes cement together the things of this world.

Pairings of all sorts, especially the gentler aspects of those more violent encounters in some of Tomlinson's poems, make for civil and reciprocal relationships, what he calls "Images of Perfection" (*The Shaft*, 289). This poem is followed by "Rhymes," which plays with varieties of perfection in sight and sound: "Word and world rhyme / As the penstrokes might if you drew / The spaciousness reaching down through a valley view" (290). Like rhyme, metaphor is a way of detecting or designing correspondence. Often, a poem builds itself around such a crucial relationship. In "The Metamorphosis" (292), for example, which appears to owe its subject and imagery to Richard Wilbur's "The Beautiful Changes," the mind perceives and transforms natural beauty, surrendering its own powers in order to swim in the illusion of metamorphosis and, by so doing, making that illusion true. Bluebellls are crowding a fellside like water; they figuratively (or is it literally?) stream across the view, raveled with grass and stems, opened and blown by the breeze. The delicate description, adhered to by a mind "in salutory confusion," at last turns inside out, when the mind itself, metaphorically swimming, "could . . . believe / Water itself might move like a flowing of flowers." (Shades of Robert Frost's

"Spring Pools"!) The following poem in *The Shaft* plays with the same sense of reciprocity. Driving "Below Tintern," the speaker looks down and away from Wordsworth, whose lines were *above* Tintern Abbey and whose farms were "green to the very door," as opposed to Tomlinson's scene, where "the river's mirrorings remake a world / Green to the clifftops." His mind swims "down and through" the towering dimness that he sees reflected in the river, which is a threshold for an inverted sky and for a mind willing to accept the momentary invitation to lose itself in and through reflection "as the car bends by" (292).

His interest in movement and change is deeply affected by and in turn strongly affects Tomlinson's syntax and his concern for that very painterly subject, the weather and its effects on sight (as in "A Meditation on John Constable"). "Weather releases him from the tyranny of rooms, / From the white finality of clapboard houses" ("Weatherman," *The Way of a World*, 168) begins a poem set in New England, whose subject could as easily be Charles Tomlinson himself as any native Yankee. The noise of migrating geese drives "the eye / Of the mind the way they go, through the opal / Changes of dawn light on the light of snow." Such changes, like Shelley's dome of many-colored glass poised beneath the white radiance of eternity, are registered as effects on nature and human witnesses. In early poems, like the homage to Constable, Tomlinson reproduces these quicksilver changes through complex syntax and opulent diction. In later work, we find the kind of simplicity of which only a master distiller is capable, as in two sonnets about moonlight. In "Moonrise" (*Annunciations*, 51), the earlier of the two, the poet and his wife are walking on a December afternoon. He points out the early-rising moon, beneath which crows return to their darkened nests, and

> Its phosphor burning back our knowledge to
> The sense that we are here, that it is now.
> Against the east, the tautness of its bow
> Is aiming outwards at futurity
> And that will soon arrive, but let it be:
> The birds are black on the illuminated sky
> And high enough to read the darkness here
> By this risen light that is bringing tides to bear.

The strings of monosyllabic words play against the delicately whispered sense of the moon as Diana the Hunter (with her "bow" within its bow shape), and the oncoming darkness has the unspoken finality of death that Howard Nemerov, to choose one obvious contemporary, also knew how to suggest without sounding grim.

"Picking Mushrooms by Moonlight" (*The Door in the Wall*, 62) is more delicate still, with the mushrooms themselves resembling little moons, a scattered crop that

> Answers to the urging of that O,
> And so do we, exclaiming as we go,
> With rounded lips translating shape to sound,
> At finding so much treasure on the ground
> Marked out by light. We stoop and gather there
> These lunar fruits of the advancing year:
> So late in time, yet timely at this date,
> They show what forces linger and outwait
> Each change of season, rhyme made visible
> And felt on the fingertips at every pull.

The poem contains a haphazardly articulated echo of Dryden's great elegy to John Oldham, "Farewell too little and too lately known" ("gather," "fruits," "advancing," "time," "show," and "rhyme" are all borrowings from Dryden). The gentleness of that allusion and the insistence on the relation between natural activity and poetic harvesting (the "O" of wonder extending from the shape of the moon and the mushroom circle; the effort to "translate" shape to sound; visible "rhyme" as itself an implicit pun on *rime*-frost which is soon-to-come) prove Tomlinson an intimate of books as well as of the external world.

I have called attention to Tomlinson's rhymes, in more formal poems (like this one) or more casual ones, where they are less predictable, less determined by poetic convention. With the exception of John Hollander, in his show-and-tell *Rhyme's Reason*, no other practicing poet has made such a cogent habit of simultaneously discussing and dramatizing rhyme.[11] The opening couplet of a signature piece, "The Chances of Rhyme" (194) (*The Way of a World*), already cited, puts the matter squarely: "The chances of rhyme are like the chances of meeting— / In the finding fortuitous, but once found, binding." What Keats called "the magic hand of chance" guides Tomlinson's poetics. Like any sonic or musical principle in poetry, rhyme is as likely to arrive by accident as by intention. But once the poet has alit upon, or been struck with, a fitting music, he has established an opportune connection for which he might express a gratitude similar to the one normally reserved for meeting one's lover or spouse. In poetry, "signifying" spells "success," "a way forward / If unmapped, a literal, not a royal succession." Tomlinson can afford to leave to chance or fate as well as to his own determination the possibilities of discovering the mot juste, the correct sound, the "successful" signifier. Such hopefulness explains the surprising appearance—in many poems without a regular rhyme scheme—of audible, chiming, repeated sounds that call our attention to the matters at hand. So, in a poem about a distant crane that unloads boulders from a boat onto the end of a harbor, we find amid the short lines a sentence like this one:

> . . . The crash
> of each stone
> brings a flash of white
> up out of the blue
> and a ripple that still has not ceased
> to spread before the next
> wedding of stone and water
> on a risen sea-bed.
> ("Sight and Sound," *The Door in the Wall*, 40)

"Crash/flash," and "spread/[wed]/bed" are especially apt in a poem that depicts things inaudible to mortal hearing; everything described takes place out of earshot, but Tomlinson makes us respond aurally to the sounds as well as the sights of the maritime scene. Although he claimed early that "art exists at a remove" ("Distinctions," *Seeing Is Believing*, 21), he evidently likes to bring home the fruits of his labors across the boundaries of removal.

In a deliciously witty poem, "To a Librettist at Liberty," Richard Howard poses a serious question based on those trifling errors of print or pronunciation (a radio announcer referring to Rossini's *Donna del Iago*, for example) that might inspire variations on old themes (e.g., a revised *Otello* with Emilia as the heroine): "what is / the sign of humanity / but making accident the means of art?"[12] In an entirely different tone, Tomlinson, too, attends to such accidents. The chances of rhyme and of meeting unfold in a small series of poems, from all stages of his career, which are based on simple acts, or accidents, of misreading. These differ from both Elizabeth Bishop's "mammoth/man-moth" mistake, which inspired her creation of a famous subterranean creature, and those poems of Wordsworth in which he misreads natural or human data only to be corrected and morally improved at the end ("Resolution and Independence," "Poems on the Naming of Places"). Tomlinson's poems locate language in the domain of landscape, as if to cement the connection between human life and seasonal change. Here, for example, are the first and last stanzas of the three-stanza "Autumn Piece" (218) already cited above:

> Baffled
> by the choreography of the season
> the eye could not

with certainty see
whether it was wind
stripping the leaves or
the leaves were struggling to be free:
. . . . . . . . . . . . . . . . . . . . . . . . . . . . . .
As the car resisted it [the force of the wind]
you felt it in either hand
commanding car, tree, sky,
master of chances,
and at a curve was a red
board said "Danger":
I thought it said dancer.

"Chances" covers natural chaos, autumnal choreography, willful and hopeful misreadings, and, of course, the unpredictable but happy rhymes in "see/ free," "hand/command," and "red/said," those stays against confusion amid natural turmoil.

In another poem ("Hyphens," *The Way In and Other Poems*, 255), Tomlinson misreads the phrase "the country's loveliness" as "the country's love-lines," with "the unnec- / essary 's'" then inspiring the restoration of a natural scene. The Hopkinsesque force behind these visual mistakes, cognitive dissonances, and rhyming schemes sounds most clearly in the bravura musical piece (and Tomlinson is seldom a bravura poet) called "Ritornello" (*The Flood*, 334), an eleven-line jeu d'esprit that begins and ends thus:

Wrong has a twisty look like wrung misprinted
Consider! and you con the stars for meaning
Sublime comes climbing from beneath the threshold
Experience? you win it out of peril
. . . . . . . . . . . . . . . . . . . . . . . . . . . . .
Abstraction means something pulled away from
Humus means earth place purchase and return.

Writing "melting" instead of "meeting" inspires a fantasy on dissolving in a poem ("Misprint," *The Shaft*, 302) that slithers down the page with no terminal period. It is followed by "Maintenant" (303), another unstopped tour de force, which begins with a bilingual pun:

Hand
holding on to this
instant metamorphosis,
the syllables maintain

against the lapse
of time that they remain
here, where all else escapes

Witty sequences like this cannot disguise the seriousness of Tomlinson's engagements with sound, or his more capacious impulse to render and amend the world by listening to, as well as watching, it. The epigraph to *A Peopled Landscape*, reappearing as the first line of its opening poem ("A Prelude," 59), is a quotation from Jean-François Millet:

I want the cries of my geese
To echo in space . . .
                                        . . . life
Under leaf, gulls going in
Behind the encroachment of the plough.

Sound and sight, like time and space, make for a synaesthetic unity. Nor is this the only allusion in Tomlinson's poetry to the relation between the turns of the plough and the poet's turn of phrase or attention to the furrows of his own verse.

Although I mentioned his traveling impulses and his satiric ones, his dealings with natural data permit us to classify him as a pastoral poet, not just in the general sense of that word but, more interestingly, in his minglings of the green world and the improved or improving world of the imagination. Tomlinson makes the serious point that Adam, having been dispossessed of Eden, can now inhabit only Arden, a subsidiary, secondhand version of paradise at one remove, but one that we are also in danger of losing. Even third-rate substitutes are fragile. The strings of similar-sounding words convey echoingly the displacement from paradise that we have been attempting to overcome since that first day:

Arden is not Eden, but Eden's rhyme:
    Time spent in Arden is time at risk
And place, also: for Arden lies under threat:
    Ownership will get what it can for Arden's trees:
No acreage of green-belt complacencies
    Can keep Macadam out: Eden lies guarded:
Pardonable Adam, denied its gate,
    Walks the grass in a less-than-Eden light
And whiteness that shines from a stone burns with his fate.
. . . . . . . . . . . . . . . . . . . . . . . . . . . . . . . . . . . . . . . . . . . . . . . . .
Adam in Arden tastes its replenishings:
    Through its dense heats the depths of Arden's springs

Convey echoic waters—voices
   Of the place that rises through this place
Overflowing, as it brims its surfaces
   In runes and hidden rhymes, in chords and keys
Where Adam, Eden, Arden run together
   And time itself must beat to the cadence of this river.
("In Arden," *The Shaft*, 305–306)

Like Tomlinson and our first parents, we are all "poised between paradise
and history." Adam is out, Macadam in: the satiric note does not lessen
Tomlinson's deeper allegiance—owing to a doubled sense of exile and rein-
tegration—to Wallace Stevens's stoic aesthetics:

From this the poem springs: that we live in a place
That is not our own and, much more, not ourselves
And hard it is in spite of blazoned days.
("Notes Toward a Supreme Fiction")

Tomlinson's descriptive prowess and his musical ear have allowed him to
read some of the runes and to reveal some of those "hidden rhymes" that
course through our precariously habitable Arden-Eden. As he announces
in another poem ("Eden," *The Way of a World*, 159), we are both given and
denied Eden; we exist in an ambiguous middle sphere, neither wholly
belonging nor entirely disenfranchised:

There is no
   Bridge but the thread of patience, no way
But the will to wish back Eden, this leaning
   To stand against the persuasions of a wind
That rings with its meaninglessness where it sang its meaning.

Bridging is accomplished, of course, by rhyme, wordplay, metaphor, all of a
poet's linguistic habits; such bridging explains both Tomlinson's technique
and his generally moderate tones. In "Against Extremity" (*The Way of a
World*, 163), he prudently demands:

Let there be treaties, bridges,
   Chords under the hands, to be spanned
Sustained: extremity hates a given good
   Or a good gained.

Such moderation must sound, to an American ear, a distinctly British note
of reserve, compromise, and politesse. The pleasures of reading or hearing

Tomlinson's poetry depend on one's willingness to appreciate, if not to share, such elegant formulations of pastoral conservatism.

A left-leaning reader might argue that Tomlinson everywhere betrays the too easy demeanor of the aesthete. In "The Garden" (*Annunciations*, 40), he takes a straight shot at those critics who fail to see the transcendent value of pastoral beyond the self-bound interests of a single class:

> And now they say
> Gardens are merely the expression of a class
> Masterful enough to enamel away
> All signs of the labour that produced them.
> This crass reading forgets that imagination
> Outgoes itself, outgrows aim
> And origin; forgets that art
> Does not offer the sweat of parturition
> As proof of its sincerity.

So much for the Marxists, New Historicists, and all the others whom Harold Bloom dismisses as the "resentniks." (On the other hand, he can mercilessly satirize "The Rich" [*The Way In*, 249], whose "favourite pastoral / is to think they're not rich at all.") Walking with friends, the poet follows and reads the work of an unnamed landscape architect (whose constructions create little rooms out of natural spots). And at last they stand "to meditate the gift we did not ask— / The work of seasons and of hands unseen / Tempering time" (41). The pastoral "meditate" (from Virgil and Milton), the faint allusion to Hesiod, and the careful rendering of a scene that everywhere breaks down the boundaries between natural growth and human plans all point to a classic performance of the pastoral impulse. Love of landscape has little to do with ownership and everything to do with appreciation of the planter's artistry:

> . . . there is nothing here
> We shall ever own, nothing that he owns now,
> In those reflections of summer trees on water,
> This composure awaiting the rain and snow.
> (42)

Such composure belongs equally to patient nature and its patient onlookers. (At an earlier point in the poem, peering through a keyhole to see a distant lake, Tomlinson becomes for a moment a British Emerson: "we are all eye.") Like all pastoralists and all poetic describers, Tomlinson comes to accept and rejoice in the happy ambiguities of "reflection" itself.

But elsewhere Tomlinson admits to a change in his own point of view, one late in coming:

> It took time to convince me that I cared
> For more than beauty: I write to rescue
> what is no longer there—absurd
> A place should be more fragile than a book.
> ("Dates: Penkhull New Road," *The Way In*, 245)

The title poem of the same volume laments the way "Bulldozers / Gobble a street up" (241), leaving in their wake dispossessed, unfortunate, poor human detritus. Tomlinson's self-assessment is accurate. Many of the early poems (in *The Necklace* especially) are brittle, "arty," self-consciously tasteful in the way of James Merrill's contemporaneous early poems. The Mediterranean "bewilders with an excessive formality," and "Art exists at a remove," he announces in two characteristic early poems ("The Mediteranean," "Distinctions," both in *Seeing Is Believing*, 20, 21). Like Merrill, Tomlinson moved away from the protective cover of aestheticism. In "Class" (*The Way In*, 248), he recalls contemptuously the Henry Higgins–like snobbism of the aesthete Percy Lubbock, for whom he briefly worked as a secretary. Like Merrill, Tomlinson could sacrifice his aestheticism without giving up his devotion to the things of this world and to the ardors of his own eye. The move from aesthete to elegist is perhaps an inevitable progress as one ages (Tomlinson was born one year after Merrill), especially for a poet whom we can now, through the wisdom of hindsight, place in the greater Romantic tradition that includes Wordsworth, Tennyson, Hardy, and Yeats, and that asks us to look soberly at, and to feel at home in, this world, however tentative or shaky our hold on it.

Yet even this sober note was sounded relatively early, in "On the Hall at Stowey," whose elegiac, semisatirical tone hardly belongs to a conventional aesthete. Instead, like the comparable poems throughout Tomlinson's work, "On the Hall at Stowey" reveals its author's working-class origins as a person for whom wastefulness, superficiality, pretension, arrogance, conspicuous consumption, and arrogance qualify as unmitigated signs of human stupidity. Not beauty alone but "proportions / Matter" ("The Art of Poetry," *The Necklace*, 11). And "proportion" includes a sense of proportion in one's own estimation of the world. In other words, even Tomlinson's late anger can be traced back to his beginnings, regardless of other changes in style or tone. His ars poetica refuses "nothing which is not elegant / And nothing which is if it is merely that." Between these two nothings Tomlinson has amassed the substantial stones of his own edifice.

But it is hardly a stony edifice. As I observed above, water, itself as transitory as weather, has a special prominence in Tomlinson's work. The first poem of Tomlinson's that I fell in love with was "Swimming Chenango Lake" (*The Way of a World*, 155), a legacy from his time teaching at Colgate University in upstate New York and certainly the best poem ever written about swimming. The poem opens with a chilly meteorological certainty before watching a swimmer take the plunge:

> Winter will bar the swimmer soon.
>     He reads the water's autumnal hesitations
> A wealth of ways: it is jarred,
>     It is astir already despite its steadiness,
> Where the first leaves at the first
>     Tremor of the morning air have dropped
> Anticipating him, launching their imprints
>     Outwards in eccentric, overlapping circles.

Constancy and movement come together. Reflection, which is wonderfully both mirrored repetition and contemplation, confers meaning on mind and world through one another. Against the depth and silence of water, as Tomlinson remarks in the title poem of *Written on Water*, we are able "to clarify ourselves." It uplifts and sustains, but is capable of submerging as well. All flow, yet all sameness, water is the only element of the four that can be seen both in itself and in its transformation of other objects. It clarifies; it distorts. As the swimmer realizes before diving into Chenango Lake, it can be read, like any natural or written text, "a wealth of ways."

Swimming is a paradigm for the relationship between man and nature, body and mind, an act of perfect courtesy and sustenance:

> For to swim is also to take hold
>     On water's meaning, to move in its embrace
> And to be, between grasp and grasping, free.
> (155)

The physical universe is the only arena for learning (see Stevens: "The greatest poverty is not to live in a physical world"). Like description, as I suggested at the end of the previous chapter, comprehension depends on literal prehension, a grasping that can never be completed. The implied contrast between noun and gerund ("grasp" and "grasping") is Tomlinson's version of Browning's wisdom about a reach and a grasp. It marks as well his relation to Wordsworth in poems like "Nutting," where a young ravager in nature sits down to listen to "the murmur and the murmuring sound" of a brook.

Effort and achievement, possession and relinquishment, tearing and healing: a whole series of antinomies surrounds the physical act of swimming. And grander oppositions mount as well: the swimmer "is unnamed / By this baptism" in an Indian lake, a medium that never fully answers the questions the body puts to it. The mercilessness of the cold waters nevertheless mercifully sustains him. As he swims through the water, the autumn sun warms and dries him:

> Above a surface a mere mosaic of tiny shatterings,
>     Where a wind is unscaping all images in the flowing obsidian,
> The going-elsewhere of ripples incessantly shaping.
> (156)

The water is a flowing mosaic. Like the Atlantic in Bishop's "At the Fish-houses" ("cold dark deep and absolutely clear"), the lake is the object and cause of knowledge. It is the medium where contraries unite, where "unscaping" and "shaping" (whose curious half-rhyme also makes a nod in Bishop's direction) coexist, and where an intransitive gerund ("going-elsewhere") and a semitransitive participle ("shaping") combine to give a sense of action caught in language.

Tomlinson construes the "geometry of water" as his swimmer moves "between grasp and grasping" with a delicate breaststroke through a chilly baptism, yielding himself to the buoyancy of a saving though cold experience that braces and sustains him physically and spiritually. When I met the poet, years after I had first read the poem, I came equipped with the assurance of a critic who has already figured things out. It struck me that only a person who viscerally understood the pleasures of New England lakes, especially in the fall, and who knew the sensation of working through, within, and on top of water, could have written such a sympathetic rendition of a physical event, even in a third-person narrative. The poem, I thought, must be a disguised autobiographical experience. I remarked with matter-of-fact confidence, "You must love swimming; you know how it feels."

"Oh, no," he replied, "I can't swim at all; I was just looking at that man. I watched very long and very hard."

*Just looking.* As Elizabeth Bishop said with equal parts self-deprecation and self-understanding, "It's just description," but watching the water is apparently as arduous as swimming through or perhaps even walking on it.

# THREE

# WHAT TO MAKE OF AN AUGMENTED THING

*Amy Clampitt's Syntactic Dramas*

Amy Clampitt looked like a tea cozy; lived like a bohemian; thought like a radical; sounded, especially when reading her own work, like an excited precocious teenager (if Marilyn Monroe had been an intellectual, this is how she would have talked); and wrote like an angel. In the fifteen years between her late but flamboyant arrival on the poetry scene and her death in 1994, Clampitt was both lionized and derided. Her admirers and detractors often agree in their characterization of her work—with its old-fashioned lushness, its frank interest in the lives and the writing of the Romantic poets, its frequent flaunting of scholarly and scientific knowledge, its playful elegance, and its unashamed reveling in language at once arcane and precise—and differ only in their evaluation of it. One critic claims that one of her longer poems "refuse[s] easy enthusiasms and guard[s] against hollow 'epic' pretensions. . . . The language is a deft compromise between narrative propulsion and lyric accretion." Others, harboring an often unstated philistine suspicion of ornament and a preference for the plain over the fancy and for the simple over the baroque, belittle the elaborate, over-burdening style that turns the poetry into "a parody of the Victorian silk that Pound sought to unravel," or mock the "bathetic enthusiasm" that emerges from the "forced" accumulations of her details.[1] *De gustibus non est disputandum.* One reader's deftness is another's bathos.

The effect of sitting down to read her *Collected Poems* is one of inundation, and certainly not to everyone's taste. Overrichness is a problem: "like a whole meal of desserts," one skeptic said to me. But now it is time to take the measure of America's oldest young poet, whose five books from 1983 to 1994 have taken cover in a single volume sympathetically introduced by the poet Mary Jo Salter.[2] It is time to praise richness and decoration, the baroque and the ornamental, the dramatic uses to which description may be put.

In her intelligent but stubborn (even wrong-headed) essay "Against Decoration," Mary Karr comes down hard on Clampitt before tearing into the true objects of her disapproval, James Merrill and some of the avatars of the New Formalism. For Karr, "[One passage] . . . could be Swinburne on acid or Tennyson gone mad with his thesaurus."[3] Karr reduces New Formalism's multiple sins to two: absence of emotion and lack of clarity. While acknowledging that Clampitt herself was never very much of a "formalist" poet, preferring stanzas or lines with a metrical base but seldom limiting herself to patterns of rhyme, Karr decides that the intricacies of Clampitt's syntax, her reliance on a difficult, obscure vocabulary, her scholarly apparatus that made as much of literary allusiveness and botanical nomenclature as of "lived" life, all remove her from the possession of the real power of what Karr considers authentic poetry.

Many readers would prefer Victorian silk to the *émaux et camées* of Poundian Imagism, and as for Clampitt's high-flown diction, her "literariness," her excited sense of wonder when confronting familiar or exotic landscapes or those places where her cultural heroes (the Wordsworths, Keats, Coleridge, George Eliot) trod, many would say, not "Basta!" but "More!" (Ironically, the beautiful sequence "Homage to John Keats" [*WTLWL*, 141–161] must be counted something of a poetic failure, as only a reader with a full grasp of the details of Keats's life and works can respond fully to the deeply referential poems.) Beside the afflatus of Hart Crane and the plainness of William Carlos Williams, Clampitt's delicately powerful mingling of high and low, big and small, fancy and fact, the extravagant and the everyday seems like an authentically revolutionary stance for an American poet at the end of her century. A poet can legitimately expect his or her readers to work toward emotion and clarity (or emotional clarity). As I show, Clampitt's poetic tropings and syntactic adventures replicate an Emersonian nature that "cannot be surprised in undress. Beauty breaks in everywhere."[4] In addition, one must acknowledge—in this era of obsession with, if not always sensitivity to, gender issues—the uniqueness of a female poet unashamedly tackling subjects and techniques that we associate more commonly with the poet who was rightfully and peculiarly Clampitt's truest precursor: not her beloved Keats, Wordsworth, or Hopkins, but Walt Whitman. Among women poets in the past fifty years, only the more flamboyantly abstruse Jorie Graham has anything approaching Clampitt's ambition.

All of her intellectual and cultural appetite is easy to miss amid the sheer gorgeousness of Clampitt's sounds, streaming, even gushing from the page as though released after years of captivity. (As everyone must know by now, Clampitt was over sixty, with several unpublished novels in her desk, when her first volume, *The Kingfisher*, appeared.) From the start she is linguistically inebriated, as when she moves eagerly from tongue to tongue, landscape to landscape, on a train into Italy from France:

> The train leaps toward Italy, the French Riviera
> falls away in the dark, the rails sing dimeter
> shifting to trimeter, a galopade to a galliard.
> We sit wedged among strangers; whatever
> we once knew (it was never much) of each other
> falls away with the landscape. Words
> fall away, we trade instead in flirting
> and cigarettes; we're all rapport with strangers.
> ("Losing Track of Language," *WTLWL*, 182)

Loss and losing, all the processes of diminishment, are the originary causes of accumulation, in whatever form. Clampitt often *builds* her poems like this signature piece, insouciantly, from an anecdotal opening that broaches major themes (language, history, and culture) in the most offhand way. The delights of experience not only balance, but also depend on, the losses we have suffered.

And Clampitt is a poet well aware of loss. The richness of diction, sound, syntax, and sentiment informing her work from the start, just like her love of Keats and the other Romantics, derives from her snowman-like center: although she did not have a heart or mind of winter, she had been cold for a long time. No one who has never known *viscerally* what it is like to be frozen to the bone can understand "The Eve of St. Agnes" (she once said in conversation) and its ravishing, compensatory dreams of sensuous fulfillment, warmth, and an escape to the southern moors. She arrived at lushness from the chill of her Iowa farmstead and from a political-religious austerity bred into her by her Quaker forebears and developed through years of political consciousness and activity. For every synaesthetic embellishment and every hothouse bloom, such as

> Mirrored among jungle blooms' curled crimson
> and chartreuse, above the mantel, diva-throated
> tuberoses, opening all the stops, deliver
> Wagnerian arias of perfume
> ("Townhouse Interior with Cat," *WTLWL*, 174)

she gives us simple declarative sentences, aphoristic nuggets of wisdom, and moral principles from which some poems proceed or to which they often lead. "A Hermit Thrush" (*AF*), for instance, begins: "Nothing's certain." Clampitt seldom uses a two-word sentence anywhere, and the stark certainty of this opening prepares us for her investigation (as throughout the entire volume) of tenuousness and tenacity, focusing on a "gust-beleaguered single spruce tree," the uncertainty of everything except "the tide that / circumscribes us," and the title figure, Clampitt's homage to the various race of Romantic birds, especially Thomas Hardy's "Darkling Thrush." The poem ends:

> . . . Watching
> the longest day take cover under
> a monk's-cowl overcast,
>
> with thunder, rain and wind, then waiting,
> we drop everything to listen as a
> hermit thrush distills its fragmentary,
> hesitant, in the end
>
> unbroken music. From what source (beyond us, or
> the wells within?) such links perceived arrive—
> diminished sequences so uninsistingly
> not even human—there's
>
> hardly a vocabulary left to wonder, uncertain
> as we are of so much in this existence, this
> botched, cumbersome, much-mended,
> not unsatisfactory thing.
> (272–274)

All of the hallmarks of Clampitt's poetry are here: the parenthetical questions that sidetrack and amplify (a lesson learned from Elizabeth Bishop); the long sentences; the personification of "the longest day" (with a reminder of its connection to her human observers, themselves taking separate but parallel cover); the skepticism in the face of happiness and wonder, tellingly arrived at in the extended adjectives of the last two lines; and the characteristic British litotes ("not unsatisfactory"), which articulates the understated happiness that Clampitt is always surprised to encounter. In a world where nothing is certain except the tide that circumscribes all human and natural activity, it is an appropriate stylistic habit for Clampitt to write *around* her subject (a disgruntled reader might even condescendingly call her poems periphrastic), circumscribing her vision of the world with sentences that attack, home in on, retreat from, and then reapproach their main objects. For her a "thing in itself" cannot exist; it will always invite another look, another "take," or it will require another, supplemental effort to describe and present it.

For all of the richness in her poetry, Clampitt is, like James Merrill, equally an elegiac poet of loss and dislocation. "Losing Track of Language" examines one kind of loss and compensatory gain; "Midsummer in the Blueberry Barrens" (*AF*, 266) begins with a nod in the direction of Wordsworth, Bishop, and Frost ("Tintern Abbey," "Cape Breton," and "Directive," respectively) by conveying a pattern of disappearance in a landscape: "Away from the shore, the roads dwindle and lose themselves / among the blueberry barrens." Clampitt is sensitive to natural erosion and encroachment for more than merely ecological or aesthetic reasons.[5] All evidence of change echoes personal instability. As early as "On the Disadvantages of Central Heating" (*K*, 17), she remarks "the farmhouse long sold, old friends / dead or lost track of." Later in that volume, in her first great long poem, "A Procession at Candlemas" (22), Clampitt alludes to Native Americans as merely one of many migratory tribes:

> . . . The westward-trekking
> transhumance, once only, of a people who,
>
> in losing everything they had, lost even
> the names they went by, stumbling past
> like caribou, perhaps camped here.

Such renderings of loss, forgetting, unwrapping, returning, and unpeeling are the essential cause of all those accumulations—in imagery, metaphor, rhythm, and syntax—that annoy or fatigue Clampitt's thoughtless or lazy readers. She always puts the weight of her style at the service of diminishments. She is, in fact, as likely to dismiss as to welcome ornament for its own sake; she disdains the merely cute, once referring condescendingly to "Guido Reni, master / of those who prettify" ("The Nereids of Seriphos," *AF*, 219). Her true Americanness reveals itself in those moments when she adheres to a Yankee's, or a farmer's, sense of value: she loves "all that / utilitarian muck down underfoot" ("The Local Genius," *K*, 62), or objets trouvés that are dear for their fragility *and* their usefulness, like the straw racks in "Stacking the Straw" (*K*, 63) that exemplify the biblical ephemerality of all flesh. Yet these "beveled loaves" also amount to "the nearest thing the region had / to monumental sculpture." Like Whitman ("This Compost"), Stevens ("The Man on the Dump"), and A. R. Ammons (*Garbage*), she bears witness to the beauty of accumulated masses of compost, as in "The Reedbeds of the

Hackensack" (*WTLWL*, 165), a bravura sestina (itself a classic form of recycling) with overtones of "Lycidas," in which she meditates on "a poetry of the incorrigibly ugly." Or she contemplates "the pleasures of the ruined" in "Salvage" (*K*, 36):

> I find esthetic
> satisfaction in these
> ceremonial removals
>
> from the category of
> received ideas
> to regions where pigeons'
> svelte smoke-velvet
> limousine, taxiing
>
> in whirligigs, reclaim
> a parking lot.

She abhors wastefulness, admiring the Darwinian elegance of destruction on the Serengeti plains, where first lions, then "down-ruffed vultures," then "feasting maggots / hone the flayed wildebeest's ribcage / clean as a crucifix" ("Good Friday," *K*, 68). On such natural selection does Clampitt build her own idiosyncratic theology.

One typical misunderstanding of ornament resents it for manufacturing false, unwarranted Sturm und Drang and for confusing mere excess with depth. In fact, Clampitt proves everywhere that "depth is not everything," as she aphoristically announces in "The Spruce Has No Taproot" (*WTLWL*, 117). We can take this arboreal example as one of Clampitt's own talismans: like all the weeds, seedlings, easily displaced persons, tribes, and species with which she identifies, it roots itself shallowly in order to adapt and to form a subtle community:

>                . . . the spruce
> has no taproot, but to hold on
> spreads its underpinnings thin—
>
> a gathering in one continuous,
> meshing intimacy, the interlace
> of unrelated fibers
> joining hands like last survivors
> who, though not even neighbors
>
> hitherto, know in their predicament
> security at best is shallow.

Such shallowness makes freedom the reward for truancy. Thus, the "poke-weed, sprung from seed / dropped by some vagrant" ("Vacant Lot with Poke-weed," *W*, 329), which seizes a temporary foothold; or, in the same group, a set of bamboo curtains, "going up where / the waterstained old ones had been, and where the seedlings— / O gray veils, gray veils—had risen and gone down," in the apartment of a Greenwich Village eccentric ("A Hedge of Rubber Trees," 335). "Nothing stays put," she announces in a poem of that title in this series that celebrates as well as laments eternal impermanence: "All that we know, that we're / made of, is motion" (339). No contemporary poet except Ammons has such a grasp on the fact, dangerous and attractive at once, of entropy as a force operating microscopically, historically, and cosmically.

Motion has political, as well as psychological, causes and effects. Clampitt cites the words of an Omaha Indian in her signature piece "The Prairie" (*W*, 346):

> *The white man does not understand America,*
> a red man wrote: *the roots of the tree of his life*
> *have yet to grasp it.*

Above all, the essence of such motion has, as it must for a poet who habitually seeks the proper form for her vision, syntactic consequences, as I discuss in greater detail in the second half of this chapter. The "inter-lace" of her spruce tree is also the right word to apply to the mesh-ings by which Clampitt, here and elsewhere, duplicates and represents those other familial, cultural, and historical reticulations, the elaborately constructed networks that enable our individual lives to flourish. Where uprooting and exile, even when temporarily denied or held at bay, pose a constant threat, the only home a poet may finally claim is a strongly built, involved, poetic structure. (A bit less compulsively than Merrill and the younger contemporary poet Mark Doty, Clampitt has a fond-ness for little stanzaic "rooms" that offer one kind of refuge. Stanzas are like description and memory themselves: efforts to separate as well as to combine the various strands of that multicolored fabric we call life.)[6] The early poem "Black Buttercups" (*WTLWL*, 125) makes the best case for the wariness Clampitt learned as a child in the face of unhousing and exile. Although she never suffered, as Merrill did, from a "broken home" (i.e., from divorce), she lost her Edenic farmstead during, but not as a result of, the Depression, when she was ten and her family moved to a different homestead several miles away. Exile and menace were the lot of her ancestors, always on the go. Even the original farmstead gave onto a symbol of final menace:

> ... the terrain began to drop (the creek
> down there had for a while powered a sawmill,
> but now ran free, unencumbered, useless)—
> that not-to-be-avoided plot whose honed stones'
> fixed stare, fanned in the night
> by passing headlights, struck back
> the rueful semaphore:
> *There is no safety.*
> (125)

Like Hopkins, Frost, and Heaney, other masters of rural pleasure and rural coldness, Clampitt knows how to brace her Latinate syntax and vocabulary with a harsh, grim monosyllabic string ("plot whose honed stones' / fixed stare, fanned in the night") for a maximally chilling effect.

Once a reader looks closely at the relationship between levels of diction or at kinds of syntax, he or she necessarily becomes aware of the consequences of Clampitt's stylistic choices. Her so-called literariness unites the political and aesthetic dimensions of her poetry: it proves that words, phrases, and even allusions are, like human beings, intricately enmeshed in greater units. Any reader, especially a younger one, who has not been trained in either Milton or (especially) in Latin, will have difficulty following the syntax of even a short poem such as "Witness" (*WTLWL*, 128), a single-sentence bus ride poem (discussed below); or understand the use of "depends from" in its literal sense of "hanging" ("Savannah," *W*, 318); or be sensitive to the combination of the laconic and the ascetic with the extensive and the embellished at the end of "Thermopylae" (*AF*, 205):

> ... we ponder a funneled-down inscription: Tell
> them for whom we came to kill and were killed, stranger,
>
> how brute beauty, valor, act, air, pride, plume here
> buckling, guttered: closed in from behind, our spears
> smashed, as, the last defenders of the pass, we fell,
> we charged like tusked brutes and gnawed like bears.

It is daring enough to make the grim epitaph of Leonidas segue into the thrilling nouns of Hopkins's "The Windhover," but to move his falcon's "buckle" into the Spartans' "buckling, guttered," and to urge a reminder of beauty's brutality in the "tusked brutes" of carnage makes an even grander— and more resourceful—literary leap. And who else these days employs the ablative absolute, Clampitt's own learning having become a naturalized part of her, with as much ease as this "old-fashioned" poet? "Our spears smashed" pushes us back into high school memories not of Leonidas and his Spartans but of Caesar and Cicero.

Far from being a merely ornamental poet, in other words, Clampitt has the artistry necessary to weigh, sometimes precariously, the trivial against the extraordinary. When thinking of the inevitable brevity of human life, she readjusts her syntax by relying on appropriate phrases instead of clauses, as at the end of her homage, "Margaret Fuller, 1847" (*AF*, 233):

> ... What did she *do*?
> it would be asked (as though that mattered).
> Gave birth. Lived through a revolution.
> Nursed its wounded. Saw it run aground.
> Published a book or two.
> And drowned.

Verbs with only an implicit subject and a glaring rhyme ("aground . . . drowned") heighten the horror of Fuller's needless early death. Clampitt snips her normally lengthy sentences to match her heroine's brief, thin-spun life. She knows, as did Yeats, that sometimes "there's more enterprise in going naked" but only because she knows the feeling of going clothed.

It is no exaggeration to call her a religious poet, not just in her allegiance to a native Quaker spirit but also in her acknowledgment of many kinds of horror that threaten to undo the inner light and inner voice altogether except in rare moments of privilege, chance, or intuition. She cites ("The August Darks," *WTLWL*, 108) a phrase from George Eliot, another of her spiritual and cultural heroes, which probably represents her own belief better than any other passage alluded to by this most allusive of contemporary poets: "If we had a keen vision and feeling of all ordinary human life, it would be like hearing the grass grow and the squirrel's heart beat, and we should die of that roar which lies on the other side of silence" (*Middlemarch*, II, 20). Always aware of "the dolor of the particular" ("High Noon," *W*, 310), from which she never shies away, Clampitt is also a sufficiently political poet to know a fundamental truth about Eliot's "roar," which she announces matter-of-factly at the end of "The August Darks": "Many / have already died of it."

That Clampitt has restored ornament to poetry I take as a signal achievement, as I do her ambitious use of civilized scholarship, scientific learning, and bookish references. In the remainder of this chapter I want to look at the interplay between the two seemingly antithetical aspects of her poems: their Keatsian lusciousness and Quaker austerity. I do so by examining Clampitt's syntax in a genre she has made peculiarly her own, the one-sentence poem, of which she has probably written a larger number than any other contemporary poet who adheres to conventional punctuation and sentence formation.[7] Of the 193 poems in *The Collected Poems*, thirty-seven are one sentence long. In at least two others, one of which I discuss below, one extremely long sentence is followed by a clipped phrase (or short sentence) or two, and there are countless poems with several *very long* sentences in them, or several equal stanzas all composed of a single sentence. The whole issue becomes slightly more complicated when one takes into account the matter of punctuation. For example, "Or Consider Prometheus" (*K*, 89) consists of two poems, each of five quatrains. Each poem has two sentences, both questions, divided by a question mark and a capital letter to signify the beginning of sentence two. Elsewhere, the same rhetorical structure is divided not by full stops but by colons or semicolons. The choice of any punctuation is, of course, not logical or natural, but neither is it merely arbitrary or conventional. A reader with a feeling for Clampitt's syntax might *hear* each of these two poems as a single sentence composed of equal parts. Likewise, in "The Waterfall" (*AF*, 271), two initial, questioning sentences are succeeded by a longer declarative one that ends without firm closure ("everywhere, existences / hang by a hair"). Even the determination of a sentence is not so easy a thing as one might think.

The whole issue of sentence formation links Clampitt to Whitman, that other Quaker Romantic, whom she resembles in more than her tendency to fuse lushness with a stern moral vision and her American commitment to the didactic properties inherent in landscape. Like hers, Whitman's sentences have the tendency to welcome us and then set us loose us amid their elaborate extensions. From this grand seigneur of poems-as-lists, Clampitt has learned to construct an entire poem, or a large portion of one, by relying more heavily on nouns and nominal constructions than on predicates and verbal ones. Like him, she often resorts to a poetic structure in which apposition or anaphora, rather than subordination, predominates. The full effect of a sometimes exhaustive (or exhausting) encyclopedic listing depends to a large extent not only on the nature of its items, but also on its syntactic arrangements. Clampitt's syntax, far from existing as a mere self-indulgent display of intricacy, possesses a powerful dramatic force.

Few critics attend to syntax anymore.[8] Some years back, reviewing two other poets, Calvin Bedient made a brilliant obiter dictum when he called it "the field of verbal action whose limits are delay and delivery, opening up and closing up, blending and separating."[9] Even more than diction, referentiality, or what used to be called theme, syntax is the field in which Clampitt stakes her claims and makes her discoveries, while forcing her readers to make theirs. (As I suggested in the previous chapter, we must see through a poet's eyes and language; our work matches what Tomlinson calls the "labour of observation.") The drama of her syntax exposes and enacts that central pair of American obsessions, the need to stay put and the need to move on, one referred to obliquely (and in an English context) by the note appended to the one-sentence lyric, "Fireweed" (*W*, 325). Clampitt quotes from Donne's last sermon at St. Paul's: "Whatsoever moved Saint Jerome to call the journies of the Israelites, in the wilderness, Mansions, the word . . . signifies but a journey, but a peregrination. Even the Israel of God hath no mansions; but journies, pilgrimages in this life." The passage is attached to a poem that defines a fast-moving weed:

A single seedling, camp-follower
of arson—frothing bombed-out
rubble with rose-purple lotfuls

unwittingly as water overbrims,
tarn-dark or sun-ignited, down
churnmilk rockfalls—aspiring

from the foothold of a London
roof-ledge, taken wistful note of
by an uprooted prairie-dweller.

Clampitt locates the fireweed within the detritus of urban blight, planting it, so to speak, everywhere in her poem but really nowhere at all. The fireweed, like the prairie-born poet, is uprooted and easy to root at the same time. To understand the poem, we must supply an ontological "is," once or more often, throughout its course. Thus, "Fireweed [is] a single seedling"; it [is] "unwitting / of past devastation as of what / remains," and so forth. The poem is itself like a journey (a continuous act of definition) and also a mansion, or a cluster of single items (as if acknowledging the truth of Donne's "We'll build in sonnets pretty rooms"); the eponymous, ubiquitous plant appears, at least linguistically, in the seven tercets as an object of appositional phrasing, a sequence of present participles but with no main verb. Journeys and mansions, centrifugal and centripetal forces, exist in a delicate balance in Clampitt's ornate descriptions.

Why would a poet write a one-sentence poem, one that is longer than, for example, a sonnet? And what are the effects of such a choice? As I implied above, with regard to the very nature of sentence formation, a reader inevitably and automatically reduces a complex, lengthy unit into shorter experiential ones in order to take it all in. Among Clampitt's one-sentence poems, two kinds immediately call attention to themselves. The first of these is visually conspicuous: the unpunctuated poem or the poem arranged with spatial designs on the page, such as "Easter Morning" (*K*, 70), which omits capital letters and a period; or "Let the Air Circulate" (*WTLWL*, 191), which lacks a real beginning and ending, but which imagines spaces of and within the air as blanks within its own typographical structure.

Another sort of one-sentence poem may be defined not by physical appearance but by subject. It is what we might call Clampitt's homage to Elizabeth Bishop: poems (like Bishop's "The Moose," whose first sentence is thirty-six lines long) about journeys, in which a long stringing-together of phrases and clauses replicates the poet's trip through a various landscape. We can locate the origin of these poems-of-process not only in Bishop but also in Clampitt's imitation of the Romantic poets in general, and Keats in particular. Examples include "Witness" (*WTLWL*, 128), in which the mind, mirroring the landscape, actually tells the landscape how it looks, as the landscape itself becomes an abstraction; or "Dallas–Fort Worth: Redbud and Mistletoe," "Iola, Kansas," and "The Subway Singer" (*W*, 286, 291, 330), the first a rendition of an airplane descent, the second of a bus ride, the third of a moving subway train. In the second and third Clampitt develops her version of the sense of community that Bishop's passengers acquire on their long divagation from Nova Scotia to Boston when stopped and confronted by that famous towering, antlerless, female moose. Like a bus or subway compartment, a sentence contains its own community, of phrases, clauses, parts of speech instead of people, although (as I explain below) this meeting place can harbor either equals or a variety of members some of whom are subordinate to others. The idea of a sentence as a community corresponds to the twin aspects of Clampitt's character and style. As a Romantic she responds to hierarchy and to highlights, whereas the Quaker in her notices the inner light shining equally through various parts of a sentence, as through a human populace.

Our most famous poet-orphan, Bishop was always deeply skeptical of happiness and wisdom in equal measure. "Iola, Kansas" is an implicit homage to the Bishop of such poems as "Arrival at Santos" and "Cape Breton," in addition to "The Moose," which square the fear of the unknown with the thrill of (even touristic) adventure, and which ask us to measure the satisfactions of a seldom achieved community of feeling against the relative unlikelihood that we should ever experience, let alone deserve, happiness, pleasure, and personal identity even for an instant.

This one-sentence tour de force, reporting an all-night bus ride through the heart of the country, actually begins by echoing "Arrival at Santos," which ends with an ominous flat statement ("We are driving to the inte-

WHAT TO MAKE OF AN AUGMENTED THING

rior") after thirty-seven lines of wittily observed details. Clampitt's journey
is more industrialized, more noun-heavy:

> Riding all night, the bus half empty, toward the interior,
> among refineries, trellised and turreted illusory cities,
> the crass, the indispensable wastefulness of oil rigs
> offshore, of homunculi swigging at the gut of a continent.
> (291)

As the bus proceeds from Texas through Oklahoma and into Kansas, it
pauses at a rest stop in the godforsaken town of the title, where the narrator, "with something akin to reverence," eats a piece of simple home-baked
boysenberry pie before piling back onto the bus with her fellow travelers:

>                   ... then back to our seats,
> the loud suction of air brakes like a thing alive, and
> the voices, the sleeping assembly raised, as by an agency
>
> out of the mystery of the interior, to a community—
> and through some duct in the rock I feel my heart go out,
> out here in the middle of nowhere (the scheme is a mess)
> to the waste, to the not knowing who or why, and am happy.

Like the bus riders in "The Moose," stopped by a giant creature in the
middle of the road and then united by a "sweet / sensation of joy" before
resuming their journey,[10] Clampitt and her companions join together in one
of those rare moments of what we can only call grace. Spiritual longing
and an awareness of "the strangeness of all there is" inspire her, in spite of
her religious, political, and emotional wariness, to be ready to relish such
moments when they do come. Rejoicing often takes place in a context of
sharing—that is, within a community of other people whose very presence
assures greater pleasure—and it takes place as well in the syntactic equivalent of community: a long sentence.

"Witness" (the very title has religious as well as spectatorial overtones)
exemplifies the difficulty of understanding punctuation and its symbolic
effects in Clampitt's work. Typically we might assume that a colon suggests
both identity (of the elements on either side of it) and linear progression.
(Ammons comes immediately to mind.) This poem, however, is somewhat
more complicated. Its three parts, divided by colons, treat what the speaker
in her bus sees first within and then outside a small town.[11] In the third section she finally suggests what it all means. The three sections are "part of an
ordinary evening in Wisconsin," somehow equivalences of one another. But

the first two sections are more than merely balanced by the third; they are offset by it. Here are the two final parts:

> ... outside town
>
> the barns, their red gone dark with sundown,
> withhold the shudder of a warped terrain—
> the castle rocks above, tree-clogged ravines
> already submarine with nightfall, flocks
>
> (like dark sheep) of toehold junipers,
> the lucent arms of birches : purity
> without a mirror, other than a mind bound
> elsewhere, to tell it how it looks.
> (128)

Everything in the first two parts of the poem comes to this: that single details add up to an abstraction ("purity"). The second colon stands at the precise midpoint between what precedes and what follows it. At the same time, the three parts of the poem are distinct, and nothing derives from or mirrors anything else, except the mind moving elsewhere, which reflects (in two senses) and "tells." In the world of these poems, things often seem disjointed, superfluous, offhand, because randomly noticed or fitfully connected, as by the metaphorical associations of ravines with water ("submarine"), junipers with sheep, and birches with human "arms."

The more difficult of the single-sentence poems can be defined rhetorically rather than thematically: they rely on the triple modes of apposition, enumeration, and subordination to bolster their observations. The first two are overlapping but different. As a trope of definition, apposition moves by discerning deeper versions of the same thing. Its form is: X is equally A, which resembles B, which reminds me of C, and so on. Enumeration, the trope of democratic equality, makes Whitmanian lists of separate items. The whole is the sum of its parts. Or it may work paradoxically by accretion and subtraction simultaneously. Clampitt herself in an early one-sentence poem ("On the Disadvantages of Central Heating," *K*, 17)—all phrasal, and with no capital letters—refers to "the perishing residue of pure sensation," a residue clarified at last by a verb that supplies a definition: "what's salvaged is this vivid diminuendo." A list poem works by accumulation. "On the Disadavantages of Central Heating" (the title suggests the list that follows) works at the same time to reduce its enumerated objects to a stripped-down version of reality, as many of its details refer to a past now "quite forgotten" or "lost track of." As forms of listing, apposition and enumeration constitute what we might label Clampitt's poetry of sensation, whereas subordination, a sentence composed of dependent and interrelated parts, produces her poetry of thought, to revert to Keats's famous distinction.

Clampitt relies on apposition as invocation (in "Athena," *AF*, 216) or on enumeration in the form of a list ("Kudzu Dormant," *W*, 283) to suggest spiritual equality. This reliance may explain why so many of her poems lack simple independent verbs, developing instead through a gathering of nouns, noun phrases, objets trouvés, and their equivalents. Like Bishop, whose astute line "Everything only connected by 'and' and 'and'" ("Over 2,000 Illustrations and a Complete Concordance"), could stand as her own borrowed motto, Clampitt often culminates her lists by articulating gratitude for simple gifts and truths. Romantic and baroque effects, rich imagery and syntactic complications (especially in the heavily subordinating poems that I discuss below) are reduced, distilled to revelation.

A typical appositive poem is "Marine Surface, Low Overcast" (*K*, 13–14). Its seven seven-line stanzas risk losing the reader in a nonstop welter of revisions, some merely a phrase, others more elaborate. The opening demands an elliptical verb:

> Out of churned aureoles
> [comes?] this buttermilk, this
> herringbone of albatross,
> floss of mercury,
> déshabille of spun
> aluminum, furred with a velouté
> of looking-glass.

All the images are equivalent ways of troping a specific scene. It is as though Clampitt has taken Stevens's "Thirteen Ways of Looking at a Blackbird," eliminated the numbers for the separate sections, and run together all of her figurations. The first three stanzas proceed with such metaphoric elaborations, and in the fourth the poem expands in two different ways:

> laminae of living tissue,
> mysteries of flex,
> affinities of texture,
> subtleties of touch, of pressure
> and release, the suppleness
> of long and intimate
> association.

Clampitt continues with her X of Y constructions, but these are now largely plural rather than singular, and they grow from sensuous specificity to a level of abstraction. By the end of the fifth stanza, the poem's first stanzaic enjambment spills us over into the sixth, impulsively heightening a steady progress. And between stanzas 6 and 7 an even more dramatic syntactic breach appears, to move the poem, at last, out of apposition and into the realm of an implicit subordination. I quote from the start of the poem's last concerted image:

> cathedral domes that seem to hover
> overturned and shaken like a basin
> to the noise of voices,
> from a rustle to the jostle
> of such rush-hour
> conglomerations
>
> no loom, no spinneret, nor forge, no factor,
> no process whatsoever, patent
> applied or not applied for,
> no five-year formula, no fabric
> for which pure imagining,
> except thus prompted,
> can invent the equal.

For all the talk of Clampitt's sensuousness (here evident in the accumulation of details, the reliance on Keatsian double-barreled adjectives, the insistent rhymes and half-rhymes), there is something ascetic about the end of the poem. Like Merrill, Clampitt sometimes omits relative pronouns or conjunctions, thereby forcing us to make sense of the missed connections above: "of such conglomerations [that there is] no loom [etc.] for which pure imagining . . . can invent the equal." Whatever else one wishes to say about the experimental nature of this sort of poem of definition, it is clear that Clampitt expects the structure of her sentence, as well as the substance of her images and the truthfulness of her thoughts, to carry the weight of the discovery she challenges us to make with her. From single noun phrases, through extended varieties of plurals and abstractions, to a more elaborate syntactic construction, this poem deepens, becoming more mysterious than any simple experiment in Imagism or list making. Having made a foray into the fog, she comes to realize the partiality of all attempts of "pure" or even impure imagining. Her poem's breathless, strung-together quality has its own expansiveness.[12]

The second type of single-sentence poems, poems of enumeration, also pays implicit homage to Bishop's and Whitman's habitual polysyndeton and anaphora, although Clampitt works less obviously, and more deviously, in her accumulations. An early enumerative poem, "Meridian" (*K*, 18), reflects the complexities of punctuation and verblessness and the duplicity of equality and process that I mentioned above. Here it is complete:

> First daylight on the bittersweet-hung
> sleeping porch at high summer : dew
> all over the lawn, sowing diamond-
> point-highlighted shadows :
> the hired man's shadow revolving
> along the walk, a flash of milkpails
> passing : no threat in sight, no hint
> anywhere in the universe, of that
>
> apathy at the meridian, the noon
> of absolute boredom : flies
> crooning black lullabies in the kitchen,
> milk-soured crocks, cream separator
> still unwashed : what is there to life
> but chores and more chores, dishwater,
> fatigue, unwanted children : nothing
> to stir the longueur of afternoon
>
> except possibly thunderheads :
> climbing, livid, turreted alabaster
> lit up from within by splendor and terror
> —forked lightning's
>                 split-second disaster.

Here enumeration is equivalent to process. Although such process often
involves physical travel, it need not. (In fact, the most beautiful of these
process poems is the one-sentence "A Winter Burial" [*W*, 315], which
chillingly charts birth, growth, death, and burial in twenty-seven haunting lines.) It is tempting to call "Meridian" a description of a summer's
day, moving as it does from early morning through noon to late afternoon,
but it really has the quality of a conjuror's trick. The title announces a
potential climax, but this is undermined by the real negation at the poem's
heart—"*no* threat in sight"—which might very well mean that noon and
then afternoon never really arrive in the poem but are merely inferred
by the poet's reflecting mind that fills in absences. In other words, the
poem seems to march through the day, but it also potentially never really
gets beyond the morning, in spite of its title. There is a hanging back
in all those hung phrases: When does "the noon of absolute boredom"
*occur* as something other than a part of an unclear deictic sequence ("*that*
apathy")? As often happens in her work, Clampitt's natural timidity or

reluctance to specify (in this case, the precise time at which noon strikes, or fails to, in the poem's time scheme) coincides with her richly inventive descriptions. A haunting absence permeates the accumulations of the sentence-as-list.

Where "Meridian" represents the peculiar poise of absence and presence in a natural process, "A Baroque Sunburst" (*WTLWL*, 107) plays with participles to skew our sense of action. Verbs, minimal in some of Clampitt's poems, are here of the essence. The title moves uninterruptedly into the first line:

> struck through such a dome
> as might await a groaning Michelangelo,
> finding only alders and barnacles
> and herring gulls at their usual squabbles,
> sheds on the cove's voluted
> silver the aloof skin tones
> of a Crivelli angel.

What initially appears to be a simple preterite ("struck") turns out to be a past participle ("[having] struck through such a dome") that leads through an intervening present participle ("finding") to the simple, present-tense "sheds": Clampitt's ingeniously deceptive verbal sequence replicates a natural temporal process.

Clampitt wants us to see things *as* process: it's the old light-as-wave-*and*-particle syndrome. Like any work of literature, an Amy Clampitt poem progresses through time; additionally, it often treats time as a subject composed of stark, successive, and often nominal moments. Abidance and movement go hand in hand. In this matter, Clampitt's syntax becomes, along with the luxuriousness of her sounds and images praised by partisans and condemned by critics, her sharpest tool, especially in the more complicated poems, which weave their way in and out of a final shape. Just as "Meridian" presented and also withheld the climax of noon, so "Man Feeding Pigeons" (*AF*, 263) gives (but more complexly) with one hand and takes away with the other. A twenty-one-line description devolves from an opening generalization: "It was the form of the thing, the unmanaged / symmetry of it." The configuration of pigeons feeding in a circle reminds the poet of angels in a Ravenna mosaic, of colorful, sculpted, Della Robbia fruit, of a "dance of freewheeling dervishes." After a colon the poem resumes but with a qualification: "it was the form / of the thing, if a thing is what it was, / and not the merest wisp of a part of / a process." And what we might have initially mistaken for artifacts, however rapidly transformed and transforming they are, are now reimagined not only as an unending sequence of events but also as a symbolic representation of spiritual conditions unrealizable except through bodily states:

> —this unraveling inkling
> of the envisioned, of states of being
>
> past alteration, of all that we've
> never quite imagined except by way of
> the body: the winged proclamations,
> the wheelings, the stairways, the
> vast, concentric, paradisal rose.

Clampitt maneuvers the colon more conventionally here. It does not sit naked, dangerously poised between two equal spaces, but snug against the word it follows and opening into that which follows it after a polite, normal break. And she makes ingenious use of her participles, present as well as past, and gerunds (with the implicit uncertainty of "being," both participle *and* gerund) to present movement without time. These pseudo-verbal words impel us into heavenly realms, those "states of being" in which we become *beings*, beyond alteration ourselves, and resembling the figures from the paradisal inner circle, "a l'alta fantasia qui mancò possa," as Dante has it at the end of the *Commedia*.

"Man Feeding Pigeons" embodies what Stephen Cushman has described as the truth-giving fiction of any poem's form.[13] We witness two takes on the same phenomenon, as though the poet wants us to feel the relative value of both but finally the superiority of the latter, in which process and spirituality transcend but simultaneously depend on, quite literally, "the form of things." Like the spirals of incoming and outgoing casual flocks of pigeons making their ambiguous undulations, Clampitt's sentence pushes us in and speeds us out. Centripetal and centrifugal motions suggest mansions and then journeys to our true, spiritual home.

Justifying his own overfondness for parentheses, Coleridge once referred in a letter to the "drama of reason" contained in a style that could "present the thought growing, instead of a mere Hortus siccus."[14] What parentheses enabled him to do, syntactic ramification does for Clampitt. Syntax (and not just in a single-sentence poem) serves a dramatic, indeed a mimetic function. For this reason, a complex poem like "The August Darks" (*WTLWL*, 108) deserves to be included among any list of Clampitt's one-sentence works. Thirty-four lines, one sentence, move to a conclusion, following which a six-word declarative sentence makes a chilling coda, climaxing and undermining the sinuous description of herring boats that set out in darkness before daylight appears.

Although I have called the bulk of this poem a sentence, it is not. Once again, Clampitt relies on the fiction of a completed utterance, but the combination of apposition, enumeration, and subordination weaves her readers through the strung-out phrasing and never leaves them in possession of anything more than glittering parts. Like Keats's "To Autumn," the most prominent Romantic poem with a grammatical sleight of hand (the invocation of the first stanza comes to an ending that is incomplete, and that must be enjambed, over a terminal period, into the second stanza: "Season of mists and mellow fruitfulness . . . Who hath not seen thee oft amid thy store?"), Clampitt's poetry of misconceived termination carries us along until we either forget our grammatical progress or mistakenly think that we have encompassed a series of discrete clauses.

Like those other poems that take as their subject almost imperceptible temporal change, "The August Darks" works by slowly transforming its scope and focus. It does so by eliminating natural connectives—not just explicit verbs but also prepositions or conjunctions that might put things in perspective for us—and by replacing them with metaphors, which subtly shift attention from one item in a sequence to the next. Here are the first six lines:

> Stealth of the flood tide, the moon dark
> but still at work, the herring shoals
> somewhere offshore, looked for
> but not infallible, as the tide is,
> as the August darks are—
>
> stealth of the seep of daylight.
> (108)

Even before stanza 2 essentially restarts it, we are aware that the poem hangs on missing statements. We must translate in order to fill the lacunae. Thus:

> Here we have the stealth of the flood tide, in which the moon is
> dark but still at work, and the herring shoals, even when looked for,
> can't be found because they and we are not infallible, whereas the
> tide and the darks are always infallible. And at the same moment
> that the flood tide and darkness are stealthy, the light is with equal
> stealth seeping into the scene.

In this depiction of first light, Clampitt's figuration complements her syntax. Just as the scene and the syntax move imperceptibly from darkness to daybreak, a central metaphor invades the poem, leaving us uncertain as to what represents what, or, in an older critical vocabulary, what term is tenor and what vehicle. The first fishing boat, ahead of the light, slips out

> into the opening aorta, that heaving
> reckoning whose flux informs the heart-
> beat of the fisherman—poor,
> dark, fallible-infallible
> handful of a marvel
>
> murmuring unasked inside the ribcage,
> workplace covert as the August darks are,
> as is the moon's work, masked within
> the blazing atrium of daylight,
> the margin of its dwindling
>
> sanguine as with labor, but effortless.

"Aorta" initially looks like a rhetorical catachresis, a term misapplied, borrowed, or wrested from one thing to give a name to something else that lacks its own, but it then merges with the actual vascular system within the fisherman ("informing" it in several senses): the invisible circulation of the blood in the ribcage parallels the external marine scene and the darkness of the moon, which is replaced by daylight in the shape of the sun, itself a bloody ("sanguine") ornament rising in the skies. Clampitt seems to have absorbed those poems of Shelley ("To a Skylark," "The Sensitive Plant") that revolve around the figure of a known but invisible lunar presence, dimmed by the sun's light. The application of "fallible-infallible" to the human heart recalls, of course, the opening of the poem and mimics the systole-diastole sequence of a heartbeat.

The paradox of an "effortless labor," as well as the vast hematological circulatory system within and between external and internal spaces, prepares us for the poem's conclusion, after an intervening description of a cruise ship on the horizon, on which a performance of *Swan Lake* might be taking place:

> . . . the heartbeat's prodigies of strain
> unseen, the tendons' ache, the blood-
> stained toe shoes, the tulle
> sweat-stained, contained
>
> out where the herring wait, beyond
> the surf-roar on the other side of silence
> we should die of (George Eliot
> declared) were we to hear it.

From the aorta of the ocean, to the fisherman's ribcage, to a stage set for dancers with bloodied feet, Clampitt ends her poem with the herring shoals with which it began, bringing it home and moving it out, by reminding us of the revelations available through what Eliot termed "a keen vision and feeling of all ordinary human life." This poem, whose theme is imperceptible borders (between darkness and light, outside and inside, work and pleasure, silence and sound), tests our sense of borders by its leisurely pacing. The interlacing of image, diction, and syntax buoys and propels the poem until it reaches its philosophical conclusion.

As often happens in Clampitt's expanded poems, however, this one retreats at its end to a statement of a simple truth in the form of an anticlimactic, sotto voce aside that balances the preceding thirty-four lines: "Many / have already died of it." After the expansion comes the reining in; after the artful spinning out of detail comes the grim simplicity of a short declarative sentence. The rhythm of opening and closing belongs to rhetoric as well as to the human heart.

One other intricate poem deserves attention. Taking a stylistic cue from its subject, "The Olive Groves of Thasos" (*AF*, 198–199) depicts, in a deeply convoluted sentence, a gnarled, entwined landscape. It, too, is both a poem of process (the harvesting of the olive crop) and a stationing, an attempt to convert a scene into an object, constantly transforming itself before our eyes. Syntax here dramatically replicates the shape of the trees and the depth of the landscape. An ongoing process of subordination submerges us so deeply in a sentence that we never quite know where we are until, at line 21, a human action begins. A human action but, as so often in Clampitt, one without a main verb: this sentence, too, has turned out to be a fragment. Beginning with a participle in line 1 ("Thronging the warped treadmill / of antiquity"), twenty lines of apposition and enumeration capture the image of the trees, "these wards of turbulence" in their "burled stupor." A procession of harvesters appears, but in a subordinate clause so far removed from the poem's opening that we have forgotten that there has been no independent one:

> when from the villages along
> the shore, where in the evenings
> we watched the fishing
> boats go out in strings
>
> of three, in trinities.
> (ll. 21–25)

From line 21 to line 46, Clampitt begins to notice the termini a quo ("villages," "hill villages," "middle villages") from which, we are relieved to learn (line 46), "the whole populace / turns out, with tarpaulins and / poles, to bring in the harvest / of these trees." And the poem ends, rounding to its beginning (as M. H. Abrams once defined the Romantic nature lyric),[15] with a series of appositives concerning the trees, but now also with a backward glance at the previous human element in the poem:

> ... this time-gnarled
> community of elders—so many-
> shaped, so warped, so densely
> frugal, so graceful a company,
>
> what more can we say, we who have
> seen the summer boats go out,
> tasted the dark honey, and savored
> the oil-steeped, black, half-bitter fruit?

In these lines that sound like a coda the humanized trees remain the genuine, permanent figures of wisdom and authority, whereas people, whether native workers or American tourists, are merely transient passers-by. Just as the poem began with the trees, so it ends with their fruit.

Clampitt seldom uses a sequence of verbs coming fast upon one another ("say," "seen," "tasted," "savored"), nor does she routinely put questions in terminal positions. I take the last line as an homage to those precursor poems that end inquisitively ("Ode to a Nightingale," "Mont Blanc," "Ode to the West Wind," inter alia). "Frugal" might not be among the first adjectives one would apply to Clampitt's art, but at this point the relatively simple syntax, the clarity of construction, and the modest evasion of moralizing ("what more can we say?") conclude the poem economically as well as gracefully. These gestures have an effect comparable to that of the short declarative sentence at the end of "The August Darks," or the abstraction of "Man Feeding Pigeons," or the clarified residue of "On the Disadvantages of Central Heating." And one might also infer that, just as there is no legitimate independent clause in this sprawling one-sentence poem, neither is there any genuine "independent" universe, scene, community, or observation that is not organically, logically, or even partially dependent for its existence on a larger commonwealth of relationships. The deep truth at the heart of all of Clampitt's poetry is her updating of Coleridge's "one life within us and abroad."

Far from spinning webs or wheels for gratuitous ornamental effect, Clampitt writes poems whose seeming overrichness challenges us to perform readerly gymnastics. If at times the exercise confuses and troubles, or threatens to lose us amid a tangle of verbal underbrush (with remembered terrors of reading Cicero in high school Latin class, or of our first forays into *Paradise Lost*), we must remind ourselves that more than any other contemporary poet—more than Merrill with his quicksilver delicacy, or Ashbery with his perplexingly seamless transitions from one register of diction to another—Clampitt *uses* her syntax to represent the entire spectrum of processes that engage us to and in the world.

Throughout her work Clampitt masterfully mingles the elegiac and the celebratory, the laconic and the baroque, the clipped and the extensive. Readers who prefer an emaciated, dour, or pared-down poetry will inevitably be put off by an initial reading. But Swinburne on acid? Tennyson gone mad with a thesaurus? Self-indulgent gush? Not at all. They should try again. Clampitt's finely honed "style," whatever that elusive term comes to mean, must ultimately be understood as her adjustment of technique to purpose. Her sensuous, deliciously embellished renditions of the natural, the artistic, and the human worlds come in many states of dress and undress. Her poetry gives more than decorative pleasures. It proves—now, when ornament seems to require a new defense against the onslaught of those who prefer their Poetry Lite—that we can applaud richness without embarrassment.

Such applause should ring more loudly because of Clampitt's turn away from syntax, indeed from language, from all sound but music, at the end. Her last volume, *A Silence Opens*, appeared just after her death in 1994. She knew she was dying as she composed much of it. For that reason as well as others, the book celebrates silence, paucity, lacunae, and diminishments as her earlier ones sometimes giddily celebrate accumulation and richness. Its opening and closing poems listen to the complexities of silence, before and after language adds meaning. "Syrinx" (363), neither Pan's nymph nor his pipe but "the reed / in the throat of a bird," reminds us that significance is really an inconsequential, fortuitous part of sound, and that "syntax comes last." This "higher form of expression . . . is, in extremity, first to / be jettisoned." Sheer breath comes first, and is last to go. At the end, the poet of vast hypotactic syntax makes a symbolic gesture. "A Silence" (432–433) abjures punctuation and, for the most part, capital letters and sentence structure. Clampitt writes with a refined wildness, delaying a main verb until the end of twenty lines of phrasal units that locate the place "past parentage or gender / beyond sung vocables" at which "a silence opens." Grace, nirvana, syncope, call it what you will: the complex religious impulse that drives poets, saints, and mountebanks alike inspires one's best efforts to define it but always at last thwarts them. The poem leaves us hanging:

a cavernous
compunction driving
founder-charlatans
who saw in it
the infinite
love of God
and had
(George Fox
was one)
great openings

*The Collected Poems* closes with this opening. The rest, of course, is silence. Such a final utterance testifies, in the religious as well as the secular sense, to Clampitt's place in American poetry. Earlier I called her an heir to Whitman. It is equally clear that her quirky, absolutely heterodox piety puts her in league with Emily Dickinson, a more austere eccentric, whose "breathless, hushed excess . . . stopped prodigies, compressions and / devastations within the atom" ("Amherst," *W*, 319) Clampitt has studied, absorbed, and reinvented, although she never resorts to Dickinson's primly syncopated versions of hymn meter. To have combined so dramatically the models of our national poetic forebears gives Clampitt another claim on our attention: she has secured a place for herself in our literary history that is, quite simply, unlike that of any other contemporary.

FOUR

# CHARLES WRIGHT AND "THE METAPHYSICS OF THE QUOTIDIAN"

. . . being unable to find peace within myself, I made use of the external surroundings to calm my spirit, and being unable to find delight within my heart, I borrowed a landscape to please it.
—T'u Lung (T'u Ch'ihshui)

The creative impulse always arises from an aching inner void, a longing for completion that only art can provide. Thus Wallace Stevens: "And not to have is the beginning of desire" ("Notes Toward a Supreme Fiction").[1] We speak of expression and fulfillment as equivalent terms even though they are linguistically opposed to each other, one an outpouring and the other an influx. But the first can produce the second and consequently stand in its place: we fulfill ourselves by self-expression. Likewise, the aesthetic and the erotic are at least in part overlapping, and sometimes virtually synonymous. From the story told by Aristophanes in Plato's *Symposium* down to Jacques Lacan's psychoanalytic theory, most Western mythographers have based their versions of Eros on some dream of finding, in a sensuous or aesthetic quest, one's better half, the "partner in your sorrow's mysteries" (Keats, "Ode on Melancholy"). In Shelley's neo-Platonic allegory "The Sensitive Plant," the titular figure "desires what it has not—the Beautiful." It is no wonder that this central "character" has often been taken as an allegorical representation of any aspiring artist, of, for example, Shelley himself.

The place of "landscape," the natural world, in such quests has usually been as a backdrop for, an external projection or a representation of the human drama played out upon or against its stage. In Charles Wright's work we find something peculiar if not unique in contemporary poetry: the use of landscape as a virtual replacement for sexuality. For all his sensuousness, he is not an erotic poet. His work is essentially neither allegorical nor symbolic, nor is it merely reportorial and empirical. It is a poetry of longing, but this longing is not directed at erotic fulfillment, social or familial coherence, or ecological sanity. The landscape, everything that comes into our view, serves different purposes for Wright from what it does for the other poets in this book. It is the only possible access to spiritual wholeness, but it offers no guarantee of anything. For Wright, the world is implicitly *not* everything that is the case, but it is all that we can be sure of. If there were a word for a style that takes the natural world as its subject without hankering after physical fulfillment, that combines lushness with austerity, visible bounty with spiritual doubt, and that proceeds by way of anecdotes that still manage to obscure important people, things, and events in the poet's present adult life, such as his wife and son, that word would be Wrighteous.[2]

In the great title poem of her 1965 *Questions of Travel*, Elizabeth Bishop wonders: "*could Pascal have been not entirely right / about just sitting quietly in one's room?*" Like traveling, through which we expect to look closely and eagerly at foreign landscapes, just examining the more domestic details of nature in one's backyard can stem from a comparably inarticulable dread, failure, or void within one's heart. The excerpt from T'u Lung above, placed carefully at the end of *China Trace*, qualifies as a legitimate epigraph to all of Charles Wright's work. Borrowing a landscape means trying to please the spirit. Other people seek and find such pleasure in the consolations of religion. Wright, too much a skeptic to believe in the Episcopalian faith of his childhood, is held too much in its sway to let it go.[3] Just as his idiosyncratic style conceals his personality and many of the details of his lived life, so his lush cravings for the spirit indwelling within the physical never point toward a doctrinal God. All is aspiration; fulfillment comes only in partial glimmers. As he said in an interview: "Roethke wrote that all finite things reveal infinitude. What we have, and all we will have, is here in the earthly paradise. . . . I'd say that to love the visible things in the visible world is to love their apokatastatic outlines in the invisible next."[4]

"Apokatastatic" comes from a man who is not afraid of abstruse, technical terms (here, the Greek word for renovation or restoration), but whose diction by and large does without such theological words, and also without the scientific terminology used by such other ardent poetic observers as A. R. Ammons, Alice Fulton, and Richard Kenney. It swerves away from the overly scintillating linguistic gestures and baroque, sinuous syntax of Amy Clampitt and James Merrill. Wright's poems often filter the lushness of Hopkins through the incomplete utterances—phrases rather than clauses—of Pound (who was Wright's first and greatest inspiration). Where John Ashbery moves in one continuous, seamless maneuver, often losing his reader in the delicate modulations of tone, gesture, scene, or subject, Wright, like Jorie Graham, seems to sputter his way hesitatingly, building a poem by accretion but with plenty of detours along the path. He has announced, "Parts are always more than the sum of their wholes" and "Poems should be written line by line, not idea by idea."[5] The second of these remarks is a variation on Mallarmé's famous advice to Degas (a poem is made not with ideas but with words), but the first virtually warns a reader not to expect a luminous, organic wholeness in Wright's poems. His negotiations with nature are unusual precisely because his poems do not progress solely along the lines of the Romantic nature lyric (written to the formula: "Here I am and this is what I see"), or those of the Whitmanian travelogue (such as the prototypical "There was a child went forth"), both of which accumulate details in order to portray a thinking or monarchic self. Nor do they sound, except occasionally, like delicate Imagist or Symbolist miniatures in which the observed data necessarily stand for an unspecified or unspecific numinous presence. Somehow Wright's poems partake of all these genres separately, or all at once, especially within the capacious boundaries of his recent "journal" works.

The most interesting treatment of Wright (as of Charles Tomlinson and Amy Clampitt, although not of Ashbery and Graham) would proceed synchronically rather than diachronically or historically. His stylistic and thematic development, though visible, is less important than the changes we might identify by examining the collected poetry as a single landscape (and attending to the landscapes *within* that landscape). Like all the other poets in this book, Wright has developed and maintained a poetic persona while often remaining unforthcoming about the merely personal details of his life. We can define him much more through his use of context, place, situation, anecdote, and natural description than through any even momentarily overt confessions. Framing himself within a recollected or perceived landscape, he enacts a pilgrimage toward self-portraiture (which means self-understanding) by painting himself *into* the landscape. In *The Southern Cross*, five poems entitled "Self-Portrait," along with "Portrait of the Artist with Hart Crane" and "Portrait of the Artist with Li Po," impart a vision of Wright, the man and the poet, just at the moment before he transforms his style from the stanzaic poems of the earlier volumes to the jagged, long-lined meditations of the journals. We observe, in other words, the poet on the verge of breakup, *sparagmos*, and poetic reconstitution.

The assembled self-portraits tremble on the margins of evanescence and disappearance. Written in the poet's midforties, the lyrics waver between past, present, and future time. The poet collects memories, stations himself in moments of contemplation, and prepares for his future dispersal and possible restoration by natural or human forces. Of these five portraits, the first is by all standards the most conventional. Three five-line stanzas begin with a realization of discovery (By whom? For what? It is not at all certain) and death ("Someday they'll find me out, and my lavish hands"). The poem continues with an accommodation in the present ("Till then, I'll hum to myself and settle the whereabouts") and ends with an invocation (rarely used by Wright) for unspecified spiritual salvation ("Hand that lifted me once, lift me again").[6]

In the three stanzas of the second self-portrait (*World*, 13), the poet in the present moment is the *hardest* thing to see. He seems to bracket himself in the blank space between stanza 1, in which he remembers Italian nights, or relives them in memory, or regards a picture of himself on his wall; and stanza 2, in which he anticipates his posthumous condition:

Charles on the Trevisan, night bridge
To the crystal, infinite alphabet of his past.
Charles on the San Trovaso, earmarked,
Holding the pages of a thrown-away book, dinghy the color of
    honey
Under the pine boughs, the water east-flowing.

The wind will edit him soon enough,
And squander his broken chords
                      in tiny striations above the air,
No slatch in the undertow.
The sunlight will bear him out,
Giving him breathing room, and a place to lie.

As if to negotiate between a collectable past and a predictable future, the poem ends in the eternal present of description:

And why not? The reindeer still file through the bronchial trees,
Holding their heads high.
The mosses still turn, the broomstraws flash on and off.

Inside, in the crosslight, and St. Jerome
And his creatures . . . St. Augustine, striking the words out.

Supposedly significant details are blurred rather than clear. What are these
reindeer accompanied by saints? It took a letter to and a reply from the poet
to certify that they are in the form of postcards that hang above his desk,
one from Finland, two from Venice reproducing Carpaccio's pictures of the
Church fathers. As a self-portrait, this poem is curiously frustrating, not
only for its failures to explain, but also for its polite depiction of a third-
person "Charles" in stanza 1, a more distant "him" in stanza 2, and a total
removal of references to him in stanza 3. The poet is his book ("earmarked"
and soon to be edited) or postcards, as Wallace Stevens, the Ariel in "The
Planet on the Table," is the collected pages of his own world.

The desire to be delivered, whether by God, ancestors, progeny, readers, or unnamed spiritual forces that will shape his ends, is apparently the
initial and transcendental motive for Wright's self-portraits. These brief lyrics reproduce the substance and much of the technique of all his volumes
taken together. It is a sign of his reticence that the third self-portrait, a
consideration of old photographs, does not even mention the poet until its
third stanza, as if getting to him randomly in a list of other people. And
signficantly, too, the self-portrait disappears as the act of pointing moves on
to other objects. What comes to portray the self is names. Or photos, postcards, and mementos. By the fourth portrait (*World*, 19) Wright settles on a
technique that he uses almost exclusively in his later work and that marks his
legacy from Pound, whom he read passionately while serving in the Army
in Italy, near Verona:

Marostica, Val di Ser. Bassano del Grappa.
Madonna del Ortolo. San Giorgio, arc and stone.
The foothills above the Piave.

Places and things that caught my eye, Walt,
In Italy. On foot, Great Cataloguer, some twenty-odd years ago.

San Zeno and Caffè Dante. Catullus' seat.
Lake Garda. The Adige at Ponte Pietra
—I still walk there, a shimmer across the bridge on hot days.

Phrases instead of clauses, names instead of actions, places instead of people, moments instead of extended linear narratives: thus Wright begins to
locate himself amid flashes, collected and set aside like candid snapshots in
an album reopened by chance or choice years later, and by the very person
whose life they constitute. He has condensed both the Whitmanian cata-

logue and the giant Whitmanian ego. In such a portrait the first-person self makes the briefest appearance, quite literally centered through a recollection of a repeated action:

> —I still walk there, a shimmer across the bridge on hot days,
> The dust, for a little while, lying lightly along my sleeve—
> Piazza Erbe, the twelve Apostles.

And then it vanishes from the poem, which subsides into a one-sentence stanza containing a single last vignette, and then retreats into the randomness of naming:

> Over the grave of John Keats
> The winter night comes down, her black habit starless and edged
>    with ice,
> Pure breaths of those who are rising from the dead.

> Dino Campana, Arthur Rimbaud.
> Hart Crane and Emily Dickinson. The Black Château.

I take this self-portrait as emblematic of Wright's newer methods of painting a self into a poem by largely ignoring it, and by attending to everything that looks initially secondary, random, or of the background. For one thing, phrases lead up to sentences, and then succeed them, just as the lyric "I" embeds itself within a recollected landscape or a series of pen-and-ink sketches never fully colored in. And, more important, the stanza itself (a staple of Wright's poetry in *Country Music: Selected Early Poems*) has begun an inexorable breakdown and expansion. From *The Southern Cross* on, the line and the paragraph will replace the pretty stanzaic rooms that have started to crumble. Like the series of self-portraits by Francis Bacon on which this sequence is based, Wright's collection dramatizes the loss of the self as a means of building it up. Just as Bacon's images ooze and flow, so Wright locates his self through the things that surround him and the things he has read, bracketing the middle three portraits with the two more conventionally confessional, external "frames." And, like Bacon's self that vanishes from the canvas, Wright sees himself in the last picture "in a tight dissolve," imploring: "Angel of Mercy, strip me down."

Such self-locating gestures in these five lyrics, or in the other two, where Hart Crane and Li Po precede the Charles Wright who makes his appearance only in their wake and as a kind of afterthought, look like a product of routine Southern politeness and of an aesthetics that forswears both self-revelation and extended narrative ("I can't tell a story. Only Southerner I know who can't," Wright once confessed in an interview).[7] Other poets in

this century, Pound most noticeably, have preached a doctrine of impersonality; it is Wright's distinctive achievement to have avoided the cryptic
coldness of Pound at his worst (or of his followers, like the Welshman David
Jones), and to have reshaped the characteristic self-centeredness of lyric by
extending it: extending its lines and stanzas quite literally and extending
the scope of its traditional concerns in order to move beyond the demands
of the ego without advancing into the larger epic forms that have tempted
most American male poets from Walt Whitman through James Merrill. (As
Howard Nemerov wittily puts it in an epigrammatic truth: most American
poets "start out Emily and wind up Walt.")[8] Charles Tomlinson also inherited Pound's "objectivist" tendencies, but he has remained solidly conservative in poetic technique. In Wright, the lyric, not the ego, has expanded,
and it has done so, paradoxically, by concentrating even more closely on
landscape and the poet's place within those landscapes he recalls, inhabits, or
symbolically recreates in the formal frames of his poetry.

In "Roma II" (*World*, 97), Wright proposes a hypothesis with the forceful
clarity he always summons up when delivering a pointed truth. He waxes
for the moment didactic and wise: "The poem is a self-portrait / always, no
matter what mask / You take off and put back on." Aphoristic plainness is
matched by a personal modesty, as the poem began with a recollection of
looking at his "mother's miniature" while living in Rome. And it continues
briefly in the pluperfect, referring to the earlier time when his mother was
alive. Then, after the epigram, it continues with a present-tense description
of Irish poets who are making a group sketch of people at a city bar: "they
draw till we're all in, even our hands." Drawing draws everyone in; the painters' hands make a metaphoric connection with the hands of their subjects.
(And they should recall for us, as well, the poet's own "lavish hands," which
I discuss above.) The self-portrait, like the lyric "I," makes only momentary
appearances. By the last stanza, all specificity has been left behind for a
mythic generality and an acknowledgment of the emptiness from which all
creative work springs:

> Surely, as has been said, emptiness is the beginning of all things.
> Thus wind over water,
>                     thus tide-pull and sand-sheen
> When the sea turns its lips back . . .
> Still, we stand by the tree whose limbs branch out like bones,
> Or steps in the bronchial sediment.
> And the masters stand in their azure gowns,
> Sticks in their hands, palm leaves like birds above their heads.

We can take this conclusion as Wright's version of Stevens's famous austere pronouncement:

> From this the poem springs: that we live in a place
> That is not our own and, much more, not ourselves
> And hard it is in spite of blazoned days.
> ("Notes Toward a Supreme Fiction," *CP*, 383)

But it is also something more. The epiphany allows him to inhabit a landscape sadly but not alone. He has transformed his Irish poet-sketchers into a combination of Yeats's Byzantine mosaic sages and his scarecrows (in "Sailing to Byzantium" and "Among School Children"), shadowed by Stevensian palm trees. The bronchial sediment recalls the reticulations of the "bronchial" trees in the second "Self-Portrait"; Wright cannot desist from simultaneously separating from and inserting himself in a landscape that contains human and superhuman figures. As a reparative elegist in the tradition of Stevens, Wright has no contemporary equal.

Such elegy takes many forms in Wright's extended work. At its simplest, it involves an exemplary vignette, as of an adolescent Charles Wright on a whiskey run with pals, fleeing from the cops and generally hooting it up with the boys. He revels in past glory and recognizes its insipidity:

> Jesus, it's so ridiculous, and full of self-love,
> The way we remember ourselves,
>                          and the dust we leave . . .
>
> Remember me as you will, but remember me once
> Slide-wheeling around the curves,
>                 letting it out on the other side of the line.
> ("Gate City Breakdown," *World*, 40)

Momentary gestures like this make Wright sound like the Wordsworth of the "Intimations" ode, lamenting "the splendor in the grass" and the "glory in the flower" that nothing can ever bring back. He also sounds like a character out of Dante, delivering what amounts to a sentimental self-epitaph and asking to be recalled by his survivors or readers in a defining moment of passionate self-abandonment.

However moving this episode may be, it is among Wright's least interesting (because most conventional) elegiac maneuvers. At his best he is a memorialist of the common destiny. Here, for example, is the pluralized and therefore anonymous small lament entitled "Snow" (*Country Music*, 112):

If we, as we are, are dust, and dust, as it will, rises,
Then we will rise, and recongregate
In the wind, in the cloud, and be their issue,

Things in a fall in a world of fall, and slip
Through the spiked branches and snapped joints of the evergreens,
White ants, white ants and the little ribs.

This poem contains the jaggedness we associate with the later Wright in the apparent evenness of an ongoing, single-sentence lyric. Its fluid hypotactic subordination keeps the poem braced along lines of tension, with a high Romantic rhetoric masking a simple statement. But the use of repetition interrupts as well as extends the rhythm of the argument. Everything ends as something else: we as dust, dust as snow, snow as white ants, trees as ribs of skeletons, rising as falling. The beauty of such considerations forswears the personal in favor of the communal, and mingles a diction of biblical cadence ("Dust we are") and romantic resignation. The lines move simultaneously in jumps, starts, hesitant afterthoughts, *and* as a nonstopped flow. Such a technique again calls our notice to Wright's effort to conjoin the spatial and the temporal (an effort I discuss in more detail below). The poem might easily be taken as a description of a little dime-store glass sphere containing a landscape, which, when turned upside down, lets loose a minisnowfall over its world. Contemplation leads here to visual description. The world ends in an image.

Whether focused on himself or on our common humanity, Wright's elegiac temper, with its associated sadness, humility, and delicacy of perception, turns a famous Coleridgean obiter dictum on its head, or at least puts a new spin on it: "Elegy is the form of poetry natural to the reflective mind. It *may* treat of any subject, but it must treat of no subject *for itself;* but always and exclusively with reference to the poet himself."[9] By one way of looking at his work we can take Wright as always the subject, even if implicit. By another, we can see that he has heeded the religious truth expressed in the adage from *The Cloud of Unknowing* that he quotes in his longest poem, "A Journal of the Year of the Ox": *Attention is the natural prayer of the soul.* By fiercely and patiently watching an external scene, even if not by the strict procedures set down by Ignatius Loyola or other saintly contemplatives, Wright manages to treat many subjects both for themselves and for their ability to absorb him within their boundaries. Depending on his mood he may express a longing for something otherworldly, a haunting by something missing and aspired to, or he may simply turn his attention with no ulterior motives to the external world, as though painting were an end in itself: "I have no interest in anything / but the color of leaves" ("A Journal of the Year of the Ox," *World,*

186). In this alternation between things for their own sake (which we can label Wright's aestheticism) and things as talismans or symbols of spiritual valences (his residual religiosity), the poems document Wright's inheritance, and movement away, from all Romantic forebears.

Like the past, the future haunts and inspires in equal measure. It provokes anxiety and strength, just as the future and the invisible paralyze but augment the poet's deepest feelings. As usual, we can compare an earlier poem with subsequent ones to chart the road Wright has traveled along (although he may often seem to have remained in the same place). "Reunion" (*Country Music*, 141) shows how the future has it in for us. It always wants to become the past. Time traps us coming and going; there is no escape:

> Already one day has detached itself from all the rest up ahead.
> It has my photograph in its soft pocket.
> It wants to carry my breath into the past in its bag of wind.
>
> I write poems to untie myself, to do penance and disappear
> Through the upper right-hand corner of things, to say grace.

Writing poems may untie and release, but such poems also reunite, join together, and commemorate. Wright sounds nostalgic for the future even though it beckons to him with a gentle menace, like the figure of Death in the medieval morality play who comes to take Everyman when he has it least in mind. This condensed lyric offers two takes, really, on death, giving the upper hand to neither. The first stanza implies the inevitable "ceas[ing] upon the midnight with no pain" that Keats contemplates in the "Ode to a Nightingale," while the second, with paradoxical counterforce, defends the poet from dissolution by getting the better of Death, making a creative assault not to immortalize the poet in the classic Horatian fashion ("Exegi monumentum aere perennius") but to dissolve him in the very act of self-commemoration.

Just a few years later, Wright reexamines his reasons for writing in the simply titled "Ars Poetica" (*World*, 38), a poem that is a partial holdover from his anaphoric and repetition-haunted earlier lyrics, but that is already moving toward the looser forms of his "journals." Once again, there is no exit, even though the rich Keatsian lushness of landscape offers its peculiar combination of temptation and frustration, fulfillment and desolation. Here the poet contrasts his present southern California setting ("I like it back here," he begins, and then repeats his proposition in a hallucinated way) with the interior space of a room (whether in California or in the South is unclear) filled with family ghosts and mementos. And the proposition proceeds almost logically. Instead of pitting one brief stanza against another, as he did in "Reunion," Wright works from thesis through antithesis to a synthesizing last section, beginning with a single, set-off line: "The spirits are everywhere." Escape is an impossibility. Once he calls those spirits down, he asks, "What will it satisfy?" He will still have

> The voices rising out of the ground,
> The fallen star my blood feeds,
> > this business I waste my heart on.
>
> And nothing stops that.

Even by the Pacific, in other words, whether by choice or destiny, the past arises, satisfaction seems unlikely, and nothing is within the poet's control.

Wright's continual quest for a poetic technique that can bear dense emotional freight involves nothing less than a refiguring of the lyric so that it can encompass the concentrated delicacy of observation that he associates with those Asian poets with whom he would like to identify; the autobiographical and historical aspects of his own life as an individual and a Southerner; and the capaciousness of meditation. In these different kinds of poetry, it is always landscape that occupies the central position, because landscape alone allows the poet to move from present to past, from here to there, and from the visible to the invisible. In "The Southern Cross" (*World*, 42), for example, a poem in the newer medley form that encourages the cross-stitching necessary to combine Wright's excursions among several genres, it is natural observation that frames and inspires his movement between the particular and the general. He wants the poem to be (like all of his "journal" poems) a combination of the three modes, so he starts with a single, ominous generalization, proceeds to four lines of individuated details, and symmetrically closes the opening section with another single-line dictum, in this case, a resignation:

> Things that divine us we never touch:
>
> The black sounds of the night music,
> The Southern Cross, like a kite at the end of its string,
>
> And now this sunrise, and empty sleeve of a day,
> The rain just starting to fall, and then not fall,
>
> No trace of a story line.

But a story line is exactly what Wright cannot avoid, even if he lacks the stereotypical Southern gift of gab and even if the line of story and poem is strung obliquely like the stars of the invisible Southern Cross. He segues immediately to recollections from early childhood, all of which lead him to the ambivalent conclusion that his "days were marked for a doom" but with the realization of "How sweet the past is, no matter how wrong, how sad. / How sweet is yesterday's noise" (43). What intercedes between the first and the second of these realizations is, once more, the natural details whose perception allows him to move from his first tentative emotional response to the next one:

> The morning is dark with spring.
> The early blooms on the honeysuckle shine like maggots after the
>      rain.
> The purple mouths of the passion blossoms
>                          open their white gums to the wind.
>
> (43)

I have picked this opening virtually at random. Other selections would make the same point: that although Wright's new kind of poetry has the appearance of casualness, it also forces us to understand his contemplative temperament as directly and intricately bound up with his descriptions of nature, into which he releases and redeems himself, and from which he then pulls himself together into new, although momentary states of thought and feeling. If at times a sense of personal failure predominates, at others visionary triumph breaks through the mundane details of the natural world. As he announces later in the poem, "the landscape was always the best part" (49).

So it may be in all of Wright's poetry. But the landscape is not the only part. Of the various strands interwoven throughout his work, we can unravel several (as I have already begun to do) to see how the whole fits together. One could collect simple aphoristic statements of failure: "Everyone's life is the same life / if you live long enough" ("The Southern Cross," 48); "The edges around what really happened / we'll never remember / No matter how hard we stare back at the past" (49); "Time is the villain in most tales, / and here, too" (51); "I can't remember enough" (52). But Wright plays off these sad admissions (in "The Southern Cross" and the other long poems) against virtually antiphonal statements of successes small and large, hopes entertained and not entirely defeated, compromises that constitute victory, sometimes with a muted Old Testament confidence or a Christian expectation of grace:

> Thinking of Dante is thinking about the other side,
> And the other side of the other side.
> It's thinking about the noon noise and the daily light.
> (45)

The Big Dipper has followed me all the days of my life.
Under its tin stars my past has come and gone.
. . . . . . . . . . . . . . . . . . . . . . . . . . . . . . . . . . . .
It blesses me once again
With its black water, and sends me on.
(45)

Everything has its work,
        everything written down
In a secondhand grace of solitude and tall trees.
(53)

It's what we forget defines us, and stays in the same place,
And waits to be rediscovered.
(54)

With an almost metronomic sway between despair and hope, Wright moves equally evenly among gnomic generalization, precise observation, and recollected anecdotes. What Keats called "a life of sensations" everywhere balances that of "thought," although Wright's poetry makes a synthesis rather than a conflict of these potentially unharmonious constituents. Both "Lost Bodies" and the adjacent "Lost Souls" (*The Other Side of the River*) bear witness to disappearances, but the best comment on all the recollections in this volume is the toneless acknowledgment that "There is no stopping the comings and goings in this world, / No stopping them, to and fro" ("Italian Days," *World*, 89). And in two adjacent sections of any long poem one can find quicksilver changes of mood: "Despair, with its three mouths full, / Dangles our good occasions, such as they are, in its grey hands," followed by

Nothing's so beautiful as the memory of it
Gathering light as glass does,
As glass does when the sundown is on it
     and darkness is still a thousand miles away.
("A Journal of the Year of the Ox," 166)

Such metaphoric visionary moments derive from and compensate for the losses, hauntings, and lassitude that often precede them. Wright makes reparations and keeps on going. "I keep coming back to the visible" ("December Journal," *World*, 209), he admits (just as Stevens keeps "coming back / To the real," in "An Ordinary Evening in New Haven" [*CP*, 471]), and in the visible he encounters things themselves and as promises, portents, even symbols of something like salvation in an undoctrinal but thoroughly spiritual realm.

"We invent what we need," concludes a largely anecdotal family reminiscence ("Arkansas Traveller," *World*, 107). What Wright generally needs
and invents—in the Renaissance sense of coming upon—is his landscapes.
These contain the "ten thousand things" of his title, each of which, according to the Chinese sages, is "crying out to us / Precisely nothing, / A silence
whose tunes we've come to understand" ("Night Journal," *World*, 147). The
ambiguous, Stevensian "nothing" that things sing to us inspires us to an
equivalent eloquence, which mingles the seen and the heard in our minds
and recreates a landscape that comes to look more like a tapestry:

> —Even a chip of beauty
> > is beauty intractable in the mind,
> Words the color of wind
> Moving across the fields there
> > wind-addled and wind-sprung,
> Abstracted as water glints,
> The fields lion-colored and rope-colored,
> As in a picture of Paradise,
> > the bodies languishing over the sky
> Trailing their dark identities
> That drift off and sieve away to the nothingness
> Behind them
> > moving across the fields there
> As words move, slowly, trailing their dark identities.
> (148)

A passage like this illustrates the shifting depths in Wright's poetry. Just as
the things of this world are transient, our words equally ephemeral, and the
next world unknowable, the very pattern of a single sentence—one perception, image, or metaphor melting into or being replaced by the next—proceeds along a double path of dissolution and accumulation. The minutest
piece of beauty is first seen as intractable, but then as evanescent. The wind
has no color of its own, but its visible effect on the fields produces mottled
colors there. A whole sequence of tropings—a metamorphosis of metaphor—moves the poem onward: a mental chip of beauty is like words, which
are the metaphorical "color" of "wind-addled" landscape, which is itself variegated like water. The natural scene then becomes a notional, depicted one
("as in a picture of Paradise"). What another poet might accomplish through
a sequence of clauses Wright accomplishes through a series of self-trans-
forming images, each turning into the next. Although he attaches himself
to the things of this world, at the same time he announces (concluding this

poem) that he would "never love anything hard enough / That would stamp me / and sink me suddenly into bliss" (149). No poet has ever so clearly resisted his own enthusiasms: to stamp means both to mark neutrally and to eradicate, to stamp out. He approaches ecstasy and then turns away from it because he cannot bear too much beauty, however mesmerizing he finds it.

Wright wants to see and to use the landscape the way one might look at a painting: first from a distance, to capture the totality of representation, the mimetic field of action, and then up close, to see the technique, the patina, the impasto, the planes of colors. First the forest, then the trees, then the branches and their leaves. For this as for other reasons, Cézanne is his great original. Although medieval and Renaissance religious art, the still lifes of Giorgio Morandi, the abstractions of Mondrian, and numerous miscellaneous photographs and sculptures frequently turn up in Wright's poems, it is Cézanne who presides as the tutelary spirit over the oeuvre. The "Homage to Cézanne" opens *The Southern Cross* and takes pride of place in Wright's poetry of the eighties. Significantly, the more recent volume, *Chickamauga*, which contains only short poems, has for a cover a sequence of photos, eleven close-ups of someone's mouth, presumably the poet's. Each poem has become the equivalent of a single, more traditional lyric utterance. The reasons for Cézanne's status as Wright's presider in the longer works from the eighties are not hard to discover. Cézanne's revision of spatial form, paving the way for the Cubists, who were his most grateful beneficiaries, has as its correspondence Wright's decision, starting tentatively with *The Southern Cross*, to break away from his earlier, smaller stanzaic units and to find suppler ways of effecting transitions in longer poems. The hemistich (the broken half-line) makes an image, phrase, or sentence *look* disjointed even when it is not syntactically so. It has the additional effect of filling in an entire printed page, which now seems to melt into its white boundaries instead of being tightly confined by them. Just as words and things (in "Night Journal") have ambiguously tangible and ephemeral realities, so the quasi-stanzaic units in the journal poems look compact and diffuse at the same time. The poems have a horizontal and a vertical thrust, as if the poet were deliberately drawing our eye along and down the page in one protracted sweep. A horizontal line has been broken up only to make us aware of it simultaneously as a vertical one.

Sometimes the cause or effect of the line break in the "journal" poems is to imitate an action described:

> The weeping cherries
> lower their languorous necks and nibble the grass.
>
> (136)

The enjambment conveys the sense of downward movement: trees are pro-
gressively, metaphorically transformed into pasturing animals. We witness a
complex pattern of figuration as the personified cherries, given their correct
name ("weeping"), become, in the second line, perhaps human, and then,
something other than human. Or:

> Last night, in the second yard, salmon-smoke in the west
> Back-vaulting the bats
>                          who plunged and swooped like wrong angels
> Hooking their slipped souls in the twilight.
> (166)

Here grammatical transposition ("Back-vaulting the bats") and an enjambed
subordination ("the bats / who plunged") produce both visual dazzle and
referential obscurity. The gymnastic bats become fallen angels, but we can
never be sure whose souls—bats' or angels'—are "hooked" in the twilight.

Sometimes the break is used in the service of a stilled description rather
than an active one:

> The trees dissolve in their plenitude
>                          into a dark forest
> And streetlights come on to stare like praying mantises down on us.
> (154)

Here the doubled prepositional phrases ("in . . . into") call attention to the
fact as well as the location of dissolution. Severed from the first part of the
sentence, the second phrase amplifies and concentrates the description.
The effect is like that of a zeugma (the yoking of two items by a single
verb or preposition), but in addition to linking two objects ("plenitude"
and "forest"), Wright also multiplies them: as the trees disappear, they are
transformed *into* a dark forest. Especially in relation to the second half
of the sentence (which details a coming into view rather than a disappearance), the divided first half serves a mimetic function. Or, here is a
different example of descriptive stillness, this time without the force of an
enjambment:

> Like the stone inside a rock,
>                          the stillness of form is the center of everything,
> Inalterable, always at ease.
> (155)

In this case, the two phrases surround the main discursive epigram, like foils
for a jewel. An independent clause, concerning the centrality of form, is itself
located—easily, unalterably—within two kinds of qualifying descriptions.

Sometimes the break makes visible a hypothetical point, but without doing violence to syntax and without any unusual enjambment:

—Structure is binary, intent on a resolution,
Its parts tight but the whole loose
and endlessly repetitious.

(136)

Or:

The new line will be like the first line,
spacial and self-contained.

(142)

The conflict between tightness and looseness, self-containment and repetition, works itself out on the page. In other words, by breaking the lines, Wright has devised a visually mimetic way of underlining his assertions. Form and fact coincide. Most of his experiments with lineation can be understood this way, with reference to localized rhetorical effects and descriptive accuracy.[10]

There may be a metaphysical reason for all of this. Like Jorie Graham, Wright longs for some ineffable presence, but whereas her recent work starts and stops and sputters before our eyes, all parenthetical asides, with less and less coherence in syntax or narrative, Wright's lines only look broken. They jolt us into a recognition of separateness but they roll fluently by. The small, the separate, the partial, and the individual all fit within the ongoing rush of the large, the whole, and the collective. Just as days strung together make a life, and as vignettes can cluster together into a biography, so the glittering pieces of Wright's crystalline observations yield a poetry of statement, observation, recollection, and aspiration.

The artistic, rather than the metaphysical, analogy for such a style, if not its direct cause, is clearly depicted on the dust jacket of *The World of the Ten Thousand Things*. Cézanne's characteristic late planes, chunks and daubs of color, are distinct *and* blurred. Even the colors themselves haphazardly melt into the unpainted areas of the canvas in a way that seems random (when seen up close) and prescribed (when seen as part of the depicted landscape). In a brief commentary inspired by the anniversary of Cézanne's death, Wright matter-of-factly summarizes his legacy: "He made us see differently, where the hooks fit, and the eyes go . . . / Nothing is ever finished" ("A Journal of English Days," *World*, 127). It all comes down, in poetry as well as painting, to the making of connections, all of which are temporary, informal, casual, even random. Like a post-Impressionist painting, Wright's long poems give the paradoxical, simultaneous pleasures of partiality and incompletion ("there is more to notice here . . . these slapdash details are random," we might say to ourselves) and aesthetic totality (we say "the whole world has been successfully epitomized"). The poem is a diary, travelogue, or record of perceptions in time; it is also a composition, a rendering of the natural world, in space. "Nothing is ever finished" is one motto; its opposite (the last line of "March Journal," *World*, 137) is "Form is finite, an undestroyable hush over all things." Through acts of description the poet stakes out his claim to a territory where finite boundaries are ever on the move:

> The landscape was always the best part.
> —
>
> Places swim up and sink back, and days do,
> The edges around what really happened
>                       we'll never remember
> No matter how hard we stare back at the past.
> ("The Southern Cross," 49)

Like Wordsworth in the opening paragraph of "Tintern Abbey," measuring his hedgerows and then blurring them ("hardly hedgerows"), seeing the "one green hue" that unifies and blurs the plotted landscape, or like Elizabeth Bishop in "At the Fishhouses," where a silver sheen covers multiple facets of a maritime scene, Wright searches for the visible form of the landscape (which he then translates for our benefit into the visible form of the printed page) as well as for the blurs, leaks, and blanknesses that appear, Cézanne-like, within it. He depicts space and time as a single synaesthetic continuum, with places on the move and even past time capable of being stared at. Parts, as he has said repeatedly, are greater than their sums.

He calls himself *"A Traveler between life and death"* and proceeds to ask himself one of those typical, unrhetorical questions that his poetry can never answer:

> Where is that line between sleep and sleep,
> That line like a wind over water
> Rippling toward shore,
>                   appearing and disappearing
> In wind-rise and wind-falter—
> That line between rain and sleet,
>                      between leaf-bronze and leaf-drop—
> That line where the river stops and the lake begins,
> Where the black blackens
>                 and light comes out of the light.
> ("A Journal of English Days," 129–130)

With such an interest in looking hard enough at the visible world to elicit a map of its "line after line after, latched untraceable line" (130) it is no wonder that Wright should achieve momentary frustrations, temporary triumphs, with nothing keeping put for long. He would doubtless approve Ammons's equivalently synaesthetic realization, in his most popular poem, "Corsons Inlet," that space and time are merely two facets of a single perceptual phenomenon, that a sand dune is as much an event in time as an organization of space, that "tomorrow a new walk is a new walk" because even more than we, nature itself is always changing.[11] It never stands still, neither in our observing nor in our remembering it. As typically happens in Wright's work, sentences that begin as meditations on place turn into ones on time. And, like Ammons's, Wright's poetry asks us to consider the line as that which binds, which leads into, and which dissolves.

"Homage to Paul Cézanne" stands vibrantly on the border between Wright's early and later technique. In its appearance and method it is all politeness: at only three places in eight pages does the poet cut a line in half, preferring to stay inside fixed stanzas, but—here's the novelty—the stanzas have differing lengths: groups of six, four, eight, two, and three lines toward the start and, at the end, a more random sequence. It is as if the poet decided on some aleatory principle of composition, an equivalent of Marianne Moore's syllabic stanzas. The poem's rhythmic forcefulness, its repetitions and anaphoric rhetoric recall Wright's earlier ways of depicting a sense of haunting. He fills the poem with images and metaphors of the dead, who occupy its space the way colors do that of a post-Impressionist landscape by Cézanne. By the middle of the poem the images actually become parts of a natural or imagined landscape:

> The dead are a cadmium blue.
> We spread them with palette knives in broad blocks and planes.
>
> We layer them stroke by stroke
> In steps and ascending mass, in verticals raised from the earth.
>
> We choose, and layer them in,
> Blue and a blue and a breath,
>
> Circle and smudge, cross-beak and buttonhook,
> We layer them in. We squint hard and terrace them line by line.
> (6)

Such a mingling of the poem's human characters and their metaphoric equivalents in a painting leads to the poem's resigned conclusion, which locates human life somewhere at the junction of death, in a landscape at once real and painted:

> What we are given in dreams we write as blue paint,
> Or messages to the clouds.
> At evening we wait for the rain to fall and the sky to clear.
> Our words are words for the clay, uttered in undertones,
> Our gestures salve for the wind.
>
> We sit on the earth and stretch our limbs,
> Hoarding the little mounds of sorrow laid up in our hearts.
> (10)

Again, where Stevens sadly announced that "not to have is the beginning of desire," Wright hoards the trials of his senses as though they were necessary preparatory stages in a creative program.

Wright's aphorisms and other abstract statements often pepper his longer poems. But such statements typically work, as I have shown, in relation to metaphor and the poet's changing perceptions of an external scene. For this reason, we must turn to a closer examination of Wright's landscapes as objects of aesthetic focus, intimations of unseen spiritual presences, and foils for the self-portraiture that he always, if obliquely, wishes to create. At times, he makes an easy equation between the ten thousand things of this world and their correspondences with the next or the other. Like Stevens, who keeps "coming back to the real,"

> I keep coming back to the visible.
>                          I keep coming back
> To what it leads me into,
> The hymn in the hymnal,
> The object, sequence and consequence.
> By being exactly what it is,
> It is that other, inviolate self we yearn for,
> Itself and more than itself,
>                          the word inside the word.
> It is the tree and what the tree stands in for, the blank,
> The far side of the last equation.
> ("December Journal," *World*, 209)

This equation comes from the poetic equivalent of an elementary algebra textbook. Statements of being are statements of self-as-other. The visible is "more than itself"; it is the tree and also a compensation for the tree. What

Wright calls in the same poem "the immanence of infinitude" (211), the relation of the "lust of the eye" (210) to what its searches lead to in the next
world, brings him to the comforting assurance that "The other world is here,
just under our fingertips" (211). Such is the Augustinian side of Wright's
temperament.

But this is always balanced by an Eastern, Confucian, or postmodern
side. There are many other moments in Wright's poetry where the two
halves of any tentative formula do not correspond, where blurs and inequali-
ties rather than one-for-one correspondence prevail. Earlier in the same volume, "Chinese Journal" (*World*, 199) begins its series of five quasi-Oriental
lyrics with a look at a Morandi sketch of bottles done in the year of the
author's birth. The artist

> Pencilled these bottles in by leaving them out, letting
> The presence of what surrounds them increase the presence
> Of what is missing,
> 
> > keeping its distance and measure.

Subtraction rather than addition becomes the measure of wisdom, as a master announces in the previous poem: "for knowledge, add something every
day, / To be wise, subtract" ("A Journal of One Significant Landscape," 198).
And as Wright himself summarizes in an earlier poem: "Exclusion's the
secret" ("Yard Journal," *World*, 122). One must put things together by taking them apart. Wright the anatomist is twin brother to Wright the syn-
thesist. The impulse to expand, through noticing and accumulating one's
responses to the external and internal worlds, must be met by an equivalent
and opposing one to reduce and let go. Thus Wright's pull (like Ammons's)
between poems large and small, or his composition of large poems made up
of separate, smaller units. Thus, also, his interest in the poetic equivalent of
painterly techniques of inclusion and exclusion, as a way of both allowing
the visible to stand for the invisible and of reminding us of the unbridgeable
gap between them. Remembering a discussion of painting with his army
buddies, he asserts "that what's outside / The picture is more important than
what's in." What he forgets exceeds what he recalls, and this polarity parallels the relation between form and formlessness in art: "nothing is ever
ended" ("A Journal of the Year of the Ox," 152).

For Wright (as for Cézanne and Jorie Graham) a focus on borders rather
than on mirroring or one-for-one correspondences may provide the truest
calculation of the currents in which we circulate. Sometimes the borders are
crisp, sharply etched; sometimes they are extended, run-over (or run-on),
and blurred. Even in spring, earthly plenitude comes with its own frustrations: "it all twists into the dark, / The not [*sic*] no image can cut / Or color

replenish. / Not red, not yellow, not blue" ("A Journal of the Year of the Ox,"
158). A zero-degree January day, detailed several pages earlier in the same
journal, provides opposite but equivalent frustrations: "How does one deal
with what is always falling away, / Returning diminished with each turn? /
The grass knows, stunned in its lockjaw bed, / but it won't tell" (154).

Wright looks to the natural world to answer such questions. At times
he is requited, at other times frustrated. As I have suggested, his questions
are never rhetorical, but even when answered, answered only for a brief
time. There is no American poet who combines so neatly the rival tendencies to summarize, epitomize, or conclude (as Wright does in his gnomic
pronouncements) and to speculate, wonder, and question. Flux provokes
the poet's eye and mind, but even when excluding things from his view he
makes no permanent or final commitments. Like Morandi with his bottles,
Wright is capable of revising the composition of his world and of his poem
on a daily basis.

Description, in other words, is a constantly changing adventure, even
though Wright's themes and tropes are remarkably persistent, indeed repeti-
tive (to the dismay of impatient readers). Other poets—Ammons and Nemerov come to mind—use perception as the starting point for discursive conclusions. With Wright one has the feeling that such speculation is never an
end in itself but a temporary stopping point, as if the poet is gathering his
breath and self-control before returning to the natural world, at once his
home and his tempter. No other poet makes the world so vividly exciting
merely to read about. Exciting and at the same time inevitable, the result
of waiting and patiently looking, as he offhandedly remarks in "The Other
Side of the River" (*World*, 80):

> I want to sit by the bank of the river,
>> in the shade of the evergreen tree,
> And look in the face of whatever,
>> the whatever that's waiting for me.

This little couplet-as-folk-song comes in the middle of one of Wright's typical maneuvers. He begins by locating himself, at Easter in southern California, and then segues to "For weeks I've thought about the Savannah River,
/ For no reason" (78). He reaches for some links, connections that appear
only to vanish: "Something infinite behind everything appears, / and then
disappears" (79). But to say that the poem merely follows Wright's standard
method of stationing himself, recalling the past, contemplating the present,
anxiously waiting for the future, combining anecdote with description and
philosophical proposition, is to ignore the interrelationship among these
various timbres and among their respective styles. In all of the registers, it is

the landscape that does the work. Here, too, that work partakes of Stevens's "way things look each day": like Emerson and Dickinson and Jorie Graham, Wright seems constantly aware that whatever he looks at is watching, and even waiting for, him in return.

His constancy of theme leads to or from a constancy of mood; in spite of glimmers of hope and confidence, Wright is our contemporary Tennyson, an anatomist of melancholy in its manifold moods, a glum examiner of his own life and its contexts. Like Tennyson he extends the Virgilian line of poets who conveniently associate melancholy with landscape details. (And like Virgil and Tennyson, as well, he is a poet of evening and of shadows.) But he is also a contemporary Rilke, one of those bees of the invisible turning the pollen of actuality into the honey of the spirit, at least at those rare moments when the numinous makes itself accessible. It should come as no surprise, then, that in terms of his dealings with the landscape he is also the premier American poet of what Ruskin scornfully dismissed as the pathetic fallacy. His landscapes are artfully viewed but also metaphorically or rhetorically humanized. As I have shown, things momentarily stand in for other things, or at least come to resemble them.

Wright employs such "fallacies" ("figurations" would be a more exact term) as the basis for an entire short poem or as one device among many in constructing a longer, looser one. The chilly "California Spring" (*World*, 30) consists of five three-line stanzas. Each line is a single end-stopped sentence. In the sameness of iteration (variations on a simple subject-predicate construction), Wright builds a description from simple observation through menacing, humanized details. So, for example, the first stanza:

At dawn the dove croons.
A hawk hangs over the field.
The liquidambar rinses its hundred hands.

After two lines of deliberate simplicity, the third sentence opens us onto a personified natural world that incorporates the human. At the end of the third stanza, a parallel image reverses the situation: "There is a spider that swings back and forth on his thin strings in the heart." So not only is nature humanized (a tree with hands), but now an arachnid image metonymically represents a human being from within. Later, as the sun rises higher, it is "caught like a kite in the drooped limbs of the tree." The common cliché ("limbs") disguises its origin as a catachresis, but by this point, if we have been properly following Wright's method, we realize the strange, not to say ominous, connections that obtain between the human and the nonhuman worlds, and between the perception of a scene and the encoding within it of suggestively animating details. The end is both shocking and appropriate:

One angel dangles his wing.
The grass edges creak and the tide pools begin to shine.
Nothing forgives.

The poem has hinted at religious possibilities from its first line, but now
we realize we have been teased out of thought. The accumulated individual
details have withheld more than we may have wanted them to deliver. Is the
angel a bird? An imagined spirit hovering over the scene? A Paraclete in the
landscape, or a figment of the poet's imagination? Light comes up as day
proceeds, and the poem ends unforgivingly with a unique two-word line of
nonfigurative, abstract language in the richly figured tapestry of description. Does the line undo everything that preceded it, or does it come as
an inevitable conclusion? The shock of the line reminds us of moments in
Rilke and James Wright; the mysteries of the pathetic fallacy prohibit any
final knowledge of our place in the observed world rather than welcome us
within it.

As an example of the same rhetoric at work on a large scale, one might
take the opening nine-line section of "The Other Side of the River" (78):

Easter again, and a small rain falls
On the mockingbird and the housefly,
                              on the Chevrolet
In its purple joy
And the TV antennas huddled across the hillside—

Easter again, and the palm trees hunch
Deeper beneath their burden,
                              the dark puddles take in
Whatever is given them,
And nothing rises more than halfway out of itself—

Easter with all its little mouths open into the rain.

Opening (as is his recent procedure) with a phrase rather than a clause,
Wright gives us two takes on his ritualized scene ("Easter again, and . . .
Easter again, and . . ."), as if acknowledging that Easter will always look
like this. The observed details are both random and willful: the unmodified
mockingbird and housefly ease us into a world where, it transpires, even the
mechanical is animated (the automobile "in its purple joy" and the antennas
"huddled"), and where the natural is humanized (the palm trees "hunch,"
the puddles "take in" the rain). The season of sacrifice, forgiveness, and
reawakening is summarized in a quasi-allegorical phrase, as though Wright
needed to end by epitomizing it: "Easter with all its little mouths open into

the rain" looks like some primitive deity, sculpted or painted. Resurrection and rebirth never seemed so banal and unpromising.

As Wright moves through a recollection of quail hunting with his brother when they were teenagers, he keeps protesting his inability to analogize: "There is no metaphor for any of this" (79), while at the same time loading all of his description with, for the most part, momentary rather than extended metaphorical gestures. He insistently returns to catachresis, the rhetorical trope of misnaming or of transferring a word to a phenomenon with no proper word of its own (speaking of the "face" of a mountain, for example, or the "limbs," rather than the branches, of a tree, as above). Thus, he mentions "the plum trees preen[ing] in the wind," "the vine-lipped face of the pine woods," and "the vinca blossoms like deep bruises among the green." And, from the other side, he undoes and de-animates living things: "quail . . . bursting like shrapnel points" and "the trees balloon and subside." Moving up and down some imaginary scale of animation (another parallel to the vertical movement on his pages), Wright takes time out in the middle of the poem to announce his main obsession, one already indicated by his figurative language:

> It's linkage I'm talking about,
> and harmonies and structures
> And all the various things that tie our wrists to the past.
>
> Something infinite behind everything appears,
> and then disappears.
>
> It's all a matter of how
> you narrow the surfaces.
> It's all a matter of how you fit in the sky.
> (79)

That last sentence ambiguously announces two of Wright's long-standing concerns, as well as the connections between the artistic and the spiritual. "How you fit in the sky" means both how you manage to depict the heavens in your version of a landscape painting, and how or where you belong in the cosmic scheme of things. Like a jigsaw puzzle, like a painting in process, like a Charles Wright poem, one's arrangements with the divine partake equally of figuring things out and putting things in. Even when he stoically concludes his poem with the sad, sentence-long realization, "So to have come to this . . . Is a short life of trouble," he is able to embed within the sentence's subject and predicate examples of the world's multiple beauties. As usual, he humanizes the natural world (n.b. the participles "whimpering," "cruising," and "thrusting" below), implicitly participating in it, and thereby mitigating his troubles and enabling his readers (if not himself) to escape from them:

> So to have come to this,
> > remembering what I did do, and what I didn't do,
> The gulls whimpering over the boathouse,
> > the monarch butterflies
> Cruising the flower beds,
> And all the soft hairs of spring thrusting up through the wind,
> And the sun, as it always does,
> > dropping into its slot without a click,
> Is a short life of trouble.
> (81)

Short, maybe; but suspended within that life as within the poem's epigrammatic conclusion are the beauties of the world, literally (as here) sprawled out across the landscape of Wright's pages. The numinous appears, amassing itself even as the poet confesses that "there comes a point when everything starts to dust away / More quickly than it appears" (80). To record the evanescence renders it permanent; the details of the observed world fill in the page just as Cézanne's squares and wriggles of color become a landscape.

Wright complicates the entire question of looking at a landscape by his mixing of genres. There are poems (like "Homage to Paul Cézanne") that skirt the edge of painterliness and that tend toward the ekphrastic while remaining faithful to the observed data in the natural, as opposed to the represented, world. Occasionally he sounds reductive and Platonic at once, as in a recent short lyric, "Morandi II" (*Chickamauga*, 67), which renders the essence of the Bolognese painter without referring to a specific painting. Instead, Wright merely names shapes ("rectangle, circle, square"), geometrical figures ("angle and plane"), painterly marks ("Scratches like an abyss") as representative "examples," before a concluding couplet that summarizes the bare contents of Morandi's oeuvre:

> Corners of buildings, bottles, hillsides, shade trees and fields,
> Color and form, light and space,
> > the losses we get strange gain from.

As I suggest in the following chapter, poems about abstract paintings are rare, but this lyric, although it concerns a representational painter, approaches the limits of abstraction. Even Wright's lists (and his general preference for nominal structures) allow him to specify items, without description or ornament, before concluding with his paradoxical summary of lessons learned.

He puts description, and painting itself, to a somewhat different use in "Homage to Claude Lorrain" (*World*, 82). A casual reminiscence about army life (Verona, 1959) recalls a Claude picture that hung on the bedroom wall: "a rigged ship in a huge sea, / Storm waves like flames above my bed." Now, however, long lost, the picture is "Trapped in the past's foliage, as so much else is / In spite of our constancy, or how / We rattle the branches and keep our lights on the right place." Time and space have merged. The past is a dense forest, and no matter how hard we try to illuminate it, the darkness seems always to prevail. The poem continues with a description of the poet's rooms before ending with a second memory of Claude's picture, which now assumes iconic and psychological power, as the poet occupies a symbolic middle space between one body of water and another, with a depicted external fire and an internalized one, and coming gradually to occupy an enclosed space as, once again, time and space come together:

> Between the sea fires of Claude Lorrain
> > and the curled sheets of the river,
> I burned on my swivel stool
> Night after night,
> > looking into the future, its charred edges
> Holding my life like a frame
> I'd hope to fit into one day, unsigned and rigged for the deeps.

Looking *at* Claude's work, Wright comes to occupy it, or some version of it, as he becomes both an anonymous picture ("unsigned") and a burning vessel ("rigged for the deep"). Figuration multiplies, in other words, as ekphrasis itself expands beyond mere description. Looking leads to absorption in space and through time. Specific detail leads to generalized significance. Often, one cannot determine which is more important to the poet: visual accuracy or abstract conclusion. Claude's picture becomes part of a gestalt, a scene, an inspiring memory.

"What matters is abstract," he remarks in a poem ("Yard Journal," 121) where the image precedes, rather than follows, the abstraction to which it is connected:

> —Deep dusk and lightning bugs
> > alphabetize on the east wall,
> The carapace of the sky blue-ribbed and buzzing
> Somehow outside it all,
> Trees dissolving against the night's job,
> > houses melting in air:
> Somewhere out there an image is biding its time,

Burning like Abraham in the cold, swept

                                   expanses of heaven,

Waiting to take me in and complete my equation:

What matters is abstract, and is what love is,

Candescent inside the memory,

                            continuous

And unexpungable, as love is.

This entire poem, cast in Wright's newer mode, allows us to see the intersections and overlappings not only between the abstract and the individual but also between the observed and the artistic. "Exclusion's the secret," as he has announced; what is visible is also what is missing. He grapples with whatever heaves into view or recedes from it, and whatever stands even momentarily still. Such struggle is another way of explaining Wright's hemistiches, his efforts to render the world continuous and stationary at once. Like lightning bugs, however, the images, details, and alphabets of the world flash on and off. Now you see them, now you don't.

Wright's poetry oddly combines particularity of observation, discreteness of detail and diction, with the haze or disjunctions caused by lineation, transitions, and other gestures that mimic the mind's transactions with external reality. As I have tried to show, many of his metaphors both clarify and mystify, calling attention to both sameness and difference in the two halves of their comparisons. The combination of simile and phrases, rather than clauses, has made many of Wright's newer, shorter poems seem like experiments in seeing and recording. Parts rather than wholes begin to overwhelm the page. Take, for example, these lines from "Meditation on Song and Structure" (*Black Zodiac*, 59):

Swallows over the battlements

                             and thigh-moulded red tile roofs,

Square crenelations, Guelph town.

Swallows against the enfrescoed backdrop of tilled hills

Like tiny sharks in the tinted air

That buoys them like a tide,

                           arrested, water-colored surge.

Swallows darting like fish through the alabaster air,

Cleansing the cleanliness, feeding on seen and the unseen.

The thrice-mentioned swallows grow throughout the stanza, first merely located, then relocated and figured in terms of "sharks," and at last refigured as "fish" in the process of action ("cleansing"). As a sentence, the stanza is officially incomplete; as an experiment in amplified troping it embraces ever larger realms of vision and descriptive possibility.

Perhaps Wright's transactions—with vision, description, and similitude—are all epitomized in a series of plangent questions in "California Dreaming" (*World*, 116): "What if the soul is indeed outside the body . . . What if inside the body another shape is waiting to come out . . . What other anagoge in this life but the self?" The search for the soul and for the truth that lies outside it dissolves into a gray area where outside/inside, body/spirit, self/world, all the distinctions on which our poetic tropings as well as our philosophies and our self-interest depend, entirely dissolve.

Later in the same poem, Wright announces what might be called the truth of all poets, namely, the gradual half-life of metaphor, the failure to abridge disparate facts, the inadequacy of language. This sad truth lies at the center of all the other failures, the mysterious hauntings and losses, in the poet's heart, precisely because it is a poetic failure. He makes his announcement significantly in a poem about his own alienation from his nonnative landscape. California was never for Wright—perhaps unique among American poets in this regard—the Golden State. Instead, it was the desert of his seventeen-year exile before his return to Virginia. Not that the South is an unmitigated paradise, but at least the poet can feel there the ties that have bound him to family, landscape, and a recognizable contour for human emotions. "Out there where the landscape ends," however, he comes to a delicate self-knowledge:

> What I know best is a little thing.
> It sits on the far side of the simile,
>
> > the like that's like the like.
>
> (116)

No wonder that lines break where syntax bends; or that flora momentarily become fauna-like; or that one memory inspires another one, however disconnected; or, finally, that the poet seems terminally melancholic. Whereas a more linear poet like Bishop uses paratactic arrangements for acts of description ("Everything only connected by 'and' and 'and,'" as her famous line puts it in "Over 2000 Illustrations and a Complete Concordance"), Charles Wright prefers hypotactic, transformative syntax, as if to say "Everything only connected by 'like' and 'like.'" And nothing stays put or unchanged for very long. Everything falls away into the depths of forgetfulness, and even what we can recollect we must give up as partial.

As I have suggested, we can measure Wright's distinctiveness by comparing his paths with those not taken. With his multiple images, his phrasal writing, his insistent anecdotes that appear only to vanish, and even his interest in nonrepresentational painting, he might have become another Frank O'Hara. But the shape of a long Wright poem differs from the "I do this, I do that" casualness of O'Hara's diary jottings. Where O'Hara is light, Wright is by turns lush and austere; where O'Hara, like so many poets in the tradition of first-person observation, gives the sense of merely following a random path of actual scenes, thoughts, and events, Wright makes everything seem both irrational and inevitable. Probably no more succinct synopsis of Wright's metaphysical stance and of his poetic method exists than the birthday entry in his year-long "Journal of the Year of the Ox" (179), a summary of his place well after the *mezzo del cammin*:

> In my fiftieth year, with a bad back and a worried mind,
> Going down the Lee Highway,
> > > the farms and villages
> Rising like fog behind me,
> Between the dream and the disappearance the abiding earth
> Affords us each for an instant.
> > > However we choose to use it
> We use it and then it's gone:
> Like the glint of the Shenandoah
> > > at Castleman's Ferry,
> Like license plates on cars we follow and then pass by,
> Like what we hold and let go,
> Like this country we've all come down,
> > > and where it's led us,
> Like what we forgot to say, each time we forget it.

With its combination of country ballad and Old Testament diction (Ecclesiastes: "the earth abideth forever"), this heartbreaking stanza reiterates Wright's central truth. Repetition—automobile-travel down an old country highway or a string of similes—leads in one direction only: toward our disappearance. The details of the road have been ravishing; the landscape takes us in and welcomes us; then we go.

# FIVE

# "A SPACE FOR BOUNDLESS REVERY"

## Varities of Ekphrastic Experience

To write of painting, or the fine arts in general, in a book about description in poetry, seems so natural as to be obligatory. An author risks thematic redundancy and the practical overexposure of already familiar terrain. Of the central poets in this book, Charles Tomlinson is a sometime painter, and the other four have all written poems about looking at pictures. In addition, the theory and practical criticism of ekphrasis have been expanded recently by the work of James Heffernan, John Hollander, W. J. T. Mitchell, Grant Scott, and others, all of whom build on the earlier pioneering studies of Jean Hagstrum and Murray Krieger.[1] For these reasons I have limited myself in this chapter to three experiments or subgenres of ekphrasis that have been more or less scanted by the critics above. First, *Recoveries*, a book-length dramatic monologue by Theodore Weiss, whose speaker is a figure *in* a painting; second, Irving Feldman's title sequence from his 1986 collection *All of Us Here*, about a show of George Segal plaster-cast sculptures; and last, a sampling of the very few ekphrastic poems about Abstract Expressionist or nonrepresentational painting made by American poets in the past fifty years. In all three cases, visual art promises what Weiss calls "a space for boundless revery,"[2] which has tempted all ekphrastic poets since Homer to dream of, through, or within the confines of a visible or imaginary material depiction. That ekphrasis is generally taken as a "verbal representation of visual representation"[3] needs some modification when one contemplates, as Weiss does, at a double remove (he imagines himself into the mouth of a figure within a picture); or as Feldman does by meditating in propria persona and overhearing conversations among fictional gallery-goers who speak from the predictable points of view of *hommes et femmes moyen sensuels*; or as the limited number of poets do who respond to nonrepresentational art by attempting to describe it or to treat it metaphorically.

## Reassuring Surprises: Theodore Weiss's Talkies

*Recoveries* (1982) is spoken by a painting, or to be more precise, a figure *in* a painting, a secondary figure in a crowd from some Florentine fresco, whose Ancient Mariner–like eye fixes a beholder, steadying him for an autobiography-meditation-announcement of which he becomes a more than casual recipient. No recent poem more forcefully depicts the marriage of the sister arts, or of viewer to scene, or the interdependence of self and world that phenomenologist Merleau-Ponty describes when he claims that any individual perceptive grasp of the world depends on and inspires a centrifugal movement that throws the perceiver back into or toward the world.[4] *Recoveries* is a poem about such collaboration, the joint acts of projection and reception, invention and attentiveness, merging and separation, on which all aesthetic experience (viewing, writing, painting, listening) depends.

As such, the poem joins classical epigraphy (in this case, a spoken transcription of what might otherwise be an extended caption or label on or underneath a real work of art) to the dramatic monologue, a genre that Weiss has always enjoyed. In his previous book-length monologue, *Gunsight* (1962), a soldier undergoing an operation gradually sinks into, and so recovers, layers of his past and the polyphonic harmonies of its depths. Refusing, years ago, to surrender, "in a proud snippety time," whole areas of the literary terrain to prose fiction, Weiss vowed to maintain a commitment, which continues here, to narrative in a sustained poem.[5] But *Recoveries* lacks the temporal and vocal opacity of its predecessor, as it tells, in a more straightforward chronology, the story of an act of creation and the history of a depicted life, with History itself as a backdrop, ending in present time as an investigation of artistic receptivity.

This does not mean that *Recoveries* is either more univocal or less obscure than *Gunsight*. On the contrary, its difficulties are simply of another sort. Given the subject matter (a talking picture), we might expect a simple Browningesque monologue—as though the Duchess of Ferrara should begin her own poem with "That's my old husband, standing by the stairs." Instead, we have an anonymous background figure speaking for himself, the life of the painting of which he is a part, and for the "master" who created them. Synecdoche is Weiss's preferred rhetorical device. The speaker is both of a scene and peripheral to it, both a living personification and a blob of impasto. The very title prepares us for layering as a theme and a technique, as it suggests regainings (improvements in health, retrievals from the depths of consciousness or history) as well as submergings (the palimpsests and pentimenti of both art and human consciousness).

It is a poem of uncovering and discovery as well. A three-page prelude in the voice of a famished poet-pilgrim brings him to the shrine of his devotion. At last, Dante-as-modern-tourist has given up picture books for the real thing:

> Pages, strewn about me, flurried so
> I, flying, seemed to land upon one site,
> another, of a church forever making.
> (1)

After ten lines, the poem settles on such bumpy syntactical patterns and ambiguous grammatical relationships, and it does not leave them until the end. Like Stevens, Clampitt, Graham, and Tomlinson, Weiss is a poet of deliberate ellipses and strenuous syntax, both of which help all of them, in Stevens's aphorism, to "make the visible a little hard to see." The obverse of their obsession with the visual, in other words, is often the peculiarity of their verbal renderings of it. Weiss can disregard word order as well as subordinate pronouns and conjunctions. His poetry has creases that we must iron out by speaking the lines clearly in order to hear and then to fill the hiatuses within. Thus: "Flurried so [much that] I . . . " But "church forever *making*"? Is this a transitive participle? Or is it intransitive? Is it applied to church or speaker? Such writing is not easy. The following lines relieve, without necessarily clarifying, the confusion:

> Making here: this church's shady, tranquil
> cool, rejecting summer, scarcely broken
> by the traffic's steady drone, I watch
> the window-filtered morning as it angles
> off these rugged stones.
> (1)

The author-speaker plays a game of reciprocities. He *makes* his way to the church, which is itself always in the process of being made, of making itself, ready to receive and to render the daylight with its own light intact, each "translucent, tiny bud / a ruddy daybreak" (2). Light clothes the morning, surrounding the fresco like a halo (and the figures within, of the same ruddy hue, are highlighted by their own painted halos). The first viewers of the fresco, the original models for many of the figures within it, engaged in a

literal relationship with the art that all subsequent viewers figuratively, or
perhaps even more than figuratively, repeat:

> . . . At last
> I, too, the fresco's every shade and shimmer
> learned by heart, the sunlight in its freshness
> sealing them, am finished with it, each—
> the fresco, I—the other's mirror, frame.
> (2–3)

The poem does not identify an actual, specific fresco. The book's dust jacket
pictures a downward-glancing, angelic figure without specifying whose work
it is. The fresco is presumably a combination of an actual Quattrocento piece
and what John Hollander has labeled a "notional" or purely invented picture.

A sudden glimmer of light calls attention to, by striking the eye of, a
figure on the wall (it has struck the poet's eyes as well), and "the good red
earth" becomes "the sighings of a rusty voice" (3). "Sighing" naturally suggests a synaesthetic, half-rhyming connection to "seeing" or "sighting." Voice
and vision overlap. And "rust" puts us in touch with the red base of the
fresco, the morning scene it depicts, and the actual rosy-fingered dawn of
the moment of viewing. And so we are off: the pilgrim now becomes the
audience, pinned by a glittering eye that translates itself into language, perhaps unused since infancy when "the paint lay wet / along my mouth" (5),
inhibiting speech while simultaneously giving life.

For fifty-six pages the painting and the figure reveal their composite
and individual destinies that come to include us within them. As a fable of
identity, *Recoveries* proves that life is relational and collective. (In his earlier
poem, "The Ultimate Antientropy," Weiss quotes as epigraph a line from
Buckminster Fuller: "Unity is plural and at minimum two.") Weiss har-
nesses puns and syntax to the demands of his primary belief, as in this early
(and too archly predictable) chord:

> I, standing in their midst, apart,
> the visible I am, the seen
> by mastery become the seeing,
> seeing become the scene.
>       And yet
> a presence not to be confined
> to names, to local time and place.
> (8)

The anonymous speaker gives voice to the mute and also to the seen, a part
speaking on behalf of the whole. He identifies himself with reference to his

central purpose. As both seen and seeing, passive and active, he constitutes a part of the full presence of a scene that moves away from local details to grander meanings. Identity opens, expands; it remains fluid and changing although confined to the two dimensions of the wall.

Like the people they represent, like Christ himself at whom they stare, the figures partake of spirit and flesh, of idea and body, of inspiration and paint. Dirt and grime have sunk into them, adding to and covering up their identities over the centuries (just as Christ himself was pressed into mortal flesh). The accumulated stares of visitors likewise complement the figures' original being, an initial X now long lost:

> . . . Lost not at all?
> Rather, I, prompting viewers
> to a greater sense of self
> and thereby to a deeper sense
> of me, more and more am that
> I am?
> (9)

One doubleness, viewer and object, matches another, that of divinity and humanity, as the speaker echoes both the Old Testament's gnomic and sometimes cranky deity and Coleridge's enigmatic recapitulation of that god in his famous definition in *Biographia Literaria* of the primary imagination (as a repetition of "the eternal act of creation in the infinite I Am.") The human representation inspires a deepening self-consciousness in the viewer, which in turn deepens his knowledge of the figure, and then the figure's own sense of self. Such transactions make up the religion of art, a legacy of the Romantic high modernism to which Weiss adheres. Art abridges or connects the human and the divine; it partakes of changeable matter and eternal truth. The figures on the wall both give to and acquire from their serious onlookers (however few) the deepening of an identity that we might mistake for the accumulating patina of time's force, did not the painting itself thoroughly implicate us in its own changing life.

Weiss worships at the altar of art nowhere more obviously than in his insistence on the creation/Creation analogy. The painting may sound at times like the ineffable divinity who resists our human attempts to placate, understand, or see him truly. But it is also, during the first of the poem's three parts, the handiwork of the artist-god who fashioned it slowly, methodically, from the red clay of its, and our, common base ("the day and night of the first day" [20]). Like the green in Wordsworth's "Tintern Abbey" or the silver in Elizabeth Bishop's "At the Fishhouses," red becomes the color of universal significance, whose origin is fathomless and unrecoverable, but whose shadings confer individuality:

> Yet, joining the rest,
> you run my fellows here and me
> together, even as you suppose
> the underdrawing's red, my mantle's
> hue, cloaks others wear, the flush
> upon the shepherd's cheek and mine
> alike.
> Like all the other reds:
> that bud burst out into a rose,
> that bird flaming across the sky,
> the sky our window lets us see,
> composing it, now roseate
> its sunrise in the stained-glass panes.
>
> All match those highlit splatterings
> upon the Christ which prove a man
> nailed to his cross can outsoar flight.
>
> Soar most as, hovering like humming-
> birds fresh nectar lures, five cherubs
> cup His each drop's sacredness.
>
> You fail to see that other acts,
> different ingredients, a past
> unique, have gone into the making
> of each red.
> (10)

The fleshing out of the human figure continues, and Weiss's ramifying syntax animates and strengthens his descriptions. The speaker's growing gaze both inspires and is fulfilled by the eye and hand of the creating artist. Reciprocity began when the first charcoal was applied and then covered by paint, which the young figure eagerly swallowed up as if for nourishment. We witness the physical allure of the creative act from the creation's, not the creator's, point of view. (It is as though the story of Victor Frankenstein's experiment were told by the Monster in the actual process of being created.) Weiss everywhere asks us implicitly to consider the sexual meanings of the verb "to make." The act of being made "resonant," "vibrant," "luminous" (adjectives that Weiss has always favored) suggests his debt to Gerard Manley Hopkins, whose "dappledness," syntactic obliquities, and strong alliterative phrasings he imitates at heightened moments:

> This day swiftly piled on days,
> a cascade dashed down mountain sides,
> far faster than the clay can dry
> my master finishes.
>               And finished,
> paints and brushes, scaffolding
> disposed of, he considers us
> well enough equipped, armed by
> his love, his craft, sealed in these paints,
> to keep us here, outwitting worm
> and wet, the worst that time can do.
>
> An offspring on our own, we're left,
> much like that Eden couple—after
> God made them, happily
> submerged within their bosky chores,
> submerged within their drowsy nook—
> uninterrupted.
> (26–27)

By such reasoning, the Fall will correspond to the moment of first sighting. Unveiled to its audience, the fresco enters time, acquires its own historical and spiritual identity from the glares and glimpses of its viewers. Left to its own silences, it abides our prying. The most poignant pages of the poem, at the end of part 1, relate this unveiling, which is both a birth and a push from the nest. All the figures attendant on the Savior have been abandoned by their human maker; they must endure their exposure, as they confront the stares of the living people who modeled *for* them and who now attend *upon* them.

Such a fall is the final enablement of being. Weiss and his speaker have added a fifth cause to Aristotle's four: a relational one. *Esse est percipi*, nothing exists but as (or until) it is perceived. Hence the importance of description in the long poem, as neither filler nor ornament: it links sensibilities on both sides of the frame. Ekphrasis itself occupies the rich middle ground between narrative on one side and meditation on the other. Not only does Weiss present the fresco's self-description, he also allows it to turn its voice toward its maker who has completed, or in Valéry's famous epigram, "abandoned" it, to achieve recovery:

The light grown silent, through this crack
and this, a portion of the fresco
missing here, the underdrawing
shows, shows what we have become.

Submissive to proprieties
belonging to our time, these drying
paints fit public faces on
us all as if an instant aging
had occurred.
                    Flesh conforms
the wiry spirit we began
with, wild as in a wind, still beating
free beneath.
                    So we stand ready
for display.
(28)

As they are themselves God's spies, the speaker and his fellows bear witness
as well to the visitation of the artist's mistress, an inspiration and perhaps a
model for some figure (the Virgin?) above them in the fresco, who comes to
them for fulfillment and self-knowledge. Like the painter and all subsequent
audiences, she too is "one of us." *De te pictura narratur*:

    . . . One time, no one
about, a hooded figure, slight
inside its wrappings, takes its station
just below.
                    Instantly I feel
that I am looking up at her,
in lengthened shadows dimly seen.
Her garments fluted like a sculpture,
huge she seems, dark to the waist,
above it radiant.
                    Her gaze,
as though set off by what it sees,
now flashes fire. Sparks of that
I felt when he first came from her?

Although we spy no part of her
beyond those unremitting eyes,
their gaze, having drunk its fill,
responsive to some thing in us

even our master failed, grows mild.
The glistening we bathe us in!
(30–31)

The next fifteen pages telescope history into a panorama of sight-seers and sights seen. Intrigue, murder, moonlit trysts, religious and secular upheaval, the Reformation, the Second World War, the Arno flood of 1966, all sweep by beneath (and in the last case, almost up to) the patient eye of our angelic speaker. The seen becomes the seer, and history a pageant for the education and entertainment of the work of art. As in *Grand Hotel*, people come, people go, nothing ever changes. Like Tiresias, the painting has seen and foresuffered all:

Such trippers flitter through. Enough
so that I can, times changed, keep time,
their costumes changed to say they are,
their gabble, echoing those gone,
the same repainted.
(41)

Dust, darkness, and neglect add to the age and wisdom of the painted figures: the dirt stirred by controversy, murder, and time itself seeps into the fresco, obscuring it while simultaneously becoming part of its identity. The act of witnessing is never value-free; the observer is implicated in the deeds below, but never really apart from, him. The repeated rituals of sacrifice chasten the speaker and teach him and us something about life and death:

...The art's renewed
that put the seal upon man's hope
by way of one Man's doom. Incarnate
it must be each age.
                    Astonished
by that sight, one act uniting
every time, we stand and, timeless,
stand.
(42–43)

Once again, dense verbal syntax bolsters the truth of the observation. "Every time" is both a direct object united by historical actions and also an adverbial reminder that nothing ever really makes any difference, as each act unites participants and observers through the ages. Every sacrifice repeats the Crucifixion.

After such knowledge, what forgiveness? Weiss has followed Eliot's multiple paths through history's treacherous mazes, but equipped with none of his master's final orthodoxies, he finds consolation only in his own cunning. The strategies of observation, description, and meditation, and the modernist techniques of dislocation (Eliot's famous term) and syntactic ambiguity conveniently allow Weiss to prove, not merely to assert, the necessary salvation that comes only from repetition. An occasional visitor like our present pilgrim or the long-gone painter's mistress startles and reanimates the fresco's figures, both figuratively and literally enlightening them with a new glance. The following lines depict, as they contemplate, the uncovering of truth, some new section of the work revealed by the sharpness of a fresh view:

> Now as near for all the world
> I have revealed to you, the heaven
> whole touch is, one instant, stroke-
> sure, vibrant, as a single meaning
> twines a complex sentence?
>                          Winds
> may revel in a grapevine so,
> its tendrils, looping, complicated
> shoots, to mine one spicy lilt.
>
> As in the workings of late Spring,
> each tree a myriad-leaf-noted
> flute that showers forth for boughs
> like staves one bird-scored harmony.
>
> Such things I feel at second-hand,
> a hand beyond my maker's. Hear
> and see them too within your words,
> your senses, your experience
> at large as much as I can know.
>
> And feel a touching through us all,
> my master, saints and demons, things
> possessed: instant recovery.
> (52)

How should we parse the first question above? Weiss intertwines phrases like the very tendrils he describes. He eliminates relative pronouns. Pushing clause on or into clause, rendering them phrasal, he transforms the hypotactic into the paratactic, eliminating, in other words, a verbal equivalent of visual depth. Like painting, his poem often seems to lack a third dimension of subordinating clauses, which we must retrieve or recover, plucking it out or risking further submergence. Each act of understanding, from which mutual salvation derives, takes a dive into the depths of history or art; it is a plumbing that is a simultaneous act of covering, repressing, dirtying.

Weiss's fascination with what is difficult (along with Ben Belitt, he was probably the last survivor of the high modernist legacy) matches an agnostic temperament that, viewing the invented fresco, worships the icons and shards of art alone rather than the religious truths the painting originally represented. In an aesthetic age, the subjective eye looks for a mirror; it seeks no miraculous Red Sea beyond its own blood, but rather only "glimpses of the human / truth, the mind and senses' moments, / earth-bound, flickering" (55). These days, artistic contemplation assures the harmonies that religion once provided. Weiss has placed himself in a tradition going back to the great Romantics. One thinks of the communion between a hopeful Coleridge and Charles Lamb at the end of "This Lime-Tree Bower My Prison," when a single rook in the evening sky unites the two men by focusing their visions, and reaching through contemporaries like Elizabeth Bishop (e.g., "Poem"). *Recoveries* promises a triple union of creator, speaking creation, and audience. Puns, which include a serious consideration of gerunds as heralds of eternal action, suggest our salvation:

> Unaware he'd draw you here,
> my master, in a sense, paints you
> in too, essential to the scene,
> the painting, so its word suggests,
> still going on.
> (57)

Not only the doubleness of "draw you here" but also the homonymic "in too / into" engages our perceptual energies. And "the painting" itself occupies an implicit double space, primarily as part of a phrase ("the painting . . . still going on"), and secondarily as the object of a preposition ("paints you / into . . . the painting"). Creation is a continual process: the nominal gerund ("painting") takes an adjectival participle ("going on"): there is no simple verb.

Beautifully cementing the continuity between seer and scene, Weiss finally returns at the end to the pilgrim's own voice, with no more preparation than a space on the page, and an expansion to a (mostly) ten-syllable line. Despite its protestations of erosion and fading, the fresco grows:

The painting going on, the latest creature,
wave insurgent, leaf, bird, star,
takes shape.
            And thus, by being wholly fresh,
it saves—by making wholly new best serves—
the treasures else forgotten which belong
to you, your master, all who once have lived.
(61)

This trio of selves, creator-fresco-audience, in continually dazzling, immortal moments that create and undo vision through a range of shades and shimmerings, renders all speculation useless. Like Anthony Hecht's speaker in "The Venetian Vespers," who thought he "might be saved by looking," Weiss asserts the saving grace of art (with a strong pun in "wholly / holy").

He ends with an appeal to our combined senses of what Keats called "negative capability" and "intensity":

Still moments matter out a monument.
And from now on, so let its moment bid,
each shade and shimmer of your fresco,
opaque, immortal moment of a red,
obliterating every argument,
every theory, doubt and terror, will
be flashing through my mind.
                    Now, into night,
the precious mine of you amassing.
(61–62)

The first sentence laconically, peculiarly, suggests the growth of the picture and its significance through a succession of still moments. Is "still" adverbial and adjectival, like Keats's "still" unravished bride? Does "matter out" mean "take matter away from" or "give matter to"? The final phrase also epitomizes Weiss's curious style. "Mine" refers to the fresco as a repository of ores and riches that grow and build continuously and are continuously pushed down farther, even as the presumed weight of carbon is required to crush and thereby to form a diamond. But the phrasal ambiguity (as well as the "mind" / "mine" rhyme) encourages us to understand the final participle as both intransitive and transitive (e.g., "you are amassing" and "I continue to amass your mine in my own mind"), and as a quasi-gerundive ("the mine of your amasssing"). We might consider this construction as an equivalent to the end of Stevens's "Description Without Place" (chapter 1):

"Like rubies reddened by rubies reddening." In "mine of you" we may even hear an echo of a Buberian I-Thou relationship, which at every step the poem has implicitly stressed but nowhere labeled as such. Mine/Me/Yours/You: with none of John Ashbery's frivolity, Weiss everywhere insists on the fluidity of pronouns. Like James Merrill, he deems his greatest treasures those that he shares.

## "If It Were Us": Art's Ghostly Improvements

The title sequence of Irving Feldman's 1986 volume is probably the strongest achievement of a constantly changing poet who, although he has won his share of the available prizes, has never garnered as wide an audience as he deserves. It provides a complex lesson in art appreciation, combining satire with a serious contemplation of art's power to provoke, annoy, and sustain. Dealing with George Segal's plaster-cast, life-sized sculptures of people in the most mundane of situations, who resemble chalky cousins of Edward Hopper's sad and isolated subjects, Feldman poses, explicitly as well as implicitly, basic aesthetic questions: Whom do these statues represent? How did the artist manage to make them? How do they make us feel? Are they any good? In other words, his speaker (in twenty poems reflecting his many moods, as well as the overheard banalities of typical gallery-goers) looks at the sculptures mimetically, formally, sociologically, evaluatively, and emotionally. He also examines them historically, for in the section entitled "Surely they're just so large" he imagines them as revenants from the plaster-cast collections that universities used for instructional purposes throughout the nineteenth century and which they either destroyed or relegated to dusty basements once slide reproductions of original works became widely available. The pieces seem to have "come racing in place from all the way back / to stand in no time at all—all of them, all of us / together here."[6] The very wonderment of the phrase "in no time at all" suggests both the eternity of art and the immediacy of the statue-creatures' hasty exit from down below. Like Weiss, whose saintly speaker stands for a brotherhood of other depicted figures, Feldman favors a first-person plural throughout his poem: the single speaker is never reluctant to speak on behalf of all of us. Part of the irregularity of the sequence's ekphrastic enterprise is precisely its handling of a whole collection, of multiple pieces, through multiple points of view.

Richard Howard has said that "the deadening hand of literalness . . . is everywhere" in this almost Kafkaesque poem, which calls into question matters of identity and of priority.[7] Like Ashbery's "Self-Portrait in a Convex Mirror," "All of Us Here" weaves its wondrous dreams through variations on the theme of a coherent self—whether of statue, viewer, or artist does not matter—all of which come to naught. Singularity vanishes: only the mass counts. We encounter them; they represent us: Who possesses, or is possessed by, whom? Everything looks like a double of something else. Nothing original survives. In numbers and in anonymity there is safety. Feldman's own easy colloquial language, a kind of deadpan vaudevillian shtick, betrays his deepest anxieties about art's relationship to experience, and even experience's relationship to identity. Nowhere have the obsessive thematic concerns of postmodernism been so lightly handled. Whatever one thinks of the Segal statues (Are they effective in their banality? Does their emptiness mirror the loss of all value and certainty in our historical moment?),[8] they are the *occasion* for serious questioning. Kenneth Gross's phrase for the sequence—"a satiric and elegiac apocalypse"—aptly captures Feldman's combination of anarchy, humor, and despair when approaching these statues that "are the shells as much as the sums of human work."[9]

Whom do these statues resemble? People we know? Human types? Ourselves? From one perspective they look alive and seem to admonish their observers: "We yield this place to them" (5). We also "acknowledge that Being (however poor) precedes / *becoming* (though swift, exuberant, fascinating, gorgeous)" (5). But from another viewpoint these statue-creatures are a "mirror of literalness" (6); because they are too easy to identify with they consequently disappoint us, like Keats's Urn and its constituent figures that speak volumes but remain eternally silent. Perhaps they remind observers unpleasantly of their own mortality, as the statues' ghastly pallor portends the common fate of the grave. Or perhaps they resemble the corpses of those people at Pompeii who were caught unaware by volcanic ash and buried in place before they had any chance to escape or even to know what, quite literally, hit them.

One feels squeamish in the presence of such death-in-life. The statues remind us "of our obtrusive, / too tedious, too obvious, too mortal selves" (7). Such mimetic art is both an occasion for self-congratulation and a reproach to our self-delusions, as unsettling as it is gratifying. The original narcissistic pleasure of seeing any human representation is quickly replaced by discomfort and annoyance. Weariness overcomes eagerness (who has not been overwhelmed by a long stretch in a museum or gallery?), and disappointment supplants hope. Feldman never allows a single response to get the upper hand for long. As in Ashbery's rendition of Parmigianino's self-portrait, the statues beckon us, and simultaneously hold us back: "what welcomes us here is only ourselves in / a sudden vision of ourselves" (7). But we encounter our own mortality and must accept our far from superior status to these dead, white, lumpish, humanoid objects. They are composed of soil, which is debris, and "of such / alluvium we are formed" (20), but "they look like coprolites" caught in "dust, pallor, drabness of the tomb" (22). In terms of representation, we think of them as the common anonymous people of our century and as "just poor people . . . whose names have been exalted into allegory: / Exile, Homeless, Refugee, Unknown, Mourner, Corpse" (32).

Even such frustrations, however, indicate the human hunger for something greater, or at least other, in life, something that only art can give. Consolations, however fleeting, are possible: "And so it's oddly flattering to feel welcomed / by being ignored, as if we belong here like stones / and trees, are features natural to the scene" (15). The milling-about living people become for a moment a "natural" backdrop for the ersatz humans whose space they have just invaded. Who is imitating whom? One plaster couple resembles a heightened, improved version of a human one:

> This couple strolling here beside the BRICK WALL
> look the way we might look if it were us
> in raincoats walking slowly in the city dusk
> —but how much better at it these figures are!
> (35)

Does art imitate nature, or the other way around? It hardly matters, for Feldman slyly reminds his readers of the implicit metaphor-making in all representation and consequently in all knowledge: "About these figures we don't ask, 'Who are they?' / We ask, 'Who, who is it they remind us of?'" (36). In other words, because they lack genuine identity or integrity they must be merely *like* something else. But if they are better than we are, then it is we, not the statues, who are the pale imitations. We are returned firmly to the realm of the simulacrum. But it is a strange simulacrum, not a mere imitation but at once an enlargement and a diminishment. Segal's three-dimensional art seems paradoxically to combine the rival strands isolated by the art historian Svetlana Alpers: the Renaissance Italian tendency toward perspective, narrative, and iconography, and the alternative tradition (mostly in the north but expanded by her to include pictures by Caravaggio and Manet) in which figures "are suspended in action to be portrayed. The stilled or arrested quality of these works is a symptom of a certain tension between the narrative assumptions of the art and an attentiveness to descriptive presence."[10]

Segal's figures are transparently mimetic and bizarrely inhuman simultaneously. Even more than most statuary they combine stasis with the appearance of activity, placed as they are amid real props, a mirror, a kitchen table, a doorway. They are versions of ourselves but also a collective memento mori.

If still life painting is *nature morte*, the statuary, a tableau vivant, is also the living, human dead:

> They were not alive and were walking in the streets,
> or they were in a bus, sitting still, and still
> were white all over, were stone in the core . . .
> This white plague expresses now the new boundary
> of death, senseless, superimposed, suddenly there,
> down, up, right here . . . unstable treacherous, *jumping*.
> (10)

The adhesive conjunctive "and" above cements their deadliness and activity: not "they were not alive *but* they were walking," to express some surprise; rather, a more banal simultaneity: they were both dead *and* mobile, just as now they are in some permanent state of aliveness but no longer really walking. *Still* white, "still unravished," one might say, thinking of Keats's bride-urn, and still *jumping*.

The poems combine general aesthetic reflection with deliberations on a particular Segal exhibit. They contain allegorical feints as well as a dramatic rendering of an entire spectrum of feelings, thoughts, and questions that an individual, or many individuals, might have in response to a specific artistic provocation. The lumpish but strikingly realistic sculptures, possessing what Feldman calls a "radiant density" (41), are, like all art, both less and greater than actual life. The last poem in the sequence, "They Say to Us," is nominally concerned with photographs, but it may as well be discussing the sculptures. In a final fantasy, the living and the dead pass family snapshots among themselves. The represented figures, whether sculpted or photographed, "appreciate under our gaze" (40), the speaker announces. A sense of satisfaction comes through at last as steady looking produces results: the figures gain in value as they are appreciated. Feldman's final contented response purges fear, pity, condescension, and even questioning:

> There they are—"little William,"
> "her brother," "the neighbor's girl"—
> all of them pressed close
> in a single pack in dark
> and radiant density.
> All of us here
> are deeply satisfied.
> (41)

Such a satisfaction has not come easily. Theodore Weiss created a talking-seeing figure for his poem. But Feldman has looked long and hard at figures who themselves have no eyes and no voice; the "sudden vision of ourselves" (7) that amuses, delights, then frustrates and disturbs, challenges him at first to think that "we," of course, shall not end up like these people.

Such vaunted superiority is a defensive and pathetic but natural response to the challenge of the statues. Because we are all composed of dust and alluvium, we fit right into the show ourselves as more than mere spectators: perhaps we "could be extras here ourselves!" (12), he sardonically exclaims. "We can't help putting ourselves in their places" (32), which means that if they are now dead they serve not only as a memento mori but also as a provocation to another, more generous kind of reimagining on our parts. We must think of them, as we invariably do of forebears, friends, and dead heroes, in their own youthful vitality. Hence the earned consolation of the last poem, quoted above, which renders an equilibrium between the living and the dead. The most banal provocation has resulted, paradoxically, in the deepest satisfaction.

## "Representational Pictures of Emotional Situations": The Possibilities for Nonrepresentational Ekphrasis

Apparently, we can never quite escape from mimesis. The English artist Howard Hodgkin, whose brilliantly painted pictures on wood evoke memories, suggest rather than portray subjects, order planes of color into luminous harmonies of spatial design, has resolutely denied his affinity with the American Abstract Expressionists. He paints, he says, "not appearances [but] representational pictures of emotional situations."[11] Even though some of their titles suggest mimetic possibilities (a portrait, a geographic location) the works do nothing to alleviate a viewer's anxieties about the relation between title and object or subject and means. The painter's hand seems to have recreated something other than *things* we can instantly recognize. Hodgkin's pictures should have provoked a wide range of "literary" responses, but only Susan Sontag has broached a meditation on his work. Even more than Matisse, De Kooning, and other inventive twentieth-century revelers in color, Hodgkin has apparently renounced design and representation entirely except through suggestive titles and occasional nuanced depictions. He has, in Sontag's estimation, "fielded the most inventive, sensuously affecting color repertory of any contemporary painter—as if, in taking up the ancient quarrel between *disegno* and *colore*, he had wanted to give *colore* its most sumptuous exclusive victory."[12] Seeing pictures such as these both provokes and inhibits response: we wish to say something, but what shall we say?

If, as Paul Fry has speculated, "poetry enviously discovers the meaning-lessness of the nonhuman in pictures," then should not abstract art offer the largest playing field of meaninglessness, the grandest provocation of generic envy?[13] No English or American poet has exclaimed so simply over the sumptuous victory of sheer color as has Garcia Lorca, albeit in a nonek-phrastic context, in his memorable "Verde, que te quiero, verde." The uni-versal silence of painting, which has traditionally inspired poets to speech and made them envious, seems to become paradoxically more silent still in the case of the nonrepresentational and the "meaningless." Or, rather, poets themselves have been by and large silent on the subject. In addition, although much has been written about the relationships between twentieth-century poets and the painters whose lives and ideas they shared (Apollinaire in France, Frank O'Hara in the United States), almost no critic has tried to deal with the understandably few poems written about nonrepresentational painting, whether Abstract Expressionist or purely geometric. As I observed in Chapter 1, poets prefer paintings of people, landscapes, people within landscapes, or still lifes. (So do critics.) We look for works to look *at* in which we can see ourselves and to which we can pose questions of identity.

With no basis for a response to a conventional character or scene, and in the absence of all mimesis, a poet confronting a painting by Pollock, Kline, Mondrian, et al. has really only two paths to follow. He or she may offer a sober, scientifically accurate "description," detailing the shapes, colors, lines, and gestures that compose a picture. Or the poet may use the painting as a springboard for reverie, reflection, or (what would be most exciting and is least done) metaphorical conjectures that would aim to translate the pic-ture's ways and means, its effects on and intentions for us, into appropriate linguistic structures. The critic Terrence Diggory suggests that an ekphrasis of Abstract Expressionist art is theoretically impossible (or at least unlikely) because one can only see, not read, the paintings.[14] But surely one could "describe" such pictures, whose invitations to speculate, to discover meaning, and to "listen" to what they may be saying are stronger even than those with a traditional iconic or naturalistic subject matter.

For reasons one can only surmise, the best descriptive renditions of non-representational paintings seem to turn up in prose. If writers traditionally respond to the sensuous immediacy of images that lack linguistic content and meaning, why does pure form thwart them? "Nostalgia for presence" is one of the great post-Romantic obsessions: if form alone is present, perhaps nostalgia for, envy of, and fascination with the visible evaporate.[15] Where the corporeality of life, even in a two-dimensional reduction, inspires poets to write poems, the incorporeality of abstract art seems to force them to express their meditations in the (perhaps more solid or four-square) medium of prose. The case of O'Hara is the best example. For all the zany exuberance of his *Collected Poems*, very few of them even try to address the paintings he so lovingly and seriously deals with in his essays. His most famous short "art" poem, "Digression on 'Number 1,' 1948," concerning one of Jackson Pollock's action paintings, does not mention the picture until line 13 (of twenty). And the aptly titled "digression" gives a reader less of a sense of the painting than of the poet-viewer, who has already proclaimed a weariness that he obviously hopes the painting will abate:

> There is the Pollock, white harm
> will not fall, his perfect hand
>
> and the many short voyages. They'll
> never fence the silver range.
> Stars are out and there is sea
> enough beneath the glistening earth
> to bear me toward the future
> which is not so dark. I see.[16]

Whatever satisfactions the painting gives the poet, or the poem gives a reader, a genuinely full or even partial vision of the painting is not among them. O'Hara reproduces more of Pollock's essence in his essay reviews, which mingle historical and biographical details with sharp and incandescent glimpses at actual pictures. When he concentrates on the paintings, he writes with memorable, often metaphorically alert phrasing. Of *White Light*, he says it "has a blazing, acrid, and dangerous glamour of a legendary kind, not unlike those volcanoes which are said to lure the natives to the lip of the crater and, by the beauty of their writhings and the strength of their fumes, cause him to fall in" (29–30). Or, of *Number 29*, a painting-collage on glass:

> [It] is a work of the future; it is waiting. Its reversible textures, the brilliant clarity of the drawing, the tragedy of a linear violence which, in recognizing itself in its own mirror-self, sees elegance, the open nostalgia for brutality expressed in embracing the sharp edges and banal forms of wires and shells, the cruel acknowledgment of pebbles as elements of the dream, the drama of black mastering sensuality and color, the apparition of these forms in open space as if in air, all these qualities united in one work present the crisis of Pollock's originality and concomitant anguish full-blown. (32–33)

Such writing pays abundant attention both to the object it describes and praises and to the audience whom the writer wishes rhetorically to persuade and imaginatively to make see.[17]

Even poets comfortable in many modes, styles, and genres seem to prefer prose, or prose poetry, as the vehicle for an ekphrastic treatment of abstract work. John Hollander concludes a lengthy meditation on a series of notional objects seen during a stroll through an imaginary museum with a one and one-half page presentation of a geometric painting (in the style of Kenneth Noland or Jules Olitski). First he describes it in a cool, scientifically measured tone. Then he animates it, giving voice to a picture that poses and next resolves a series of questions concerning figuration itself. The picture cuts to the ontological heart of formal enigmas:

> "I know what you are asking me: Am I not a representation of the very problem of picturing what I represent? A physical metaphor, too blue, too objectlike, to be any more than a picture of my circle; yet that gross blue periphery itself dreams of a gentler touch, a frailer penciled way of getting at the immaterial form, as if at any moment the inner dream of what a circle truly is could be erased in a kind of waking. Oh yes, circles are a problem."[18]

Whereas Weiss listened to the voice of a human figure in a fresco, Hollander goes two steps further: not only does he hear an entire picture speak but he also gives voice and soul to a resolutely nonhuman shape, in this case, a pair of concentric circles. Apparently, the clarity of prose best matches the austerity of the painting's subject and its ontological reveries about the very "problem" of circles.

Kenneth Koch's whacky "The Artist," a tour de force that successfully predicted forty years ago various movements still to come (Pop Art, Site-Specific Art, Cristo and his wrappings), manages to be a poem (albeit a very prosy one) that briefly "describes" works of art, but largely because of their entirely notional status. (Koch can invent objects to describe, but it is apparently more difficult for him, and his contemporaries, to describe actual ones.) The hero confronts the problem of every artist: What to do next. He goes from work to work with dizzying energy and playful panache:

> To bring things up to date: I have just finished *Campaign*, which is a
>     tremendous piece of charcoal.
> Its shape is difficult to describe; but it is extremely large and would
>     reach to the sixth floor of the Empire State Building.
> I have been very successful in the past fourteen or fifteen years.[19]

More prose than poem, "The Artist" stands out as a rarity in many ways. Another proof of my thesis concerning poets' reluctance to approach non-mimetic subjects, especially in a poem, is Edward Hirsch's recent anthology of writers *on* art. It includes only four nonrepresentational painters (Jasper

Johns, Anselm Kiefer, Li-Lin Lee, and Piet Mondrian). Of these, Johns's *Corpse and Mirror II* (with no recognizable corpse or mirror visible in the painter's famous cross-hatchings) inspires the poet John Yau to a prose meditation, troping on the painting's titular objects but not the painting itself.[20]

In the absence of either human figures with explicit or implied narrative and psychological potential, or landscapes and other material objects that might stimulate concentration as well as reverie, most poets shy away from an attention to the nakedness of sheer form. Jorie Graham, whose early poem "For Mark Rothko" I discuss in Chapter 7, uses a Rothko color-block painting as a starting point for an understanding of shades of redness within a natural field of vision. The painting itself is an originating Muse for empirical and psychological responses to another kind of scene. It is more like a memory or recollection than an actual presence the poet is confronting on the occasion of her poem.

Richard Howard, who has focused his own devotion to the fine arts largely on the characters and procedures of artists themselves, has performed a remarkable feat in the title poem from *Like Most Revelations*:

> It is the movement that incites the form,
> discovered as a downward rapture—yes,
> it is the movement that delights the form,
> sustained by its own velocity. And yet
>
> it is the movement that delays the form
> while darkness slows and encumbers; in fact
> it is the movement that betrays the form,
> baffled in such toils of ease, until
>
> it is the movement that deceives the form,
> beguiling our attention—we supposed
> it is the movement that achieves the form.
> Were we mistaken? What does it matter if
>
> it is the movement that negates the form?
> Even though we give (give up) ourselves
> to this mortal process of continuing,
> it is the movement that creates the form.[21]

An homage to Morris Louis and his long vertical strips of dripping color, the poem is rare for Howard in its own tightly insistent lyricism and its quatrains in which "form" appears twice, rhyming only with itself, and as the object of a series of rhyming though contrary verbs ("incites/delights," "delays/betrays," "negates/creates"). This poem and its unspecified but

archetypal Louis painting, like most other revelations, force us to give ourselves up to a process that creates by first negating, that delights by inciting,
that achieves by deceiving. The series of statements are really questions in
disguise about the process and results of a Morris Louis painting, whose
seductively vibrant colors either undermine or, in a final irony, affirm its
form. Action painting has inspired an appropriate sort of action poetry. In
both, *lines* give substance and subject to the final product. Because each of
Howard's quatrains contains both enjambed and end-stopped lines, we are
reminded that we experience painting and poem as sequential and continuous, but also as discrete and partial.

"Digression," O'Hara's term for his own ekphrasis about abstract art,
suggests that the Pollock painting is even more an occasion for reverie away
from, rather than about, itself than for an act of homage through accurate
description. Far from wishing to compete with the painter, who always has
the advantage of silence, the poet takes as a given the silence of noniconic
shapes and weaves from them either a dream—with barely discernible
connection to the original provocation—or a series of abstract reflections
occasioned by a depicted abstraction.[22] Howard subtitles his poem "After
Morris Louis," another indication of a movement away from an originary
provocation.

Douglas Crase's "Blue Poles" also moves away from a specific picture
(Pollock's enormous 1953 oil, whose title refers to a partially representational
detail within the action field), but his meditation implicitly works as a metaphor rather than a pure description or an effort to solve problems from aesthetics. It opens by turning away from the painting and by suggesting its
resemblance to a landscape:

> What we bring back is the sense of the size of it,
> Potential as something permanent is, the way a road map
> Of even the oldest state suggests in its tangled details
> The extent of a country in which topography and settlement
> Interrupt only at random into a personal view.

The painting—its lines, colors, random patterns that when looked at long
enough cohere into a semblance of order—has as its central organizing motif
the poles at the title, with which the poem ends:

> . . . Serene and adamantly enlarged,
> Seismic totems arranged at the rim of day, they advance
> On the waking extent of the world, what it knew.[23]

By treating the painting metaphorically as a map, Crase moves between an
actual description and a "digression." "Blue Poles" is less *after* Pollock (as

Howard's poem is after Louis) than a recreation of his picture and a demonstration of how one might make sense of purely abstract phenomena.

Perhaps the most interesting recent ekphrastic meditation is Charles Wright's "Summer Storm," originally included in Hirsch's anthology and later reprinted in the poet's 1995 volume *Chickamauga* but significantly without the accompanying illustration of Mondrian's *Composition—Gray Red* (1935):

> As Mondrian knew,
> Art is the image of an image of an image,
> More vacant, more transparent
> With each repeat and slough:
> > one skin, two skins, it comes clear,
> An old idea is not that old.
>
> Two rectangles, red and gray, from 1935,
> Distant thunder like distant thunder—
> Howitzer shells, large
> > drop-offs into drumbeat and roll.
> And there's that maple again,
> Head like an African Ice Age queen, full-leafed and lipped.
>
> Behind her, like clear weather,
> Mondrian's window gives out
> > onto ontology,
> A dab of red, a dab of gray, white interstices.
> You can't see the same thing twice,
> As Mondrian knew.[24]

Wright's poem is a three-stanza fantasia. It includes—seamlessly, as part of a single experiential *take* on its titular subject—an abbreviated description of the actual painting, a theoretical point of view, and an imaginative recreation, through various layers of abstraction, of what the painting *might* be representing. It begins and ends with aesthetic generalizations about the nature of seeing and depicting. Despite the easy, colloquial philosophizing that Wright has made recognizably his own, the poem implicitly provokes questions: Exactly what does it describe? What Wright thinks Mondrian represents or sees? What the geometry establishes or signifies? What Mondrian saw from a window and then transcribed? Or, rather, a summer storm during the composition of the poem, not the painting?

Only two lines refer directly to the canvas; we must take the rest as a merging of Mondrian's vision with Wright's own. What a reader cannot tell from the poem is what the painting actually looks like: its red and gray rectangles occupy a small part of its lower right-hand corner, while the entire canvas, divided regularly by Mondrian's characteristic thin black lines, might represent four panes of a window, the top left pane matching the gray of the rectangle at the lower right. We have, then, metaphorically two windows: Mondrian's painted one and Wright's actual one, through which he looks at both the maple tree in his own backyard and a print of the abstract picture, while hearing distant thunder on a summer day. Mondrian—his vision, his picture, and his inspiration—opens us to the study of being itself: a claim asserted though hardly proved by the poem. The poet uses his tropes, a simile within a metaphor, to compare a thing to itself as well as to something else (thunder to thunder, thunder to gunfire), or to expand a field of reference (maple tree in Virginia to African sculpture). The poem is an act of repetition as well as of reflection. It makes its own images out of Mondrian's original one, sloughing a skin like a snake, getting farther away from an original (and becoming an image of an image of an image) while simultaneously revealing the new skin underneath. What disappears (the snake's skin, the former image, Mondrian's window or even his entire picture) is replaced by a new work: Wright's window, his backyard, *his* ontology, his poem.

If representational art encourages description of both its technique and its subject matter, nonrepresentational art forces a different kind of descriptive and emotional response. Rilke's comment that in *Neue Gedichte* he expressed "not feelings, but *things* I had felt" (my emphasis), prepared the way for what Frank Kermode subsequently labeled the "Romantic image,"[25] an icon bearing psychological, emotive, and conceptual weight, and also the whole idea of materialism in modern art. "To feel things" instead of feelings is rather like Howard Hodgkin's claim to represent "emotional situations." It is the necessary antithesis to Wordsworth's conjecture that "the soul, / Remembering how she felt, but what she felt / Remembering not, retains an obscure sense / Of possible sublimity."[26] The processes of feeling and recollection loom large in Wordsworth's speculation, whereas Rilke's evokes something like a hard residue. Poets and painters of the past two centuries might be divided between those whose bias falls on the side of the process, and those whose falls on that of the *thing*. We can, therefore, see exactly why so few contemporary poets have taken up the cause of nonrepresentational painting: to write about it requires an equal commitment to action, process, the "how," and to product, material, the thing-itself.[27] When Randall Jarrell played the role of Devil's advocate in his essay "Against Abstract Expressionism," he spoke on behalf of the world's own materiality as well as the artist's obligation to praise it by reproducing it: "Doesn't the world need the painter's praise any more?" he asked despairingly.[28] But the materials of Mondrian's painting (or those of Hodgkin, Louis, Pollock, et al.) do not turn away from the world, or from the human relationship to it. Far from resisting the world, these painters have reimagined it and represented it in a language whose syntax, vocabulary, and grammar we have yet to learn. Merleau-Ponty remarks provocatively that "the world is *what we see* and . . . nevertheless, we must learn to see it." Such a world contains the pure essences of color, shape, pattern, and their energetic depictions in paintings that have but seldom been "listened to" by our visibly attentive poets.

# SIX

# JOHN ASHBERY'S HAUNTED LANDSCAPES

Including John Ashbery in a book about description, indeed, labeling him a descriptive poet (or any other specific *kind* of poet) may seem presumptuous or simply special pleading, as it has been his fate to have evaded easy categorizing ever since the publication of *Some Trees* in 1956. Nevertheless, Ashbery's descriptive urges and gestures can furnish readers with a handle or a possible entry into the vague morass, the swamps and thickets of the verbal terrain that he has mapped out for half a century. Ashbery's poems often seem like verbal equivalents of a kaleidoscope that contains different parts of speech instead of rapidly whirling colored particles. Amid rambling speculations, syntactic confusions, obscure references, missed connections, layers of magnificently mottled diction that sometimes fail to cohere, his descriptions are often the first things that deviate into sense. They suggest that he is observing the world steadily if momentarily, and they prove the ineluctable modality of the visible as one strand, among many, in his various trains of thought.

Description is the glue that helps to keep the poems together. Presenting Ashbery as a landscape poet, or a descriptive one, casts light on a sizable proportion of his poetry—even if only parts rather than wholes, let alone volumes. It is especially as a watcher of the world that I wish to consider him. He appropriates the domain of the seen, painting as well as nature, as his province and the occasion for many of his most moving utterances. What often seems his true subject is the contest or marriage between the writing person (or instrument) and the objects of his (or its) attention. Although the sense of the "personal" is slight in Ashbery, as he himself has confessed in interviews, many critics have noticed his connections to British Romanticism, which constitutes one great tradition in the contemporary poetic scene. I wish to draw out that strand and take a deeper look at the "haunted landscape" of a poet haunted by the very idea of landscape.[1]

A landscape haunted by what, and for what reason? The phrase comes from the title of a poem in *As We Know* with an ominous, mysterious, but also inevitable conclusion: "Now time and the land are identical, / Linked forever."[2] As readers have long been aware, in Ashbery time seems to flow seamlessly as he ticks along through life, registering the phenomena of consciousness as they flicker through his brain. Past, present, and future are equally accessible, melting into one another; so are persons, an "I," a "we" flowing randomly into a "he" and a "you." But the third part of Ashbery's current appears in his use of space, specifically a landscape always changing and always heaving into the present tense through the radiant illumination or foggy mists of nostalgia. Time, consciousness, and landscape are his primary subjects. Ashbery is a poet nostalgic for space as well as time. In "Haunted Landscape," everything changes before our eyes: the poem ends with a haunted house, before which it has presented an abandoned mountain landscape and a farming scene somewhere down South. The poem extends from pastoral to georgic to domestic gestures. At the midpoint of its thirteen stanzas comes a three-stanza sentence, typical of Ashbery's experiments with syntax and image, and of his pondering the usefulness of the landscape itself:

> They were thinking, too, that this was the right way to begin
> A farm that would later have to be uprooted to make way
> For the new plains and mountains that would follow after
> To be extinguished in turn as the ocean takes over
>
> Where the glacier leaves off and in the thundering of surf
> And rock, something, some note or other, gets lost,
> And we have this to look back on, not much, but a sign
> Of the petty ordering of our days as it was created and
>     led us
>
> By the nose through itself, and now it has happened
> And we have it to look at, and have to look at it
> For the good it now possesses which has shrunk from the
> Outline surrounding it to a little heap or handful near
>     the center.
> (262)

All of nature unfolds through geological layers of time. The phrase "uprooted to make way / For" implies a forward move into capitalist real estate development rather than a backward one toward topographic upheaval. We look back on our memory of the farm, nostalgia for an Eden that is a center, as the chiasmus of "we have it to look at, and have to look at it" makes clear. Such a haunting memory surrounds us, all the time and everywhere, even while it exists as a mere heap of images near the center, whether in actuality or in another chamber of the mind. A panorama of visual details overwhelms Ashbery's poems and his speakers, sometimes charming them, sometimes depressing them.

"It sure was pleasant to spend a day in the country," announces the cartoon-inspired narrator of "Farm Implements and Rutabagas in a Landscape" (106), a sestina in which Popeye and his family cavort, talking in pseudo-Elizabethan accents. Popeye speaks for all of Ashbery's quasi-characters, who seem to know that a rural retreat, whether in a Renaissance pastoral or a contemporary comic book, is at best a partial answer and a momentary stay against urban blight, civilized traumas, adult fears, and political disarray. Here, as elsewhere, Ashbery reminds us of the impossible dream of home. Physical locations resemble what he calls in another, mocking context "centers of communication" ("And *Ut Pictura Poesis* Is Her Name," 235), those semipersonified fields for which other people abandon us. There is neither a center that can hold nor a periphery that can be reached. Flux is all, which is why a permanently desirable pastoral landscape always evades us, and why the constantly interrupting, dallying details of the cityscape engage as much of Ashbery's imaginative energies as the refinements of the green world. His central question, never explicitly asked, always hovering over every page, is the same as that of Elizabeth Bishop: Where is our home?

Because Ashbery has almost no "self," he has almost no self-pity. Still, he sadly writes, in the middle of "A Wave" (328–329), while describing a place at "the other end of the bridge . . . the place of power, / A hill ringed with low, ridgelike fortifications":

> . . . And so because it is impossible to believe
> That anyone lives there, it is we who shall be homeless,
>    outdoors
> At the end. And we won't quite know what to do about it.
> It's mind-boggling, actually.

Ashbery conceives of home as Bishop does in "The End of March": as something distant and unstable, like her rickety cabin on stilts, and never to be reached, however much it is dreamed about. The goal recedes, mirage-like, and we return down the beach. Ashbery may very well allude to Bishop's poem further on in "A Wave" when, depicting a kind of dream cabin of his own, he describes a time "when hours and days go by in silence and the phone / Never rings, and widely spaced drops of water / Fall from the eaves." At this point, he says, one can rejoice "That the years of war are far off in the past or in the future, / That memory contains everything," and one can contemplate the self, memories, "and move on refreshed" (332–333). The same nostalgia surfaces in a later section when the "you" speaks of a dream landscape:

> "I was lost, but seemed to be coming home,
> Through quincunxes of apple trees, but ever
> As I drew closer, as in Zeno's paradox, the mirage
> Of home withdrew and regrouped a little farther off."
> (339)

This is the dream of the prodigal son returning to the father's home. John Shoptaw analyzes this as Asbery's Oedipal drama, but even without the biographical information one can see in Ashbery's handling of the landscape something akin to Bishop's. Or like Stevens's in "The Auroras of Autumn," which opposes the sheer dramatic theatricality of the boreal heavens, their constant change and color, to a lonely cabin on the northern shore and to the dream of both mother and father. Ashbery would agree with Stevens: "The house is of the mind and they and time, / Together, all together."[3]

Among the many qualities that tie Ashbery, through Stevens, to the Emersonian line in American literature, the most salient is surprise. An Ashbery poem follows no predictable course; its landscape cannot be foreseen, just as its scenario, theme, dialogue, and syntax meander through a linguistic territory that keeps us always off guard. Ashbery ends the fourth long paragraph of "Self-Portrait in a Convex Mirror" with a poignant analysis of one's own amazement at noticing a snowfall that has occurred while one was napping in the afternoon. Such an ordinary event has nothing to recommend it but the fact that now, with day ending, "it will be hard for you / To get to sleep tonight, at least until late." When fully responding to Ashbery's poetry, we run the risk of radically disturbing life's diurnal rhythms. Day and night; waking and sleep; up and down; inside and outside: all the old, rigid binaries are juggled, or sometimes jostled, but within a seamless flow of language that keeps us buoyed, dumbfounded but not threatened. Like Parmigianino in his self-portrait, Ashbery startles but he does not shock. And the effect of his provocations has everything to do with the steadiness of his tone over and above the transformations in his sentences or his semifarcical, semisentimental experiments with diction.

In his notes to *West-Östlicher Divan*, discussing metaphor in Arabic poetry, Goethe observes that "to the Oriental, all things suggest all things, so that, accustomed to connecting remotest things together crosswise, he does not hesitate to draw contrary things from one another by small changes in letters or syllables." Language is, in this mode, inherently poetic; the "Oriental" poet can move easily and freely from primary tropes outward to more daring ones.[4] Although the sentiment has connections to Dr. Johnson on the wit of the metaphysicals, it is also an accurate description of Ashbery's poetry. One thinks of Emerson ("Nominalist and Realist"): "No sentence will hold the whole truth, and the only way in which we can be just, is by giving ourselves the lie." Or (from *The Conduct of Life*): "The feat of the imagination is in showing the convertibility of every thing into every other thing."[5] In Ashbery's poetry of process, all things suggest all other things. Goethe associates such dreaminess, in which sensations flow seamlessly if illogically together, with the Orient. For Ashbery, another analogy is closer to home. Ashbery looks like an avatar of Gaston Bachelard, for whom poetic reverie "functions with inattention." And because of this, "it is often without memory. It is a flight from out of the real that does not always find a consistent unreal world. By following 'the path of reverie'—and a constantly downhill path—consciousness relaxes and wanders and consequently *becomes clouded*."[6] Writing about the equally dreamy Walter Pater, Denis Donoghue refers to this as "the faculty of mind that escapes mere intelligence." In his peculiar way, Ashbery combines Emersonian pragmatism with Paterian aesthetics. What does not escape is his wishful attachment to landscape or other visible data rendered through descriptive language.[7] In the pages that follow I distinguish between Ashbery's attentiveness and his inattention, the two polar points of his compass. The first we can label his Romantic heritage, the second his postmodernist leanings.

Ashbery muses upon the charms and the annoyances, the pleasures and frustrations, of a world in which the freely roaming mind surveys a series of landscapes, taking them in, revising them and then ignoring them, spurning them for new ones. It makes a rival world of forms elsewhere. His landscapes shimmer and vanish. Landscape and syntax are, for him, the same. For Ashbery as for Pater, stability and identity are impossibilities. In commenting on Pater, Donoghue might as well be describing Ashbery: his "claim to 'deal with the conditions of modern life' means only that he evades their obduracy by seeming to rearrange them, making new semblances more congenial than the ones that beset us. What else can art do? Nothing, in sober fact." Or: "Pater's sentences ask to be read as if they wanted to be looked at, not merely to be understood."[8]

Accepting the tacit invitation to "look" at Ashbery's sentences, we often fail to "understand" them, precisely because they wind their way between thickets and clearings, alternately offering and denying clear referentiality or simple "subject matter." Like Stevens (and as Coleridge said about Shakespeare), Ashbery gives us the sense of watching poetry happen while we are experiencing it.[9] Landscape and description more generally provide a temporary resting place for emotion and intellection. It comes as a relief to alight for a moment on a sentence like this, in which we *look* at landscape and sentences together:

> Everything is landscape:
> Perspectives of cliffs beaten by innumerable waves,
> More wheatfields than you can count, forests
> With disappearing paths, stone towers
> And finally and above all the great urban centers, with
> Their office buildings and populations,
>     at the center of which
> We live our lives, made up of a great quantity of
>     isolated instants
> So as to be lost at the heart of a multitude of things.

This excerpt from "French Poems" (*DD*, 39) might be a paradigm of all of Ashbery's work. It mingles at least a temporary grammatical integrity, or the illusion of coherence, with a deeper wonder at the inherent mystery of all connections or of all appearances of integrity. The flat (perhaps self-mocking) diction of the newscaster ("the great urban centers") lets us down after the rhythmically alive, Latinate rolling of "perspectives of fields beaten by innumerable waves." Finally, there's the Wordsworthian shape of the whole unit, ending with a simple announcement of our loss situated at the heart of a multitude of things. Ashbery's sentences are like the landscape he describes here, although seldom as simple. They reproduce a sense of inundation from waves or from uncountable wheat fields and disappearing paths, in the midst of which we lose our isolated selves. We are located but hard to spot, just as the features of the landscape are difficult to enumerate.

Ashbery has already posed, in part 2 of this poem, a central question about the fullness as well as the mystery or the unavailability of external nature:

> But the existence of all these things and especially
> The amazing fullness of their number must be
> For us a source of unforgettable questions:
> Such as: whence does all this come? and again:
> Shall I some day be a part of all this fullness?
> (38)

The "I" is, presumably, not now a part of the scene but an observer of it. But Ashbery is always changing his position, sometimes looking out and sometimes looking in. He offers us the equivalent of a Cubist painting's multiple perspectives. Likewise his landscapes: sometimes one has the sense that he is primarily a city poet, commenting on the cityscape and its shifting visual panorama and sounds. At other times he elicits country images, childhood memories or bits of data from his Hudson River Valley farm. It might be most accurate to call Ashbery a suburban poet (see "Sunrise in Suburbia," *DD*, 49): everything is on a periphery, everything is on the move. As in the United States, where contexts fluctuate or have positively disappeared, in Ashbery's poetry the lack of a center signifies the lack of a centered self and of a central culture.[10] From Emerson and Stevens, with their insistence on the central man and the centrality *of* man, Ashbery veers, darting glances at the landscape, feeling at home everywhere and nowhere at once.

Ashbery's poetic practice reflects his existential anxieties. Long, rambling meditations alternate with shorter, pithier, and more intense lyrical utterances. When reading Ashbery one often comes upon moments—stanzas, extended passages, single sentences, sometimes intensely compacted images—that make graspable, immediate sense and offer, however temporarily, an opening into the murkier opacities of the rest of a poem. These rich nuggets, more often than not in a high, nostalgic, sensuously romantic mode, usually perform acts of description (primarily of landscape, sometimes of interiors). In other words, Ashbery *uses* the landscape, and the general availability of external data, to focus our senses and to steady us momentarily within or on top of the shifting sands of his spatially and temporally unlocatable terrain. He has returned description to its classically sanctioned—and occasionally suspect—position (see Chapter 1) as an interruption of narrative. For Ashbery, description constitutes both dilation and centrality.

Here are the last lines of "The Gazing Grain" (*Houseboat Days*, 215):

... That which is given to see
At any moment is the residue, shadowed

In gold or emerging into the clear bluish haze
Of uncertainty. We come back to ourselves
Through the rubbish of cloud and tree-spattered pavement.
These days stand like vapor under the trees.

Time and space exist together in a hazy landscape composed of perhaps unequal parts of brilliance and vagueness. The gold shadows the residue; the bluish haze of uncertainty is, paradoxically, clear. The city street in which our consciousness emerges, and by which we can take its measure, is spattered: neither clarity nor cleanliness belongs in the urban landscape, just as our days are occluded with vapor.

For sheer splendor, little can compare with the last stanza of "As One Put Drunk into the Packet-Boat" (164), not strictly a landscape per se but a composed description coming in a place of closure:

> The night sheen takes over. A moon of cistercian pallor
> Has climbed to the center of heaven, installed,
> Finally involved with the business of darkness.
> And a sigh heaves from all the small things on earth,
> The books, the papers, the old garters and union-suit
> > buttons
> Kept in a white cardboard box somewhere, and all
> > the lower
> Versions of cities flattened under the equalizing night.
> The summer demands and takes away too much,
> But night, the reserved, the reticent, gives more
> than it takes.

We could take the final couplet as a token of Ashbery's entire method. Night gives by flattening, blurring the distinction between one gesture and its opposite. In this scene, the night behaves like Ashbery himself, who demands our attention but, always reticent and reserved with his own persona, withholds and stations himself at a distance. In the high Romantic mode, Ashbery has—almost but not quite—personified his "night" as a sexually enticing and generously spiritual presence. Natural description often intricately affirms the possibilities of sexuality in Ashbery's poetry, as it does here. A careful attending to the external world suggests sensitivity to erotic nuance and ultimately to the possibility of spiritual vision. In this regard, one might compare him with Charles Wright, who, at least as I have presented him in Chapter 4, moves directly from landscape to spirituality, eliding sexuality along the way.

How does Ashbery perceive, describe, and use the natural world? It is relatively easy to anchor "Self-Portrait in a Convex Mirror" to the Parmigianino picture that occasions it, and to which it returns over and again. But landscape and description in general are more varied in Ashbery's other works, both long poems and shorter lyrics. For my purposes, it will be useful to categorize Ashbery's descriptions under four different rubrics, or as four tropes: plenitude, partiality, change, and closure.

Let us first consider plenitude, wholeness, and the embodiment of excess:

> This love of beauty is Taste. Others have the same love in such excess, that, not content with admiring, they seek to embody it in new form.
>
> The creation of beauty is Art.... A work of art is an abstract or epitome of the world. It is the result or expression of nature, in miniature.... Nothing is quite beautiful alone: nothing but is beautiful in the whole.... The world thus exists to the soul to satisfy the desire of beauty.[11]

Emerson's hopeful encouragement to the artist to embody his admiration of nature and thereby to redeem his soul and simultaneously to complete nature has offered one traditional justification for the grandeur of American poets' ambitions and achievements. Acknowledging the commerce between the individual and nature during which "all mean egotism vanishes" has had the paradoxical result, of course, of enabling some of our vastest, most egocentric productions: the work of Whitman, Pound, Williams, and the long poems of Ammons and Ashbery come to mind. But a nostalgia for the organic wholeness promised by prophets of Romanticism has given way, with the distrust of all modes of integrity and harmony that too often look like hegemony, totalitarianism, or self-delusion, to myths of postmodernism and other crises of representation. Fredric Jameson might well be talking about Ashbery when he defines the general conditions of postmodernism as "what you get when the modernization process is complete and nature is gone for good.... [or an] absolute and absolutely random pluralism ... a coexistence not even of multiple and alternate worlds so much as of unrelated fuzzy sets and semiautonomous subsystems whose overlap is perceptually maintained like hallucinogenic depth planes in a space of many dimensions."[12] What matters in Ashbery, however, is not that "nature" is gone for good but that it is omnipresent. Our perception of it is partial, jagged, and comes to us through a winking eye. Nature itself sublimely disorients and destabilizes (as Emerson, in different moods, would attest), as does language itself. We have both of them, always at hand, always ensuring our vertiginous, momentary consciousness of wanting to belong in a place.

As Ashbery off-handedly acknowledges:

> . . . Yet it's wonderful, this

*being*; to point to a tree and say don't I know
> you from somewhere?
Sure, now I remember, it was in some landscape
> somewhere,
and we can all take off our hats.
("Musica Reservata," *HL*, 25)

The goofy understated recognition that nature has been here all along, that landscapes may change but that the idea of landscape does not, and that *being* is a condition for knowing one's place within a world of things gives Ashbery in his most expansive moods a cause for celebration. His position is an analogy to the sober philosophizing of Emerson and Heidegger that he wishes to salute through trope, gesture, and energetic banalities. Emerson above all: "The way of life is wonderful: it is by abandonment,"[13] whereas for Heidegger, thinking is like dwelling. Ashbery fits more snugly into an American situation than a continental one.[14]

Abandonment is hardly the first thing one thinks of when confronting the accumulated oeuvre of our most unparaphrasable poet. As Julie Ellison has said of his precursor, Emerson's prose "accumulates but does not progress."[15] Even to mention plenitude, as I do above, is to risk certain pitfalls. First, there is the matter of organic integrity. Ashbery's poems, especially the largest ones like *Flow Chart*, meander, and even the shorter ones often lack coherent centrality. What A. R. Ammons calls "good poems, all those little rondures / splendidly brought off, painted gourds on a shelf" make infrequent appearances in Ashbery's work.[16] And often, these are poems that share "the dream of a unified field" with Jorie Graham's equally strenuous and disjunctive poems. In two exemplary, adjacent poems, "The Whole Is Admirably Composed" and "By Forced Marches" (*HL*), Ashbery uses the described details of landscape to offset a personal sense of disengagement, alienation, and unspecified sadness. "I am all I have. I am afraid. I am left alone" ("By Forced Marches" 31) is the premise on which both of these poems, like many others, may be said to rest.

In "The Whole Is Admirably Composed" (*HL*, 29) the art appreciation tone of the title represents nostalgia for the kind of fullness nowhere available to any human subject in Ashbery's poems. A menace suggestive of film noir informs the opening stanza, and against this menace the landscape interjects itself:

In rainy nights all the faces look like telephones.
Help me! I am in this street because I was
going someplace, and now, not to be there is here.

So billows pile up on the shore, I hear
the mountains, the tide of autumn pulls in
ever thicker like a blanket of tears, and

people go about their business, unconcerned
if with another.

Any possibility of human aid or even communication has been forestalled;
the speaker magically vanishes from "there" to "here" as he removes agency
and place simultaneously. The "so" that precedes the trio of natural "images"
leaves us wondering whether to take it as a sign of metaphor ("just so") or
resignation ("and therefore"), but in its vagueness there adheres Ashberyian
sense. "Billows pile up" repeats the plenitude of "all the faces," and "I hear
/ the mountains" ironically offsets the uncommunicative, unspeaking tele-
phone-like faces of people on the street. Even the "tide of autumn" recalls
the "rainy nights" and "billows," and it also prepares us for further natural
and human indices of tears (a "room of sobs and of grieving" in the second
stanza, and "water from the / falls" in the third).

Ashbery seldom comes clear in his depiction of the vectors of human
emotion; he prefers to let observed data stand in the place of such explorations, as he does here, when he requires something like a landscape painting,
admirably composed, to do the work of human exposition. The middle of
the poem alludes mysteriously to unspeakable sadness in past and present
time, but Ashbery gives us a resting place at the end, an appropriate closure
to human emotion and artistic "composition":

There is more to inconstancy than you will
want to hear, and meanwhile the streets have dried,
tears have been put away until another time, and a smile
paints the easy vapor that rises from all
human activity. I see it is time to question trees,
thorns in hedges, again, the same blind investigation
that leads you from trap to trap before bargaining
to forget you. And this is only a bump
on the earth's surface, casting no shadow, until
the white and dark fruits of the far pledge be
wafted into view again, out of control, shimmering
in the dark that runs off and is collected
in oceans. And the map is again wiped clean.
(29–30)

"Don't I know you from somewhere?" he asked a tree earlier in this volume,
and now he acknowledges that this inevitable, repeated questioning con-

stantly tempts and frustrates us. The young Wordsworth on his way home from school had to grab at a tree or some other external object to recall himself from the abyss of idealism and to restore contact with external reality.[17] Likewise, whatever unspecified disappointment or "inconstancy" prevails in the human realm, we have those unresponsive but ineluctable *things* that connect us to the world, although never to one another or to themselves. Both human tears and human smiles ("all human activity" and emotion) are "a bump" because all perception and feeling are momentary. The map of a landscape, a slate of consciousness, and a tear-drenched face can all be "wiped clean" before the next act of composing (a face, a self, a painting) begins.

This poem encourages us to think of Ashbery's plenitude as a form of compensation for unspecified disappointments and threats of emptiness. In this regard, landscape serves the same function it does for Coleridge ("This Lime-Tree Bower My Prison"), who must make do with both a real and an imagined scene to protect himself against his exaggerated fears of abandonment; and for Elizabeth Bishop (in "Poem"), who makes contact with a dead relative by observing, via his painting, a landscape they both "know." Ashbery has liberally if inadvertently prepared the way for his readers, in the early poem "The Instruction Manual" (5), a proleptic allegory of method. Here we have an invented description of a place the speaker can only pretend to see. Trapped in his office, chained to a desk, he dreams of Guadalajara as compensation for current boredom. Another early poem, "In the Dusk-Charged Air" (54), Ashbery's Whitmanian catalogue of all the rivers in the world, also predicts the capacity of his later long poems to flow seamlessly along a stream of consciousness; the amassing of detail seems to constitute an assault on emptiness. When he asks, in "French Poems" (*DD*, 38), "Shall I some day be a part of all this fullness?" he is both wistful and wry, for surely he knows at some level that he already belongs to the fullness he documents. The desire for plenitude, whether it accompanies confidence or regret, always balances a knowledge of paucity, as Ashbery ruefully acknowledges in a paragraph from his prose poem "For John Clare" (103):

> There ought to be room for more things, for a spreading out, like. Being immersed in the details of rock and field and slope—letting them come to you for once, and then meeting them halfway would be so much easier—if they took an ingenuous pride in being in one's blood. Alas, we perceive them if at all as those things that were meant to be put aside—costumes of the supporting actors or voice trilling at the end of a narrow enclosed street. You can do nothing with them. Not even offer to pay.

Having already claimed "There's so much to be seen everywhere" and "There is so much to be said, and on the surface of it very little gets said," Ashbery desires a poetry of total immersion, involvement, and participation that might turn him into a version of Wordsworth's Lucy, who is "rolled round in earth's diurnal course." He has expanded this immersion through the accumulations of *Flow Chart*, although in his several succeeding volumes he has retreated from tropes of plenitude and returned to modes of disjuncture.

But for his first three decades at least, abundance or plenitude was his major figure, and details of observed, imagined, or depicted landscape helped the poet to put on the mantle of monarch of all he might survey. We cannot take him at his word, in the passage above: his largesse wants to put nothing aside, because he can make use of everything. Admirably composing a whole often begins with descriptive details, anchoring a poem—or the reader at poem's start—before it heads off into other, uncharted or abstruse territory. A quartet of examples will suffice: "Summer," "Scheherazade," "Grand Galop," and "Pyrography." The tantalizing beginning of each prepares us for unsettling directions later on.

By using the terms "plenitude" and "partiality" to categorize the way Ashbery tropes with and on description, I mean that there are some poems in which description offers discrete segments, resting points (as I have suggested) between other divagations. These are the equivalent of arias amid recitative. In others, however, such as the typical quartet above, landscape or description permeates the whole, serving as a ground for other motifs (the drama of human consciousness and the play of language, above all) with which it is interwoven. "Summer" is like the earlier poem "Spring Day," which is addressed to a "you" who is in part the titular day, in part one of those mysteriously meant referents of Ashbery's pronouns. In "Spring Day," cityscape and landscape details merge into a gestalt, a "dream" through which the narrator focuses his attention: "Gracious and growing thing, with those leaves like stars, / We shall soon give all our attention to you" (85), he claims at poem's end. He bestows his attention so lightly and variously that nothing receives it for very long. (This is why he has become our preeminent poet of weather.) "Summer" tackles themes from Shelley's "Hymn to Intellectual Beauty" and Keats's "To Autumn" to reflect growth, transience, and the consciousness of death, but it does it so fleetingly (more in the manner of Shelley than of Keats) that all discursive unity and referential stability have been displaced in favor of syntactic ambiguity and referential vagueness.

It is for this reason that the descriptive details serve as more than momentary points of coherence. Beginning with "that sound like the wind / Forgetting in the branches that means something / Nobody can translate," and complementing sound with sight ("the shadow is ample / And hardly seen, divided among the twigs of a tree" [90]), Ashbery alludes to, but hardly specifies, our consciousness of death and endings, which makes us nostalgic for those times when fate seemed to be our servant of fullness ("summer, the ball of pine needles") and of premonition ("and winter, the twitter / Of cold stars at the pane, that describes with broad gestures / This state of being that is not so big after all"). Ashbery approaches death as a phenomenon negotiable only through such recognitions and through the narcissism of seeing one's face "reflected in the water" at the end of a flight of steps going down to a narrow ledge. Details offer menace and solace, in inverse proportion to the propositional truths or philosophical propositions he refuses to extend.

One reason to count the title poem in *Self-Portrait in a Convex Mirror* as Ashbery's masterpiece is that it integrates observation, speculation, and ekphrastic description within the poetics of reverie. But several of the shorter lyrics surrounding the central poem suggest how hard-won, or willed, is the triumph of the longer one. "Scheherazade" begins by taking details of a setting for the infinite suggestiveness of Scheherazade's stories. (A similar poem, "Variations, Calypso and Fugue on a Theme of Ella Wheeler Wilcox" [94], takes a trite moral—"For the pleasures of the many / May be ofttimes traced to one / As the hand that plants an acorn / Shelters armies from the sun"—as terminus a quo for rhymed nonsense and other variations.)

So the poem opens with simple detail:

> Unsupported by reason's enigma
> Water collects in squared stone catch basins.
> The land is dry. Under it moves
> The water. Fish live in the wells. The leaves,
> A concerned green, are scrawled on the light. Bad
> Bindweed and rank ragweed somehow forget to flourish here.
> An inexhaustible wardrobe has been placed at the disposal
> Of each new occurrence.
> (169)

Such mysterious coolness sets the stage for evocations of stories and our parts in them. Liberated or trapped as we may be, we play major and minor roles. The "description" does not really cohere, in spite of the simplicity and brevity of the individual sentences. Like his eponymous heroine, Ashbery wishes to weave a spell, inviting us to participate in a world of make-believe. At the poem's midpoint comes the revelation (of Ashbery's methods as well as those of his Scheherazade):

> The greatness in the moment of telling stayed unresolved
> Until its wealth of incident, pain mixed with pleasure,

Faded in the precise moment of bursting
Into bloom, its growth a static lament.
(170)

Precisely because Ashbery wants to balance outside against inside, as Wordsworth does in his majestic formulation of "an ennobling interchange / Of action from within and from without,"[18] he needs to weave into the rhetorical flourishes of his narrative gestures a reminder that an outside actually exists. It is not coincidental that he compares storytelling to the blooming and fading of an unspecified plant. When we listen to some enchanting bedtime story, our own attention rises and then falls, just as it does when we read an Ashbery poem.

Because the ontological status of all objects outside the self is highly questionable throughout Ashbery's poetry, referentiality per se barely exists. The promise of such referentiality can frustrate hostile and impatient readers ("Unsupported by reason's enigmas"?), but it can also enchant. So, "Grand Galop" begins with a proposition to which it then keeps coming back: "All things seem mention of themselves / And the names which stem from them branch out to other referents" (172). The thesis continues in the mention of the eponymous weigela (i.e., a plant named for its discoverer) doing "its dusty thing / In fire-hammered air." And the poem proceeds, as a "galop" in fact, through a typically Ashberyian panorama of space and time, to reach its principal idea: that an accumulation of random details, first noticed and then put to use, "drifts away in fragments":

And one is left sitting in the yard
To try to write poetry
Using what Wyatt and Surrey left around,
Took up and put down again
Like so much gorgeous raw material.
(177)

For all his refinement, Ashbery sometimes seems to belong to the school of the raw rather than of the cooked, as sense data, like natural events or poetic shards and remnants, occur suddenly, randomly, and with little effect. As in "Scheherazade," data "branch" out in garden and poetry alike. Like Whitman, Ashbery identifies himself with the debris as well as the beauties that litter the natural and political landscapes ("The lies fall like flaxen threads from the skies / All over America," 177–178). And the debris includes his Anglo-American literary heritage, conceived as a garden (an anthology or florilegium) that provokes two responses.

He addresses Surrey again at the end of the poem's penultimate stanza:

Surrey, your lute is getting an attack of nervous paralysis
But there are, again, things to be sung of
And this is one of them, only I would not dream of intruding on
The frantic completeness, the all-purpose benevolence
Of that still-moist garden where the tooting originates:
Between intervals of clenched teeth, your venomous rondelay.
(178)

Then he suggests two paths he might follow, which, mutatis mutandis, are the same that Elizabeth Bishop might have considered: the route of nostalgia and the route of fearful adventure. Under "*angst*-colored skies," frightened, he realizes how little time has changed:

One has traveled such a short distance.
The styles haven't changed much,
And I still have a sweater and one or two other things I had then.

Such comfort to be derived from the past (which for Ashbery, as for Bishop, involves memories of home and safety) is offset by the menace of a final detail: "But now we are at Cape Fear and the overland trail / Is impassable, and a dense curtain of mist hangs over the sea" (179). As Bishop does at the end of "Cape Breton" ("an ancient chill is rippling the dark brooks") and "Arrival at Santos" ("we are driving to the interior"), Ashbery increases the level of menace and mystery, refusing closure in a major key in favor of a fade-out in a minor one. Landscape stands in for the less visible human being stationed—or trapped—within it.

The Whitmanian "Pyrography," commissioned by the Department of the Interior for the 1976 Bicentennial to accompany a traveling display of landscape paintings,[19] moves through three related subjects: time and history, a progress across the American landscape, and the development of both personal and national consciousness. As I mentioned at the start of this chapter, time, space, and personal identity (or shifting layers of consciousness) are Ashbery's three overlapping interests. The poem begins as invitation, continues as adventure, and ends in acceptance; it displays all of his usual frustrating manipulations of reference and connection. But it also maintains satisfactory coherence precisely because it successfully interweaves its three thematic strands, never stringing its sentences so far along a path of obscurity that they, and their reader, become enmeshed and lost.

The opening sentence mingles specificity and vagueness: "Out here on Cottage Grove it matters" (212). Ashbery's deictics—themselves a subject in need of fuller treatment—veer between the seemingly graspable (Cottage Grove) and the tantalizing (what is "it"?). I take "it" to refer to the art display and to the still grander project that it symbolizes: the very idea of America. ("This is America calling: / The mirroring of state to state," Ashbery announces in ll. 4–5). "Pyrography" charts, somewhat haphazardly, the travel of show and people across a continent that is both hastily assembled (it's hard to know exactly where we *are* at any given moment, although Warren, Ohio, and Bolinas, California, get a mention) and lovingly described. He takes a satiric stab at the artificiality of America itself, its architecture and its ideology: "The land wasn't immediately appealing; we built it / Partly over with fake ruins, in the image of ourselves" (212). Here, more than anywhere, Ashbery tries to pay homage to his ideal of getting it all in, and he self-mockingly uses cliché to suggest the unreality of his own ambitious project:

> . . . if we were going
> To be able to write the history of our time, starting with today,
> It would be necessary to model all these unimportant details
> So as to be able to include them; otherwise the narrative
> Would have that flat, sandpapered look the sky gets
> Out in the middle west toward the end of summer,
> The look of wanting to back out before the argument
> Has been resolved, and at the same time to save appearances
> So that tomorrow will be pure. Therefore, since we have to do our
>      business
> In spite of things, why not make it in spite of everything?
> (213)

The "flat, sandpapered look" is what Ashbery's poems half reject and at least half invite. The phrase adequately describes both a kind of landscape and a texture of the poetry itself. Getting everything in will reduce everything to unappealing sameness, however democratic the design might be. But modeling details—Ashbery's own eye for individuation never fails him—provokes an almost unutterable feeling of sadness. He ends with the "parade . . . turning into our street" (i.e., the celebration of the Bicentennial, the arrival of the exhibition), but fear and nostalgia now unite to give a sense of the darker side of whatever we mean by "America":

> The look, the way things first scared you
> In the night light, and later turned out to be,
> Yet still capable, all the same, of a narrow fidelity
> To what you and they wanted to become:
> No sighs like Russian music, only a vast unravelling

Out toward the junctions and to the darkness beyond
To these bare fields, built at today's expense.
(214)

Unraveling, bareness, and darkness elide the present in a landscape of past
and future.

Gestures such as this conclusion, which the Emerson of "Experience"
might label "oblique and casual" (Emerson, 473), often stabilize the
meaning and effect of Ashbery's poems. But just as often they do not, pro-
ducing a beauty not explicable in terms of a poem's setting, tone, or nominal
subject. In these cases, Ashbery's "descriptions" assume the status of synec-
dochic parts, glittering but fragmentary jewels lost in an otherwise unvary-
ing foil: what I mean by "partiality." When, in the middle of *Flow Chart*,
Ashbery announces—apropos of who knows what—"THIS IS AN ILLUS-
TRATION OF SOMETHING" (*FC*, 178), he is self-mockingly reminding
us, and himself, that meaning becomes almost incidental by comparison to
effect, tone, and the sheer pleasures of randomness (or what Stevens would
call "merely circulating"). As it is often the sentence, the stanza, the paragraph
(the part, in other words) rather than the whole that is his unit of meaning,
the total effect, especially of the longer poems, depends on the rhythm that
builds up between and through these parts. Where Ammons veers between
centers and peripheries, for Ashbery there is no center, no substance, only
discrete particulars: "And these marginalia—what other word is there for
them?—are the substance of the text, / by not being allowed to fit in" (37).
Exclusion is the surest way to call attention to something; things that do not
fit in are automatically noteworthy because they have evaded the "flat, sandpapered look." As he wearily puts it in the last line of "Cop and Sweater,"
"From the universal boutique each of us stumbles on" (*HL*, 23).

Although it is tempting to read Ashbery as a gloss on much of Emerson, one must be careful. Emerson begins "The Divinity School Address"
with an intense description of "this refulgent summer," a perfect world that
converses with us, engaging all of our senses and happily displaying nature's
mysteries. He continues with the human application of his surround: "But
when the mind opens and reveals the laws which traverse the universe and
make things what they are, then shrinks the great world at once into a mere
illustration and fable of this mind" (75). He is clear in his sense of what illustrates what. Ashbery cannot be; details threaten to overwhelm and confuse.

The Emersonian inheritance has taken hold, if not transcendentally
then at least stylistically. As Barbara Packer, one of Emerson's best readers,

has observed specifically of *Nature*, but in a judgment applicable to practically all of his salient work, "The succession of competing style—rhapsodic, lapidary, lyrical, detached—is often so rapid as to leave the reader giddy." As opposed to Thoreau, Emerson "effaces" himself in his text, leaving us with no clue as to how to interpret or define him.[20] Like Emerson, emerging from a Protestant tradition that scrupulously respects each person's (or each reader's) identity, Ashbery celebrates what Emerson praised in Walter Savage Landor: "the merit of not explaining,"[21] or, rather, not connecting. Like Emerson's prose, Ashbery's poetry moves, but it seldom progresses.

This is why the interpolated "descriptions of nature" perform a valuable, stabilizing function. Ashbery would agree with Emerson that "a beauty not explicable, is dearer than a beauty which we can see to the end of."[22] The endless pseudo-lectures to which he is given (one thinks of Gertrude Stein's calling Pound "the village explainer") seldom contribute to our understanding of a poem's total form, except as a collection of objets from the universal stylistic boutique. Randomness, whether accidental or surreally deliberate, has made him a preeminent poet of contingency, of the inessential.

Let us say, then, that Ashbery never explains, but he always describes, or details.[23] If "everything is landscaped / for one's greater peace of mind" (*FC*, 209), order exists as a gently redemptive palliative, but even without such order, Ashbery admits that "I've too much respect for the junk we call living / that keeps passing by" (*FC*, 213). Thus, he tries to take it all in: "I have seen it all, and I write, and I have seen nothing" (*FC*, 214). Writing becomes a version of landscape arrangements, a recompense for reality (as in "The Instruction Manual" or similar set pieces redolent of travel brochures, such as the western landscape in *Flow Chart*, 110–111). But writing also attempts imaginative reconstructions of "home," a resting point, however temporary. Reading itself is a kind of dwelling, just as "composing" prepares both a text and a ground:

Any day now you must start to dwell in it,
   the poetry, and for this, grave preparations must be
         made, the walks of sand
raked, the rubble wall picked clean of dead vine stems,
         but what
if poetry were something else entirely, not this
         purple weather
with the eye of a god attached, that sees
inward and outward? What if it were only a small,
         other way of living,
  like being in the wind?
(*FC*, 145)

The second alternative, the "small . . . way of living," never holds too long an appeal for Ashbery, prisoner as he is of the seigneurial "eye of a god," the image he inherits from Stevens, Whitman, and Emerson. He admonishes himself to "look sharp, and sharply, at what is around you" (*FC*, 201), and such sharpness accounts for the persistent move from margin to center, the landscaping of his own pages:

> Organize your thoughts in random lines and, later on
> down the road, paginate them. You'll see the bluebells
>     and cowslips on every hill; even
> dragonflies will have become a thing of wonder, as long
> as you don't get too close, and let water run through
>     it all. What the hell! We're
> in here having a fine time, our satisfaction pierces
>     heaven's summit, and there are only
> a few more who need to be drugged or convinced. As long
>     as we're on this planet
> the thrill never ceases.
>     (*FC*, 159)

Like Emerson, Thoreau, and Whitman, Ashbery seems to be a loner, but his main theme—like that of Ammons and James Merrill, his polar opposites in many ways—may be our mutual dependencies. The landscape of his work and the landscapes *in* his work wax and wane; only filaments, webs, randomly and temporarily held connections, count for much. To his chagrin, but more often to his delight, as he announces in a shorter poem, "We too are embroiled in this scene of happening" (*HL*, 3).

Nature and our observation of it are Ashbery's analogy for the act of writing, and a compensation or escape from it as well. Thus, in an extended riff in *Flow Chart* (94–96), he poses as a daffy library researcher, straining his eyes on "useless newsprint," for whom going outside offers the cliché of a release:

> . . . the streetscape
> always looked refreshingly right, as though
>     scene-painters had been at work, and then,
> at such moments, it was truly a pleasure to walk
>     along, surprised yet not too surprised
> by every new, dimpled vista. People would smile at me,
>     as though we shared some pleasant
> secret, or a tree would swoon into its fragrance, like
>     a freshly unwrapped bouquet

from the florist's. I knew then that nature
    was my friend.
(94)

The cliché, a sentiment verging on sentimentality, betrays a sporadically recurrent sensation throughout Ashbery's work: watching the world, and being watched *by* it in return, may threaten disequilibrium but just as often hold out the promise that the world "guides us / through the passes, the deserts, the windswept tumult that is to be our home / once we have penetrated it successfully, and all else has been laid to rest" (*FC*, 96).

Such Wordsworthian gestures ("we are laid asleep / In body and become a living soul" is too great an affirmation for Ashbery to make) enable Ashbery to "assemble / landscapes" (*FC*, 55), in his ongoing effort to establish temporary residency if not permanent dwelling: "Isn't it all going to be a fiction / anyway, and if so, what does it matter where we decide to settle down?" (*FC*, 83). The turns in Ashbery's longer poems always amount to returns: the "relief" of coming back "to the beloved home with its misted windows, its teakettle, its worn places on the ceiling, / for better or worse" (*FC*, 115). Houses offer both comfort and confinement; external nature gives liberty but also the threat of inundation.

Moving away from the amiable meandering of *Flow Chart*, I wish to look at several examples of Ashbery's reliance on tropes of partiality in smaller poems, where descriptive data play a proportionately larger role. Although his long poems (not just *Flow Chart* and "Self-Portrait in a Convex Mirror," but even the minor and more opaque "Clepsydra" and "The Skaters") may be more typical, the short ones are the more polished. Ashbery has three basic modes of speech: the *abstract*, or elevated (philosophical or pretentious diction amid syntactic tangles); the *colloquial* (efforts to render or imitate the spoken language by attending to cliché and varying figures of speech, and generally enlivening "les mots de la tribu"); and the *descriptive* (a precise though sometimes dreamy evocation of the things of this world). We may align these with his three major thematic parameters: abstraction corresponds to time, colloquialism to personal identity, and description to place or space. In many poems, the last is the bridge between the first two, and when in a short lyric all three modes come together, he achieves a balance containing none of the predictably frustrating disjunctions of his larger articulations.

Ashbery puts to good use his decorative impulse in "Forties Flick" (166), not so much a description per se as an evocation of a generic film noir. The Hopperesque mood is deftly handled with a few strong brushstrokes in the opening stanza:

The shadow of the Venetian blind on the painted wall,
Shadows of the snake-plant and cacti, the plaster animals,
Focus the tragic melancholy of the bright stare
Into nowhere, a hole like the black holes in space.
In bra and panties she sidles to the window:
Zip! Up with the blind. A fragile street scene offers itself,
With wafer-thin pedestrians who know where they are going.
The blind comes down slowly, the slats are slowly tilted up.

The poem turns on a ritual of looking: we watch the woman (one imagines
Mary Astor, Ruth Roman, Barbara Stanwyck, or some other smoking doll)
watch a street scene and pull down the curtain on it. But "watch" is of course
an artificial word, as all we are actually doing is reading a verbal description
of an imagined scene. This sense of artifice stands out more prominently in
the poem's second half, an evocation of finality, quiet, discomfort, and all the
things that go into a genre film ("knowing what important details to leave
out / And the way character is developed").

Ashbery ends with equally icy, eerily evocative details:

                                    . . . Things too real
To be of much concern, hence artificial, yet now all over the page,
The indoors with the outside becoming part of you
As you find you had never left off laughing at death,
The background, dark vine at the edge of the porch.

The film has metamorphosed into a written text, as the reader finds he or
she has never really left the page, and indoors and outside have been swallowed up by and into the perceiver. Art conveys a heightened sense of reality,
at once individuated (as in the artifice of the opening details) and omnipresent ("all over the page"), just as the cityscape of the poem's opening has been
exchanged for what looks like a rendering of a country, or at least a suburban
house at the end. The exotic, the distant, the noir have all been absorbed
into the domestic: the menacing dark vine seems on the verge of strangling
human efforts to keep house.

Ashbery applies such decorative touches in many poems where they
serve essentially narrative functions. "Street Musicians" (207), the first
poem in *Houseboat Days*, uses what John Shoptaw calls "a humble narrative" to construct "a myth of origins."[24] Again, descriptive details perform
the work that another poet might handle by linear storytelling. One stanza
in the past tense suggests breakup, breakdown, or separation. The season
is the index:

> . . . Farther than anyone was ever
> Called, through increasingly suburban airs
> And ways, with autumn falling over everything.

And in the second stanza, the poet continues his seasonal reference in order to depict the alienation of the other musician, who is now alone:

> . . . the year turning over on itself
> In November, with the spaces among the days
> More literal, the meat more visible on the bone.

From the present, the poem ends with a backward look to a moment of togetherness if not happiness. Landscape becomes the metonymic embodiment of human relations:

> Our question of a place of origin hangs
> Like smoke: how we picnicked in pine forests,
> In coves with the water always seeping up, and left
> Our trash, sperm and excrement everywhere, smeared
> On the landscape, to make of us what we could.

The conclusion seems to work in two directions: human and natural agencies are in conflict, as it is unclear whether the last infinitive phrase modifies the trash or the human picnickers.

The descriptive details in these two poems exemplify Ashbery's decorative and quasi-narrative methods. His poetic scenes become, in other words, expressionistic or metonymic figures for human drama and consciousness. Those of "Mixed Feelings" (182) enact epistemological and phenomenological dramas. They become part of an allegory of discovery, allowing us to locate ourselves with respect to an observed scene (in this case, an old photograph) and to the history of the past half-century. Although the descriptive details are here fewer and apparently more casual, they are in fact more meticulously embedded into the conversational elements that constitute an equivalent historical marker in the poem. The breezy tone animates a different kind of forties flick, one full of American confidence and optimism. "Mixed Feelings" really means "mixed scenes" or "mixed lingos," as the opening photograph of "girls lounging around / An old fighter bomber, circa 1942 vintage" in California sunlight suddenly is transformed into a rendezvous on the opposite coast:

> Let's go on and out, somewhere
> Through the canyons of the garment center
> To a small café, and have a cup of coffee.

Mixing scenes requires mixing variations of the *koine*: the tired bureaucratic clichés of the present day ("How to explain to these girls, if indeed that's what they are, / These Ruths, Lindas, Pats and Sheilas / About the *vast change* that's taken place / In *the fabric of our society*" [my emphasis]) with yesterday's now faded slang: "Aw nerts, / One of them might say, this guy's too much for me."

At his finest, Ashbery mixes feelings, scenes, and levels of discourse as a way of presenting our own progress through time and space, coming upon the past as by surprise and negotiating a response to the present only with reference to the histories we all bring with us. Appropriately the poem ends, as do so many of his, with a descriptive detail that offers an index of change and stability. A part (in this case, the single last line) comes to stand for a whole. We may meet these girls again "in the not too distant future," he says,

> They looking as astonishingly young and fresh as when this picture
> was made
> But full of contradictory ideas, stupid ones as well as
> Worthwhile ones, but all flooding the surface of our minds
> As we babble about the sky and the weather and the forests of
> change.

"Babble" is, of course, what we all do when we meet old friends or make new ones, and talk of the weather becomes a staple in Ashbery's poetry, as in social discourse at large, as both an evasion and a stand-in for other kinds of language. "Forests of change" sounds an appropriately conclusive, though ominous, note: like the "fields of sleep" in Wordsworth's "Intimations" ode, it calls into question the very nature of its phrasing. How does the genitive work? Does change emanate from the forests? Are the forests themselves constantly changing? Like the surface of our minds, inundated with new and contradictory ideas, our conversation, like the layers of language that compose it, is susceptible to radical, sudden shifts. Changes in tone, diction, and pitch provide an index to Ashbery's linguistic maneuvering. Changes in landscape provide an external symbol of the same phenomenon.

Nothing offers a greater model for change than the weather, and Ashbery, for whom so little ever remains in place, relies on meteorology as a source for tropes of pervasive change. Like Charles Tomlinson, another ardent watcher of the skies, Ashbery merges time and space, but unlike his British contemporary, who adheres to the fictions of objectivity and neutral observation, he uses changes in the weather as a parallel to the ever-shifting changes in feeling and personal identity of his garrulous speakers. As a precursor text we might consider the characteristic second stanza of "Sunday Morning," in which Stevens's heroine imagines "measures destined for her soul" as coming from an interchange of outer and inner weathers, of a seasonality with human counterparts:

> Divinity must live within herself:
> Passions of rain, or moods in falling snow;
> Grievings in loneliness, or unsubdued
> Elations when the forest blooms; gusty
> Emotions on wet roads on autumn nights;
> All pleasures and all pains, remembering
> The bough of summer and the winter branch.[25]

The generative force of the prepositions animates the picture, maintaining a rhetorical balance between outer and inner states. "Passions of rain" allows for objective, subjective, and possessive genitives, where "moods in falling snow" suggests both those moods felt *by* the woman during winter and the general moods provoked, universally and externally, *by* the snow itself. As the phrases expand ("unsubdued / Elations when," "gusty / Emotions on"), and nouns are separated by line endings from their antecedent modifiers, so does the sense that the woman is participating in a greater external process even as she internalizes that very process. The equation grows and then diminishes: divinity *is* passions, moods, grievings, elations, emotions, and finally "all pleasures and all pains" as the last, loosely referential participle ("remembering") returns us to the woman as the focus of attention. "Remembering" comes to mean "reconstituting," "absorbing," and "reliving." From plurality the stanza reaches the elegant isolation of single Wordsworthian metonymies, the "bough of summer," the "branch" (a bough denuded of foliage) of winter. Weather isolates the natural landscape details, with which the stanza ends; parts represent the whole.

I have paused at Stevens's stanza because it offers a contrastive model for Ashbery's own dealings with the weather. He can invoke it with a cliché and personify it, developing it as a trope for poetry and landscape, as well as personal identity:

> It's this crazy weather we've been having:
> Falling forward one minute, lying down the next
> Among the loose grasses and soft, white, nameless flowers.
> People have been making a garment out of it,
> Stitching the white of lilacs together with lightning
> At some anonymous crossroads.
> ("Crazy Weather," 221)

The weather has become as unpredictable as a clown, as natural as a land-scape, and as useful as a piece of cloth. "This poetry of mud" comes out of the crazy weather, so we can no longer hope to "approximate" the old dignity poetry once enjoyed, except perhaps in some "rare, / Uninteresting speci-men" that might be growing somewhere else. This little allegory of Ash-bery's own method (his poems change as mysteriously and unpredictably as the weather itself) suggests as well the course of poetry as a quasi-natural force. In its rapidly changing fullness the weather becomes the model for all kinds of change.

These are personal as well as historical. In "The System" (137), the larg-est section of *Three Poems*, Ashbery expands on Stevens's suggestion that inner and outer weather maintain a permanent congruity, when he describes "latent," as opposed to "frontal," happiness through the extended simile of weather:

> We all know those periods of balmy weather in early spring, some-times even before spring has officially begun: days or even a few hours when the air seems suffused with an unearthly tenderness, as though love were about to start, now, at this moment, on an endless journey put off since the beginning of time.

Only the mysteriousness of the air, an element equally ephemeral and tran-sient, can stand in for the promise and impermanence of love and happiness. "Crazy" weather, indeed: by definition, all weather is crazy, unpredictable and unreliable. Time always threatens, as in the lovely lyric "Le Mensonge de Nina Petrovna" ("as one hand of the clock homes / in on its chosen numeral" [*HL*, 75–76]), where time and cosmological forces conspire against human aspiration:

> as through an enormous pastry tube
> clouds ooze around the stars, lest
> (so brittle and unimportant are they)
> the wherewithal be lacking
> to bring earth into some semblance
> of unity under the sky
> that mocks us and will never
> let us be entirely
> all that we were someday to be.

Ashbery refuses to allow human aspiration to appear as more than ridicu-lous cliché ("the wherewithal be lacking," "be . . . all that we were . . . to be"), but even his defensiveness cannot conceal the nostalgia implicit in such aspiration; the clarity and prominence of the descriptive details—oozing clouds, mocking sky—grant forceful activity to personified external forces because human subjects have been reduced, dissipated, and rendered will-less.

Like Stevens and the heroine of "Sunday Morning," Ashbery and his "characters" may lack will, especially compared to the unfathomable surrounding forces of time and weather, but they maintain consciousness. He cannot use tropes of fullness except ironically, nostalgically, or briefly, because like any postmodern skeptic he knows too much. Time takes too much away from us all. "There was never any fullness that was going to be," he ruefully announces in "Poem at the New Year" (*HL*, 83), which takes a sad, regretful look at the hopes for plenitude that are defrauded by winter. And even the beginning of the following poem, "Central Air" (*HL*, 84), resumes the same acknowledgment that the change of season and weather inevitably disappoints rather than fulfills: "Not all the buds will open, this year or any year." If anything, consciousness of change allows Ashbery occasionally to accommodate his major tropes simultaneously, as in the title poem of *As We Know* (259).

The poem encourages an interrogation of the relationships among my trio of topics: time, landscape, and knowledge or consciousness. These are unstable at best, mysterious and threatening at worst. The poem begins by mingling time and space:

> All that we see is penetrated by it—
> The distant tree tops with their steeple (so
> Innocent), the stair, the windows' fixed flashing—
> Pierced full of holes by the evil that is not evil,
> The romance that is not mysterious, the life that is not life,
> A present that is elsewhere.

There follow two stanzas of erotic suggestiveness, guilt and paranoia, sunlight and the hope of getting home "one of these days." Landscape, consciousness, sexuality, and one's sense of time merge seamlessly:

> And further in the small capitulations
> Of the dance, you rub elbows with it,
> Finger it. That day you did it
> Was the day you had to stop, because the doing
> Involved the whole fabric, there was no other way to appear.
> You slid down on your knees
> For those precious jewels of spring water
> Planted on the moss, before they got soaked up

And you teetered on the edge of this
Calm street with its sidewalks, its traffic,

As though they are coming to get you.
But there was no one in the noon glare,
Only birds like secrets to find out about
And a home to get to, one of these days.

And the poem ends with a stanza of abstraction, of meditation under the aegis of changing light and visionary possibility:

The light that was shadowed then
Was seen to be our lives,
Everything about us that love might wish to examine,
Then put away for a certain length of time, until
The whole is to be reviewed, and we turned
Toward each other, to each other.
The way we had come was all we could see
And it crept up on us, embarrassed
That there is so much to tell now, really now.

To Yeats's great question "How can we know?" Ashbery seems to say: "We always have known." But *what* it is that we know? The fact of knowledge is clear, its content less so. Charles Altieri has persuasively discussed the poem's erotic situation and the complex temporality implied by the last line: "A moment becomes *really now* only *as* two sensibilities contour themselves to it."[26] I should like to complement this reading with some questions and observations to place the poem more securely in the Romantic line of vision and skepticism and to locate Ashbery's descriptive details at the center of that skepticism.

The poem's unstable pronouns and deictics (commonplaces of Ashbery's method, and also a nose-thumbing gesture directed at Romantic nature lyric) are supplemented by indiscretions or confusions of tense ("You teetered . . . as though they are coming to get you," "then put away . . . until the whole is to be reviewed") that destabilize the narrative. Time seems to be of the essence, but only casually. Space is unequally undone, as is the lesser category of materiality: after all, neither jewels nor drops of water can be planted, and the hapless seeker after redemption/grace teeters off in quest of an unavailable home. The last line expresses both multiple temporality ("now, really *now*"), and a flippantly gay twist, a nod or giggle ("oh, *really* now"), of an entre nous sort that maintains the casual camaraderie of the title. The poem begins and ends with suggestions of a private arrangement between consenting and knowing adults, adults who know the score.

The paranoia of suspicion and embarrassment, another staple of Ashbery's poetry, is easy to equate with a gay sensibility, but it adduces the poem's epistemological in addition to its erotic domains. The penetrating "it" that extends throughout the poem is not only love, however conceived, but also an updated version of Wordsworth's "sense sublime / Of something far more deeply interfused" (here penetrating in a phallic way, rather than overflowing in a traditional Romantic one). What Altieri labels the deep-buried, alienated self—an unnamed it, whether submerged id, mysterious agency, or erotic excitement—could also partake of the Romantic sublime, especially because it "creeps" like Shelley's winds that represent the unseen shadow of an unseen intellectual beauty.

Even such a sketchy landscape as this one places Ashbery in the descriptive tradition our literary culture has inherited from the English Romantics. Although undermining their tropes, he is always recalling them. I would say, finally, that neither temporality nor eros is the main subject of the poem, but rather consciousness: the Ashbery speaker may be paranoid or suspicious, but mostly he is world-weary with the force of too much skepticism. What is it that penetrates, that permeates, that contradicts even itself, a life not life, an unevil evil, a familiar romance? It is the "sentiment of Being spread / O'er all that moves and all that seemeth still," as Wordsworth has it.[27] The present is a temporal category (*really now*), but it is also a gift, like grace perhaps, that exists out of our reach, *elsewhere*. Details of landscape, architecture, climate, and light function here neither as synecdoches nor as stopping points at which the reader can regain bearings; rather, they become part of the drama of consciousness, things one notices on the page as in life. Background and foreground merge, just as the ambiguity of "embarrassed" (does the epithet refer to "us" or "it"? Is "it" the same as the preceding "way," or merely a neutral pronoun beginning a new proposition?) calls into question the nature of knowledge. Knowledge and people constantly change, like the so-called external world.

&

It is appropriate to end with endings. Whatever skepticism Ashbery maintains in regard to objects outside the self,[28] his residual romantic faith allows us to broach the issue of closure in his poetry. Many of his most memorable pieces of description, even when seemingly arbitrary or unconnected to what precedes them, come at the end of poems and lend a note of muted, almost redemptive hope or triumph. Partly this phenomenon has to do with the association he makes between landscape (and other kinds of description) and his own nostalgia for homecomings. As he says wistfully in "The Bungalows" (114): "They are the same aren't they, / The presumed landscape and the dream of home." And home and death, in this tender poem, combine to effect a meditative ending:

> Who cares about what was there before? There is no going back,
> For standing still means death, and life is moving on,
> Moving on towards death. But sometimes standing still is also life.
> (116)

Such rhythmic and, in this case, meditative certainty shows how Ashbery's endings, even when not directly concerned with descriptive detail, often possess an old-fashioned ring. The early "Glazunoviana" from *Some Trees* (11), a miniaturized picture composed entirely of descriptive details and questions about them, ends with three sentences whose lilting triple rhythms complement the encroaching, mysterious, and possibly threatening loveliness of those details:

> Lovely tribes have just moved to the north.
> In the flickering evening the martins grow denser.
> Rivers of wings surround us and vast tribulation.

Whatever one feels or wishes to say about these lines one must admit that they *sound* climactic, as do the rhyming and the visual detail that grow toward abstraction at the end of "The Ice-Cream Wars" from *Houseboat Days* (242):

> A few black smudges
> On the outer boulevards, like squashed midges
> And the truth becomes a hole, something one has always known,
> A heaviness in the trees, and no one can say
> Where it comes from, or how long it will stay—
>
> A randomness, a darkness of one's own.

Musical gestures (sound and rhythm) augment descriptive data as Ashbery builds toward endings that often sound a note of finality.[29] For all the apparent, maddening randomness and divagation within the structure of a poem, a paragraph, or a sentence, Ashbery's endings seem thoroughly "composed," enabling a feeling of composure in the reader.

Earlier in this chapter I quoted the last stanza from "As One Put Drunk into the Packet-Boat," the opening poem in *Self-Portrait in a Convex Mirror*. Here we have a luminous example of Ashbery's reshaping of the traditional Romantic nature lyric. It begins empirically: "I tried each thing, only some were immortal and free" (163). It then moves from a single to a plural subject, from past to present (and implied future) tenses, and from one place to another, all the while making a nod toward illumination, expectation, and daylight: "Elsewhere we are as sitting in a place where sunlight / Filters down, a little at a time, / Waiting for someone to come." Like "As We Know," the body of the poem details a drama of nervous energy, fear of exposure, hopefulness, delay, and disappointment. It ends with the gorgeous depiction of the "moon of cistercian pallor" that climbs the sky as "the night sheen takes over." Whenever Ashbery's eye gains control of his consciousness and his articulation, as it does here, his poem powerfully mingles particularity, observation, and material detail with abstraction, deliberation, contemplation, and theoretical generalization. In "And *Ut Pictura Poesis* Is Her Name" (235), that pedagogic jeu d'esprit (his version of an ars poetica or "How to Write a Poem" that so many contemporary poets have tried), Ashbery advises us on what kinds of details, language, and poetic stances to include in a poem. He ends on a note of pure discursiveness. Something "Ought to be written about how this affects / You when you write poetry," he says:

> The extreme austerity of an almost empty mind
> Colliding with the lush, Rousseau-like foliage of its desire to
>     communicate
> Something between breaths, if only for the sake
> Of others and their desire to understand you and desert you
> For other centers of communication, so that understanding
> May begin, and in doing so be undone.

An embarrassment of riches counters and fills the Lockean tabula rasa of the mind, just as it fills the blank page of the poem. The greedily receptive eye sees too much, takes too much in. It is the precarious plight of the seer. External nature can become the mirror image of internal reality as well as the material that fills it, as Ashbery allows in this section of "A Wave" (324):

> . . . And the mind
> Is the beach on which the rocks pop up, just a neutral
> Support for them in their indignity.

Waves and dreams coincide, both necessary and "useless," "more trees in a landscape of trees" (325). As Ashbery has it in "Down by the Station, Early in the Morning" (*A Wave*, 14), nothing exists "until you name it, remembering." Such naming results in "magic, then terror, then pity at the emptiness, / Then air gradually bathing and filling the emptiness as it leaks." It is a conjuror's trick: air replaces emptiness, which leaks—like air!—from the balloon of consciousness.

    Ashbery's endings, for all of their variety, usually offer catharsis, a fulfillment that is simultaneously a draining, a climax that also subdues. "Down by the Station" (*A Wave*, 14; written during recovery from illness) ends with reminders of both "As One Put into the Packet-Boat" and Ashbery's masterpiece, "Self-Portrait in a Convex Mirror":

> . . . And so each day
> Culminates in merriment as well as a deep shock like an electric one,
>
> As the wrecking ball bursts through the wall with the bookshelves
> Scattering the works of famous authors as well as those
> Of more obscure ones, and books with no author, letting in
> Space, and an extraneous babble from the street
> Confirming the new value the hollow core has again, the light
> From the lighthouse that protects as it pushes us away.

Merriment and shock, climax and destruction, illumination and dispersal, protection and aversion, above all, the relationship between depth and surface, go hand in hand. For all the attention critics have given to Ashbery as a poet of consciousness who registers or reflects the meanderings of a mind moving in worlds unrealized, they have scanted his own equivalent attention to the surface of *things*, Wordsworthian and otherwise. When all cores prove to be hollow, when depth proves to be an agreed upon fiction at best or, at worst, a delusion, then only surfaces remain, and our attention must remain squarely upon them.

Such attention explains why "Self-Portrait in a Convex Mirror" is Ashbery's most important and most characteristic poem. Precisely because it combines two significant genres that Ashbery has always favored, the meandering Romantic nature lyric in the mode of "Tintern Abbey" and the ekphrastic meditation that has become a staple of contemporary verse, it offers the clearest evidence of his methods and of the uses to which he puts description. Description glides in and out, as one among many of the forms that consciousness takes. Looking intently leads to a dissipation of concentration as the eye shifts, the mind wanders, and things come and go, in and out of focus. The stream of data matches the stream of consciousness.

"Self-Portrait" succeeds in part because Ashbery integrates objective details of ekphrastic description, embellishments, his memories of seeing Parmigianino's picture in Vienna, and quotations from Vasari and Sydney Freedberg on the subject of the painting. He then augments his objective sightings with internalized reveries prompted by the painting or by his turning away from it. The first landscape (i.e., data that proceed from a single detail, a windowpane, in the painting) appears as Parmigianino's soul merges with some other, like that of the viewer or reader, in a contemplation of entrapment and sadness:

. . . The soul has to stay where it is,
Even though restless, hearing raindrops at the pane,
The sighing of autumn leaves thrashed by the wind,
Longing to be free, outside, but it must stay
Posing in this place.
(188–189)

"This is what the portrait says," Ashbery concludes. But the picture says no such thing, any more than Keats's Urn tells us that "Beauty is Truth." The conclusion is merely a first hypothesis that is immediately modified ("But there is . . ."). The temporal movement of a mind thinking fits in neatly with Ashbery's perfected didactic tone—inherited from Auden and appropriate to the museum-going he is engaged in—as he reminds us that "le temps" means both time and weather. (Another reason for, and example of, his constant entanglements of time and space.) Both are equally unpredictable, unchartable, and desolate. Today is "our / Landscape sweeping out from us to disappear / On the horizon" (192). Seeing *is* believing (as Charles Tomlinson puts it), but belief changes along with perception; responding to external stimuli gives us our most reliable frequency for understanding ourselves and our world.

Not people, but landscape and weather constitute the largest proportion of the "otherness" with which all aesthetic watching is designed to put us in touch. They help to define the self, not merely to complement it. This is what "gets included in the most ordinary / Forms of daily activity, changing everything / Slightly and profoundly" (201). We can see it in the mirror, in the painting, in the surround, or within the depths of memory and imagination. Just as New York "is a logarithm / Of other cities," so landscape with its "filiations, shuttlings" (195) is the algorithm by which "soul" or "self" can take its measure. And Ashbery carefully pits such an aestheticizing gesture against all of the "big theor[ies] to explain the universe," none of which can "tell the whole story," because, finally, "it is what is outside . . . That matters."

He means what is outside the mind, the individual, or whatever else offers enclosure (a picture, a frame, a room in a picture or in a museum). Nowhere else does Ashbery's description offer such liberation as in "Self-Portrait." He comes down clearly on the side of "surface," than which nothing more exists. Any core, like that in "Down by the Station," is inevitably hollow and disappointing, because impermanent. It is as though Ashbery has heeded Wittgenstein's famous dictum and replaced analysis with the clear-headedness of description: "The surface is what's there / And nothing can exist except what's there" (190).

Because all is surface one must attend to external details even though one is never able to take them all in. One moment of attention necessarily excludes others. As Parmigianino works and as we enter the process of his self-depicting, we are tricked into thinking his reflection our own: "We have surprised him / At work, but no, he has surprised us / As he works" (195). And the details of such involvement and forgetfulness lead then into one of Ashbery's loveliest renderings of weather and of our sudden awareness of what we might almost have missed:

> . . . The picture is almost finished,
> The surprise almost over, as when one looks out,
> Startled by a snowfall which even now is
> Ending in specks and sparkles of snow.
> It happened while you were inside, asleep,
> And there is no reason why you should have
> Been awake for it, except that the day
> Is ending and it will be hard for you
> To get to sleep tonight, at least until late.
> (195)

Dreaming delays all sense of an ending, as it also deflects—through time—attention to the weather, which always escapes definition precisely because it is always happening, never finished. Regardless of the effort of our attentiveness, completion and satisfaction are never to be achieved. Looking *at* or *through* a frame, a window, a painting, or a consciousness can lead only to disappointment, for capture is possible only through the act of painting, not of responding to a finished work. Ekphrasis is doomed to end in the disappointment of removal or retreat. Ashbery urges Parmigianino to withdraw his hand, his "shield of a greeting" (which at the beginning was said to "protect / What it advertises"). The poem began by noticing parts, and it ends the same way.

Ashbery called attention first to the painter's "right hand / Bigger than the head" in the poem's opening sentence fragment. This led to the first full sentence:

> . . . A few leaded panes, old beams,
> Fur, pleated muslin, a coral ring run together
> In a movement supporting the face, which swims
> Toward and away like the land
> Except that it is in repose.
> (188)[30]

From two kinds of fragments—a bodily part used as a synecdoche, and a fragment in lieu of a clause—the poem opens into a fuller utterance, a complete sentence that also begins a descriptive enumeration. Thus the poem begins its investigations. By the end, however, as disappointment sets in, the ekphrasis diminishes, and the sardonic allusion to the end of Keats's "Ode to a Nightingale" ("the 'it was all a dream' / Syndrome" [203]) implies that Ashbery as narrator–describer–museum-goer wishes to abandon description. Looking and transcribing reach a claustrophobic point of no return: "the action is the cold, syrupy flow / Of a pageant" (204). The insinuated frustration in such confinement encourages termination, as the poem subsides into gestures of farewell and burial:

> . . . The hand holds no chalk
> And each part of the whole falls off
> And cannot know it knew, except
> Here and there, in cold pockets
> Of remembrance, whispers out of time.
> (204)

Epistemological questions are at the heart of Ashbery's oeuvre: What do we know? And how? They make one last appearance here as the hand of painter or poet drops its instrument and gets neatly tucked into a metaphorical pocket, the repository of material and temporal leftovers. This is the spot where what he called "all the small things on earth" ("As One Put Drunk into the Packet-Boat," 164) become involved in "the business of darkness." Only intimations remain in this Wordsworthian gesture: shadows and coldness replace, then preempt the glory and the freshness of a dream.

Those final "whispers out of time" suggest ambiguously that the whispers are *made* out of time but also that they exist *beyond* time. The poem has promoted and eschewed acts of enclosure (another name for acts of description), and now it ends with an act of melting and relinquishment, an escape from paradise. We leave a temporary center and are cast adrift once more on an ocean of life, consciousness, and departure. Ashbery's descriptions are part of his attempt to capture what can never stay still, as he so delicately acknowledges in "Syringa" (246), another of his great "art" poems:

> . . . For although memories, of a season, for example,
> Melt into a single snapshot, one cannot guard, treasure
> That stalled moment. It too is flowing, fleeting;
> It is a picture of flowing, scenery, though living, mortal,
> Over which an abstract action is laid out in blunt,
> Harsh strokes.

What the English painter Howard Hodgkin said of his own paintings, that they are "not appearances [but] representational pictures of emotional situations," corresponds to Ashbery's effort to reproduce an expanse of time ("memories of a season") within a single "stalled moment." Time, like "scenery," is, however, always bidding us adieu. "Blunt, / Harsh strokes" are those acts of description with which the poet attempts to square the circle, to capture the essence of a reality that his better judgment realizes is uncapturable. Both Ashbery's rhythm and his diction attest to disappointment. The monosyllabic conclusion of the sentence ("is laid out in blunt, / Harsh strokes") slows down his earlier "flowing" syntax. To "lay out" is at least in part to prepare a corpse for burial. Like a snapshot, a poem is a version of still life, *nature morte*, no matter how fluid its meanderings. For Ashbery, all description both animates and deadens. Never was such a keen eye aware of the dangers it posed to the objects of its vision.

# SEVEN

# JORIE GRAHAM'S "NEW WAY OF LOOKING"

I n the richly laconic aphorisms that make up the "Adagia" in Wallace Stevens's *Opus Posthumous*, we come upon two that might serve as points of entry into the alluring, stern, fiercely defiant sensibility of Jorie Graham:

> The thing seen becomes the thing unseen.
> The opposite is, or seems to be, impossible.
> . . . . . . . . . . . . . . . . . . . . . . . . . . . . . . . .
> Description is an element, like air or water.[1]

Like all good epigrams, these nuggets provoke questions more than they provide answers. "Becomes" means "complements" as well as "turns into"; Stevens, sympathetic student of Emerson and Baudelaire, intuits a constant symbolic relationship between the natural world and the world of the spirit. Even more ambiguous than the meanings of "becoming" are its processes. When the visible turns into the invisible, it logically disappears from sight: it evaporates, escapes notice. But we must qualify the tentative second half of Steven's pronouncement: things *previously* unseen can heave into view, making themselves visible before finally vanishing. Angels and all otherworldly emissaries come and go at will. For his part, the poet demands a disciplined attendance on the "thing seen," with a hope of capturing or rendering its essence through an act of accurate observation in order to put himself in touch with the circulating currents of the invisible. The act of "description" becomes a significant element, although not the only one, in his task. Stevens chooses his elements cunningly: not earth and fire, the two most capable of being seen, but air and water, the first invisible, the second translucent. One might as well try to catch the wind as try to describe anything.

The frustrations inherent in such efforts mark the continuing explorations by the one contemporary poet who is most drawn to the visible world and distrustful of it in equal measure. If the major tradition of poetic description has meant keeping one's eye steadily on one's subject (the line that runs from Wordsworth through Hopkins down to such diverse lookers-on or lookers-at as A. R. Ammons, Gary Snyder, and Charles Tomlinson), then Jorie Graham has alighted upon a new vantage point, one that refuses to look evenly and patiently, and that makes its maneuvers by nervously cross-cutting from one item, gesture, scene, or thought, to another. For all her intensity, Graham is not really an intimate poet. It is hard to get to know her, just as it is sometimes hard to know what one of her poems is literally "about." Her difficulty has everything to do with how she looks at the world and then renders her vision in her poems. Description is a central element in her work, but like air and water, it is a medium often invisible or dark.

Where John Ashbery has fashioned a poetry that moves seamlessly along a flow chart, recording all sensations at all frequencies and in as many tones, moods, or layers of diction as possible, Graham proceeds by interruption and asides, with a flickering glance that makes (in another nod to Stevens) the visible a little hard to see. Even her syntax differs from that of Ashbery, whose long sentences are structurally sound, although the references may be opaque (the form remains intact, but the subject disappears from view), as well as from that of Amy Clampitt, whose old-fashioned Miltonic, sinuously baroque tendrils reproduce, microcosmically, a plentiful world of flora and fauna. In a famous letter to Thomas Poole, Coleridge once observed that the use of parentheses signaled the very drama of thought, which showed the thought growing and ramifying and made of the words on the page a living process rather than a *hortus siccus*, a vibrantly Gothic (i.e., English) rather than a deadeningly classic (i.e., French) style.[2] Graham's drama of thought is jagged, unreticulated, looking more often like blips on a computer screen than branches gracefully arching away from a central stem. Especially in her most recent books the parenthetical remarks, visible lacunae, syntactic interruptions, experiments with phrasing and lineation, and the pull of the line against that of the sentence all lead to one inevitable conclusion: that what she calls, in the title of one poem, "The Dream of the Unified Field" (*Materialism*, and repeated as the title of her 1995 Pulitzer Prize–winning anthology of her own work) must remain a dream only, never a fact, whether in the provinces of painting and physics, or within the human psyche, or in the universe of the seen and the unseen. Buckminster Fuller's observation—"Unity is plural and at minimum two"—has special resonance for

Graham, as her rival tendencies, to unify and to diversify or shatter, have political, philosophical, and, above all, aesthetic causes and consequences in her poetry.

Graham courts the unexpected. Some later poems demonstrate satisfying closure just as some earlier ones do not. Her poems move mysteriously, using—indeed, enacting—description as part of their quest for adequate form. Making the visible a little hard to see begins with her covers. On the dust jackets of eight of her volumes are reproductions of paintings, all of which call into question the nature of seeing. *Erosion*, with a photograph of the poet on the cover, is the exception, but even here the picture extends *beyond* its overlaid framing lines. The Mark Rothko painting on *Hybrids of Plants and of Ghosts* insists on the ways one shade of color blurs into another. The half picture of a naked woman by an open window on *The End of Beauty* divides Eric Fischl's painting and tantalizes us with a frame (the dimensions of the cover) imposed upon an abbreviated image. A version of Mantegna's *Christ Descending into Limbo* on the cover of *Materialism* depicts a swirling, caped figure seen from behind, with leg and hair the only visible body parts. Figures from a fresco by Giotto are seen in profile at the bottom of *Swarm*; five people in clear profile stand out from the undifferentiated others who melt into the background or the left-hand border. *Never* reproduces a small portion of Vermeer's *The Astronomer*, showing two hands, one globe, and a window. The symbolism is clear: a miniaturized world confronted not by a complete human being but only by his grasping, measuring hands.

Most telling of all is Francis Bacon's *Study of a Figure in a Landscape* on the cover of *Region of Unlikeness*, where the blurred outlines of human likeness dissolve into the surround of a field. What Graham calls "the great *thereness* of being" in this volume ("Untitled," 17) suggests that reality, essence, and identity exist at a remove, and that the attempt to capture them is inevitably doomed. Magritte's painting of Pascal's coat on the cover of *The Errancy* is complete, but the coat itself is tattered and ripped, exposing the city and sky behind and beneath it. In all these cases, you *can* judge a book by its cover: the illustrations refuse to come into focus, into a neat box or frame, and even when the illustration is complete, as are the Rothko and Magritte pictures, it poses questions of representation. The exception (i.e., a completed picture without explicit irony) proves the rule: *The Dream of the Unified Field* reproduces Bartolo di Fredi's *The Creation of Eve*. Adam's wished-for unification involves sleep and then the birth of Eve by an act of separation from his own body. Like Adam, Graham dreams of a unity that can occur only through fracture. Her poems, like the covers of her books, assay figural description and landscape painting but refuse completion. It is as though Graham wishes she were Poussin, inserting human figures in a pastoral landscape, but is prohibited from doing so. All paradises are, if not lost, at least inaccessible.

In *Materialism* Graham announces with uncharacteristic nostalgia her longing for an old-fashioned Romantic organicism:

> ... Reader,
> wind blowing through these lines I wish were branches,
> searchlight in daylight, trying as I
>            am trying
> to find a filament of the real like some twist of
>            handwriting glowing in the middle
> distance—somewhere up here, in the air—.
> ("Young Maples in Wind")[3]

She wants to find a filament of the real, but she also tries to create one in the twist of her handwriting. A poem like this invites instructive comparison with the work of Romantic forebears and contemporaries like the late Howard Nemerov, a great reader of natural hieroglyphics and unlettered poetry, who takes an easy fanciful notice of alphabets inscribed in the air by blue swallows or incised by skaters' blades on frozen ponds. But Graham, almost everywhere else, even more surely thwarts such comparison.

Nemerov was always clear in his doubleness. Looking at the swallows "divide the air / In shapes invisible and evanescent," he tempts himself and us with the possibility of meaning in nature:

> Thus helplessly the mind in its brain
> Weaves up relation's spindrift web,
> Seeing the swallows' tails as nibs
> Dipped in invisible ink, writing.

But his mind, trained by William of Occam, knows it must look at the world "emptied of speech" because "the spelling mind / Imposes with its grammar book / Unreal relations on the blue / Swallows." To read the world as the *liber naturae* is a dream whose usefulness has long since passed, but Nemerov constantly entertains such nostalgias. He wants to see writing everywhere (in the invisible ink of swallows, in skaters' blades on ice), and where he sees writing he wants meaning (in Chinese ideograms he cannot understand). He loads his potent epigram pregnantly: "Still, the point of style / is character" ("Writing").[4]

Graham frustratingly spurns the discursive clarity of Nemerov and his entire generation. Regardless of the genuine, wrenching, and dramatic changes that she has made in her books—correcting, undoing, and revising earlier work—one element remains constant: her visual delight in the world is matched by an opposing resistance to the visible. She has revived the grand ambitions of poets like Wordsworth, Eliot, and Stevens but has also undercut the very ground that made those ambitions possible. She asks us to see the world anew. Description is one element among many, but one she will neither rely on wholly nor do without.

Just when a reader might think that Nemerov's blue swallows or their cousins have appeared, Graham works a turn on the Romantic preoccupation with bird flight and birdsong. She devotes as much energy, throughout her poetry, to looking at birds as to listening to them, thereby evincing at least an equal sensitivity to the visible as to the audible.[5] Here, for example, is the beautiful ending of "Existence and Presence" (*Materialism*, 142) in the same volume, in which she conducts a soliloquy on a hillside and seems to see at twilight the figure of Diana the huntress, followed by ambiguous flocks:

An alphabet flew over, made liquid syntax for a while,
diving and rising, forking, a caprice of clear meanings,
right pauses, unwrapping the watching-temptation—
then chopped and scattered, one last one chittering away,
then silence, then the individual screeches of the nighthunters
at dusk, the hollows sucked in around that cry.

Failing even to identify the kind of bird, Graham jumps instinctively to the level of the abstract, the intellectual. She does not so much "describe" the flock as attempt to "read" it, but whatever clarity of meaning it possesses goes unspecified and finally disappears. The experience of the event is more important than its accurate description. And not only does she refuse to describe but she also, characteristically, refuses to moralize or to mourn. Seldom has the experience of the natural world resulted in so little human emotion.

Even writing itself suffers a fate worse than in Nemerov's lovely dreams. In "Penmanship" (*Hybrids*, 31), the alphabet becomes a landscape on the page in the eyes of the young learner, each letter contributing to the ongoing development of a visual image that metaphorically resembles a natural one. For a moment in midpoem, Graham loses herself in an imagined seascape ("flooded lowlands, topsoil gone downstream, the ocean / flashing her green garments, many-stemmed and / many-headed") before personifying the twenty-six letters as a school of fish whose major impulse "is for normalcy, marriage," that is, for correctness. But poet and poem drift off into an inconclusive reverie (with an explicit allusion to the labials and gutturals in Stevens's "The Plot Against the Giant"), as if to acknowledge that such dreams can never be realized:

these labials and gutturals narrowing their aim,
shedding the body for
its wish, a pure idea, a thought as true as
not true, water

lilies, water-
striders. . . .

Regardless of the real, wrenching, and dramatic changes that Graham has
made in her books, each of which corrects, undoes, and revises the previous
ones, one element remains constant: she must discover or grapple with ways
of handling her ambivalent responses to Romanticism and its American
modernist inheritors.

The title of the first poem in Graham's first book ("The Way Things
Work," *Hybrids*, 3) might invite thoughts of celebration, on the principle of Richard Wilbur's "The Beautiful Changes"; instead, the poem moves
from fluidity, transition, a Romantic principle of harmony, to electricity,
mechanics, tangibility. The first line extends from the generalized title:

is by admitting
or opening away.
This is the simplest form
of current: Blue
moving through blue;
blue through purple;
the objects of desire
opening upon themselves
without us;
the objects of faith.
The way things work
is by solution,
. . . . . . . . . . . . . . . . . . . . . . . . . . . .
The way things work
is that we finally believe
they are there,
common and able
to illustrate themselves.
Wheel, kinetic flow,
rising and falling water,

ingots, levers and keys,

. . . . . . . . . . . . . . . . .

The way things work
is that eventually
something catches.

Admitting, solution, belief, catching: the poem ends on a note of almost random chance. Eventually some hook or ratchet takes hold, stapling us to a
universe that might as well do without us. Whereas most interested observers
of the processes of the natural or physical world tend to take delight in the
manifold operations of a clockwork universe, or of an organically unfolding
unity, of the visible evidence of an indwelling spirituality, Jorie Graham has
maintained so skeptical a stance from the beginning (beneath all the stylistic
changes in her poetry) that we may reasonably call her the least hedonistic,
least delighted, least sensuously fulfilled of descriptive poets in spite of the
lush outpourings of gorgeous details and ecstatic feelings that fill her work.

Like all but one of her books, *Hybrids* has a cover illustration by a painter.
In this case, it is one of Mark Rothko's color-field oils. Graham has always
been drawn to painting as a subject and an analogy, but "For Mark Rothko"
proves that from the start Graham has never tried to be a conventionally
ekphrastic poet. Instead of "describing" one of Rothko's paintings—a challenge to any poet's potential wish to represent the nonrepresentational (see
Chapter 5)—Graham makes an homage to him by proceeding deductively
from the idea of a color in Rothko to the specific scene she observes from
her window:

Shall I say it is the constancy of persian red
that permits me to see
this persian-red bird
come to sit now
on the brick barbecue
within my windowframe.
(36)

Nature, we assume, imitates art or, rather, one kind of experience (the memory of a Rothko painting) prepares a viewer for another kind of sighting, one
that changes before one's eyes as the bird disappears from view:

When I look again he is gone.
He is easy to imagine
in flight: *red extended flame,*

I would say, or, *ribbon*
*torn from a hat*
*rising once*

*before it catches on a twig,*
or, *flying painted mouth*
but then how far
have we come?
He could fly now
into a moment of sunlight

that fell from the sun's edge
ten thousand years ago,
mixed in with sunlight
absolutely new.
There is no way to understand
the difference. Some red

has always just slipped from
our field of vision, a cardinal
dropping from persian to magenta to white so slowly
in order that the loss
be tempted,
not endured.
(36–37)

The idea of color dominates the poet's imagination, as does the way color slips from shade to shade, moment to moment in time, and along a visual spectrum in space. Something comes into view and then vanishes, leaving imagined traces in the perceiver's eye. The last stanza suggests vision's eternally transitional qualities, so beautiful that they invite us to repeat the process of perception and memory (one possible implication of the verb "tempted") rather than lament the loss of beauty. As in "The Way Things Work," where blue moved through blue through purple, here Graham refuses to settle for an elegiac response to change and loss.

The visible world has always inspired in Graham a deeply ambivalent set of responses. On the one hand, it attracts her; on the other, she deeply distrusts it. As I mentioned in Chapter 1, seventy years ago, in his famous introduction to the idiosyncratic *Oxford Book of Modern Verse*, Yeats claimed that he and his generation wanted to revolt "against irrelevant descriptions of nature." Graham hews to the same path of resistance: "irrelevant" may be for her synonymous with "perceptually accurate" or "deeply committed" or "carefully witnessed." Her contemporary Mark Doty poses and answers the question: "What is description, after all, / but encoded desire" ("Description," *Atlantis*), and in another poem from the same volume ("Two Ruined Boats"), he makes a comparable gesture of reparation and restitution: "Description is itself a kind of travel, / And I can study all day in an orient / of color."[6] Such ease of formulation, clarity of purpose, and delight in sensuous participation must appeal to that part of Graham's temperament and upbringing that comes from years in France and Italy, dedicated looking at real and painted landscapes, and physical self-awareness. But increasingly she has come to resist the orient of color in favor of blanknesses, interstices, gaps and lacunae. Here, for example, is the opening of "Room Tone" (*The End of Beauty*, 73):

> Turn around (wind in the sycamore).
> Did you see that did you hear that (wind in the
> _____ _____ _____?) can you touch it,
> what *can* you touch? will you
> speak back to me,
> will you look up now, please?
> Dear reader, is it enough for you that I am thinking of you
> in this generic sort of way,
> moving across the page for you that your eyes move,
> moving in and out of these rooms that there be a *there*
> for you?

Leaving things out rather than putting them all in—omission instead of inclusion—becomes as much a tool for the wordsmith as the painter, as both John Ashbery (at the start of *Three Poems*) and James Merrill (in such experimental lyrics as "Losing the Marbles" and "Self-Portrait in Tyvek™ Windbreaker") have proved.[7] The source of such flamboyant economies in the twentieth century has been the Ezra Pound of mock-imagism, but in excerpts such as this one Graham shows how omission, like fragments and asides, possesses its own dramatic usefulness. In this case, Graham wishes to reconstruct an earlier scene, an erotic pairing of lovers (one of them, perhaps, the poet herself, who remains, however, curiously removed from her own reminiscence), but what resonates most powerfully is her inability to retell, to reimagine, to describe with anything like fluency. Like John Ashbery and Charles Wright, Graham uses narrative (which is an element like air or water, or description) in her poetry but never tells a story in its entirety.

Instead, interruption, echoes from *Paradise Lost*, repeated phrases, hallucinated questions of and reminders to the reader amass almost musically to inhibit, frustrate, and finally to destroy all sense of both narrative and description itself. The poem ends:

> and here is the daylight now, look,
> and this a lifted hand up into it,
> and a name repeated slowly to indicate _____,
> and here the one (half-cup of?) breath being exchanged by the two
>            two bodies,
> the one breath back and forth and back and forth until they're dizzy
>            they're
> making themselves sick, in the white room, in the
> (as in the land of darkness yet in light) white room, so white,
> (and fansie that they feel
> divinitie within them breeding wings) how white? (wherewith to
>            scorn
> the earth)
> and freedom (click) and minutes (click) and
> (under amazement of their hideous change)
> something like what's called *being-born* (click, click
> (75–76)

Leisurely storytelling and description have given way to the nervousness of candid snapshots. Whether such a technique can ever be judged as more than experimental or other than frustrating to either poet or audience is less important than its temporary usefulness to a woman who resists the very impulses that most strongly inspire her: the impulses to narrate and to describe. Graham wishes to achieve depiction through other means.

The goal of beauty becomes, in this transitional volume, its completion, and Graham tries to use the "end" to justify several radical means. Her perverse daring allows her to title a poem "Description" (*End of Beauty*, 11) and then to locate a natural sight within a frame constructed of both experience and myth, and to animate the whole as though it were a story narrated or filmed. The poem seems to deposit Tristan and Isolde in an industrialized, midwestern blight. And yet it begins as a sight caught from a passing train window (a frame, in other words, that always resists stasis):

> Meet me, meet me whisper the waters from the train window and
>            the small skiff adrift
> with its passenger, oarless, being pulled in by
> some destination, delicate, a blossom on the wing of
> the swollen waters.

The passenger is floating "down through the air-killed reeds, / past the refinery," and only the echo of Wagner-filtered-through-Eliot ("Waste / and the empty / the sea") tells us that the poet's mind has invested the scene with mythic possibilities by reading into a glimpsed vision some mythic adjustments.

But even this focus needs readjusting, as the poet ends by losing sight of the skiff and its passenger and also by merging Tristan and Isolde with the figures of Orpheus and Eurydice, another pair of lovers referred to throughout the volume:

> . . . Westward strain the eyes,
> eastward the ship flies, the rudderless boat, the sleepy
> passenger mortally
>
> wounded. How far will he go pulled in by the listening of that far
>     shore?
> And as she approached, unable to see any body
>         within,
> she heard to her heart's delight a lovely harp,
>     a sweet voice,
> and as long as he harped and as long as he sang
>     she never stirred to
>
> save him.
> (13)

The provocative breaking-up and breaking-down of story and scene has for Graham a psychological analogy: the volume contains five partial self-portraits, each of which figures the author in terms of a mythic pair: Apollo and Daphne, Adam and Eve, Demeter and Persephone, Orpheus and Eurydice, and (a variant) Penelope weaving and unweaving. Identity is fragmented, doubled, reconditioned; neither self nor story retains the satisfying fulfillments that we expect myth and description to provide.

Graham has apparently forsworn discursiveness. Even other kinds of continuities, especially syntactic and grammatical ones, have evaporated in *The End of Beauty* (to be restored, partially, later on). In an interview she attempts to justify her experiments with endings and her wish to move beyond Western notions of language and eschatology: "I'd like to find a kind of language—or *action* in language (form, in other words) which would . . . be more like the painting or the stage-event than the label to it. The ritual rather than the *use* it's put to."[8] Although many poems from all of her books retain titles that seem more like labels ("Self-Portrait," for example) or explanations than events, it is also clear that Graham wishes to push language into realms analogous to those explored and then created by the action painting of Pollock and other Abstract Expressionists. Whether a poet can ever realize this dream of a field of linguistic action is doubtful: if the experience of reading such jagged, partial, often uncompleted utterances yields only a sense of action or ritual, but no sense of ending or purposeful-ness (even Kant's "purposefulness without purpose"), then the dream serves a need for the dreamer but not for the recipient.

Even to frame Graham's purpose in terms of dreams takes us to an area of intersection with a poet whom we would not immediately think of as a stylistic precursor: Elizabeth Bishop. Once more, the comparison with so devotedly a "descriptive" poet as Mark Doty brings out Graham's peculiar manipulation of her poetic inheritance. Where Doty actually pays homage to Bishop's marine scenes (replacing Provincetown for Nova Scotia) and to the famous seal of "At the Fishhouses," everywhere gently insinuating his allegiance to Bishop's famous observant eye and her painterly spirit, Gra-ham attaches herself to the darker, existential side of Bishop's temperament: not to her imagery, her syntax, or her humor, but to the failures that lie on the other side of her successes.[9] Acknowledging the liminality of Bishop's poetry, its preference for border states (one thinks of "Cape Breton," "The Bight," "At the Fishhouses," "In the Waiting Room," inter alia), Graham responds to these poems' enactment of the ways "the ineffable erodes the known, and the known makes inroads into the ineffable."[10] There is no great leap from Stevens, at the intersection of the visible and the invisible, to Bishop—or Graham—at the threshold between the known, the knowable, and the unknown. *Erodes*, of course, is a Graham word, not a Bishop one. What to Bishop were ideologically innocent acts of description becomes for her successor something else: "Description is an attempt to go out into it and come back changed. . . . [Not in description itself] but in the cracks of it, the thing emerges. You have to undertake an act which you know is essentially futile, in the direct sense: the words are not going to seize the thing. But leaks in between the attempts at seizure *is* the thing, and you have to be willing to suffer the limits of description in order to get it."[11] Graham sug-gests that all meaning is accidental and beside the point, a thing uncovered during the adventure.

Graham makes reading difficult deliberately, in part for political rea-sons. We have been inured, she says, to the possible distortions and lies of language through politics and advertising. She is as skeptical of labels and "uses" as she is of terminations. Paradoxically, this postmodern skeptic, who distrusts Western notions of closure, and eschatology in general, sounds like an echo, at century's end, of T. S. Eliot at its start: she aims for "the dissoci-ated sensibility restored to wholeness by the act of reading. . . . [I] had to go back to the line, had to contend with all the implications of the line, not just the sentence."[12] But Graham extends an even older tradition than that of Eliotic high modernism and its nostalgias for a premodern temper of wholeness of culture and personality. As with the great English gardens of the eighteenth century, modeled after the paintings of Poussin and Claude, themselves based on the pastoral imagery of Theocritus and Virgil, in much of Graham's poetry the look of landscape often seems filtered through, or *as*, the look of painting. Where the field of action and observation is strenuously, though often opaquely, depicted, we cannot be sure whether we occupy a reading space intended to put us in mind of or within the frame of a painting or an external scene. Graham manages to internalize all of her spaces even while seeming to respond to something outside of herself.

For Graham, "reality" itself is liminal: the real exists *between* or *among*, never *within*. Thus her series of self-portraits as X and Y. And thus, also, her sympathy with Eurydice ("Orpheus and Eurydice," *The End of Beauty*, 18):

—what she dreamed

was of disappearing into the seen

not of disappearing, lord, into the real—

Because, as Helen Vendler has observed, the present is the time of lyric, everything in Graham seems to rush into a continuous present even in those moments when she adheres to a narrative impulse to recount past events.[13] Nothing can be caught entire; nothing can be seen, understood, or transcribed entire. The impulse to describe and to narrate gives way, breaks down, and surrenders to greater forces, because time moves more swiftly than one's ability to capture or even register it. "Here it is, *here*, the end of beauty, the present" ("The Lovers," 64): the origin of the title phrase of this volume presents ending and culmination as always in medias res, unreachable, unstoppable.

Nevertheless, Graham contains within herself both a closet painter and a closet metaphysician. She wishes to capture a scene, especially to register the connections, however tentative, between the visible and the invisible (which we may read as the "spiritual"). When Persephone emerges from the underworld (in "Self-Portrait as Demeter and Persephone," *The End of Beauty*, 62):

The first thing she saw when she surfaced was the wind
wrapping like a body round the stiff stripped trees
that would bend more deeply into that love if they could
to accompany its eagerness young wind its rage
if they weren't so perfect if they weren't so shorn.

Such Romantic wistfulness seems like an updating of both Shelley ("Hymn to Intellectual Beauty") and Keats ("In Drear-Nighted December"). What Shelley calls "the awful shadow of some unseen Power" emerges as Persephone, fresh from the embrace of Pluto, imaginatively populates the natural world by seeing the unseen as an erotic force, enwrapping and inspiring the trees that want to respond, but that in their early spring leaflessness cannot open themselves to the wind's caresses. Like Keats, Graham looks on vacancy and performs an imaginative act of reparation, in this case, an anticipation of later fruitfulness when the wind, though still not literally visible, will fulfill—and be fulfilled by—the responsive, clothed trees.

The poem registers an act of reparation, of discovering and then filling emptiness. "Pollock and Canvas" (*The End of Beauty*, 86–87), a medley of speculations, reflections, and quotations from the painter, quotations from God to Moses, an envoi from a Renaissance lyric, epitomizes Graham's wrestling with the problem of description, of technique in general, in painting and, by extension, in poetry. The theme is fullness and emptiness, completion and separation; the technique is simultaneously aggregative and disjunctive. Unlike William Blake, who adoringly welcomed the binding line that gives form and shape, whether in drawing or in epigram, Graham can neither accept nor fully evade the confinements of ending. The third part of the poem begins:

> Where does the end
> begin?
> where does the lifting off of hands become
> love,
> letting the made wade out into danger,
> letting the form slur out into flaw, in-
>
> conclusiveness? Where does the end of love
> begin? (Where does *that* love begin?)
> And then He rested, is that where the real
> making
> begins—the now—Then He rested letting in chance letting in
> any wind any shadow quick with minutes, and whimsy,
> through the light, letting the snake the turning
> in.

The question exists on the artistic, the erotic, and the religious planes. For Graham, all creation (God's, Pollock's, her own) starts with the promise of satisfaction but invariably ends with the admission of the serpent into the garden. Form slurs into flaw; inconclusiveness is itself broken between lines, spilling over linguistic borders. Graham fears both beginnings and endings. "Form's what affirms," says the self-parodying James Merrill in his "The Thousand and Second Night,"[14] but for Graham form oozes, melts, blends, drips, in the way Pollock's paintbrush never touches "at any point, / the still ground" (81). Graham's quicksilver forms affirm the shadowy boundaries between speech and writing, self and other, narrative and lyric, center and periphery, finitude and expansiveness. The arena of her poems exists, like that of Pollock's drip paintings, in the great gap "between." Frames exist to be broken.

When Ashbery announces, in "Self-Portrait in a Convex Mirror," that "Today has no margins, the event arrives / Flush with its edges, is of the same substance, / Indistinguishable," he embodies the charming—sometimes goofy, sometimes exasperating—random continuum of his own work and its renderings of time's fluidity.[15] If time is his central element, space is Graham's: her painterly obsession inclines her to an experience of the world that both visualizes (attempts to see) and surveys (attempts to map) it through lineation. In the same way that Charles Wright's extended and broken lines reproduce the canvasses of Cézanne, Graham's even more jagged syntax and lineation approximate the thoroughly nonrepresentational effects of Pollock and other Abstract Expressionists.

Her readers have always sensed that Graham's turn toward open forms, longer lines, less "organically" composed and ended poems has liberated her from the more artful closure of the lyrics in her first two volumes. What interests me, on the other hand, is the constancy of her ideas rather than the changes in her techniques. As Elaine Scarry has written, with reference to a letter from Coleridge to William Godwin in 1800, "The end of the century is a period in which the performative and the descriptive often become for a time indistinguishable."[16] In her ongoing performances, Graham has been unable to avoid description.

Even in *Hybrids* the problem could not be solved. And it was—as it remains—intimately allied with the nature and notion of framing. As counter to the frame, that which binds, surrounds, limits, and defines, Graham has always posed what we may call the "blur," which is not just something that smashes a frame but, instead, any principle of occluding, oozing, or dimming crispness of perception. She evidently takes seriously Stevens's aphorism that the poem must make the visible a little hard to see. Forms and color, like perception itself, melt. Voice interrupts; parentheses interrupt.[17]

Graham does not see: if she did, she would have clear direct objects of vision. Instead, she must look *at, toward,* above all, *through.* "To look" is never a transitive verb, no matter how much one wants it to be. The prepositions make a frame. Graham began her career as a poet who wanted to look through, at, and toward, and occasionally she used her looking as the means of reaching an ending, of coming upon moral certitude. In "I watched a snake" (*Erosion*, 34–35), she performs a maneuver so characteristic of another *kind* of poet that its unusualness in her oeuvre stands out. Here is a poem thoroughly within the Romantic or neo-Romantic tradition, in which observation leads to emblem making. The snake, threading its way through the grass behind the house, visible then invisible, becomes a conventional simile:

> This must be a perfect progress where
> movement appears
> to be a vanishing, a mending
> of the visible
>
> by the invisible—just as we
> stitch the earth,
> it seems to me, each time
> we die, going
> back under, coming back up. . . .
> It is the simplest
>
> stitch, this going where we must,
> leaving a not
> unpretty pattern by default.

The human analogy allows her to end on a note of triumph, with the kind of generalization that her later work eschews, along with conclusion:

> . . . Passion is work
> that retrieves us,
> lost stitches. It makes a pattern of us,
> it fastens us
> to sturdier stuff
> no doubt.
>
> (35)

Everything about this poem is easy: the Romantic move from observation to application to moralizing; the clarity of simile; the offhand diction ("it seems to me," "a not / unpretty pattern," "no doubt"); the effort to allow description to convey human passion by sequestering the observer much as the snake sequesters itself in its work to capture a "blue- / black dragonfly"; the epigrammatic nugget ("Desire // is the honest work of the body, / its engine, its wind") that would sit more comfortably in the finished work of Nemerov or

Richard Wilbur than in Graham's later, more explosive confrontations with nature, with description, and with herself.

Looking at something, especially within a frame or from the protective backing of a frame (a speaker gazing outside *through* a window), is a standard procedure in Graham's poetry and is often complemented by an insistence on "being looked at" or being seen. Always, as she announces at the start of "Framing" (*Hybrids*, 35), "Something is left out, something left behind." Only by framing does history occur. Looking at an old photo of herself, seeing herself through the frame of a portrait and a temporal one as well, Graham also enjoys looking out, where she cannot be seen, as in "Self-Portrait" (46), a love poem in the same volume:

> After fresh snow I'll go up to the attic and look out.
> My looking is a set of tracks—the first—
> a description of the view
> that cannot mar it.

New snow occasions metaphoric action—writing—an assault on the landscape. She inscribes her traces on the snow without (or so she thinks) physically altering the scene but affecting it anyway. The provocation of the snow distinguishes Graham from Ashbery, who is always more passive a persona and a respondent in his poetry. In "Self-Portrait in a Convex Mirror," for example, there are the beautiful, unexpected lines about snow following upon the discovery that whereas we think we have "surprised" the painter, or the work of art, in actuality it's the other way around ("he has surprised us / As he works"):

> . . . The picture is almost finished,
> The surprise almost over, as when one looks out,
> Startled by a snowfall which even now is
> Ending in specks and sparkles of snow.
> It happened while you were inside, asleep,
> And there is no reason why you should have
> Been awake for it, except that the day
> Is ending and it will be hard for you
> To get to sleep tonight, at least until late.[18]

Unlike Graham, Ashbery feels no need to make actual or metaphorical tracks in the snow, which has come unannounced, silent and secret, interrupting our sleep patterns but proffering warmth and minor comfort. Ashbery is a poet of reverie; Graham, a poet of engagement.

As she announces in "Still Life" (*Hybrids*, 51), looking out from a window at a wintry scene beyond:

For at the windowpane
we are the heroes
leaving home to journey out over the visible, that trusty fabric,
and are the heroines

staying behind.

For Graham, whose Rilkesque pronouncement "the patience of the visible
/ is the invisible" ("The Slow Sounding and Eventual Reemergence Of,"
*Hybrids*, 58) exposes both her spiritual longings and her impatience with
waiting, the poet seems a still, free spirit attached to the world but never
quite at home in it. The final poem in *Hybrids*, summarizing her various
obsessions throughout this book (and the later ones), shows us the shifting
panorama composed of external nature, internal reality, and the invisible
spiritual world to which both aspire through a painted or depicted world.
An elaborate image emerges linking birds, their feathers, pens, writing, protection against and aspiration to the invisible, in a form that echoes nursery
rhyme as well as scripture. Although not nominally a "descriptive" poem,
opening with a categorical equation ("The bird is an alphabet"), "A Feather
for Voltaire" (66–67) presumes looking and describing as the basis for the
connections and turnings it makes. Graham concludes her first book with a
statement of heroic, almost theological purposefulness:

A feather,
pulled from the body or found on the snow

can be dipped into ink
to make one or more words: *possessive, the sun.* A pen
can get drunk,
having come so far, having so far to go—*meadow,*
*in vain, imagine*
*the pain*

and when he was gone then there was none

and this is the key to the kingdom.

Writing may well be both the best revenge and also the only access we have
to the invisible. Emptiness, as in a wintry landscape, or a feather left by a
now departed bird, or a solitary woman, invites or demands filling, first by a
looking, then by an assault on the invisible through writing. These assaults,
though nominally changed in their form, provide the basis for Graham's
subsequent books.

I have already termed "being looked at" the obverse of looking. At its most inviting, such an impulse from the natural world inspires our assaults upon it, as in Graham's offhand remark: "the day tries harder to be *really /* seen" ("Event Horizon," *Materialism*, 51). But as it does, it also can quietly menace us as a kind of payment for our own emotional disequilibrium. In the remarkable, sonnet-like "Act III, Sc. 2" (*Region of Unlikeness*, 66), a climactic dramatic moment between two people is figured in terms of their surround. "Look she said this is not the distance / we wanted to stay at": her request for intimacy is unheeded, met with silence, "*waiting*," and even her casual "Look" at the start of line 1 turns out to anticipate the intensity of looking, and being looked at, that stills the couple literally at the midpoint of the action (e.g., III, 2), which is also the poem's end:

Then the you, whoever you are, peering down to see
   if it's done yet.
Then just the look on things of being looked-at.
Then just the look on things of being seen.

That things being looked at have their own "look" means either that an animism underlies the world, or (at least as likely a possibility) that Graham's speaker (here and elsewhere) displays the kind of paranoia that would inspire her to look and suspect that the external world knows it is being looked at. Dickinson's field of gazing grain and Stevens's "the way things look each day" are her transcendental forbears. It is significant that the poem that succeeds this one is entitled "Immobilism" (*Region*, 67) and begins with an act of vigorous looking that is stopped in its tracks:

The eye in its socket sweeps over the withered field.
It slides over the still place.
Stays.

The "fast" eye, neither "translator" nor "intruder," according to Graham's denials, although a "prisoner," works hard to survey the wintry landscape, running, leaping, counting, and astounding nature. That which "cannot look back" at one moment becomes animated the very next when the clicking-camera-eye surveys the landscape it "owns": "The two white metal chairs look at each other" (69). Such diction must do more than mean simply that the two chairs face one another (as if even "facing" ever obliterates the animation implicit in the things of this world); instead, it gives us, as do the nervous pace, lineation, and syntax of this rendition of surveillance, the potential sense of our being looked at in return by those things we are observing. Graham chose as epigraph to this section of *Region of Unlike-*

*ness* an appropriate aphorism of Nietzsche: "It is a sad, hard but determined gaze—an eye that looks out" (63).

The work of looking, of trying to connect the world to God's shadow, admits of no conclusion. Like Graham's unhedged boundaries and broken frames, the poem is open-ended because the quest for sight is like the quest for salvation, and the poet is as skeptical of aesthetic finalities as she is of religious certitudes. The poem ends as it had begun. The eye (never absolutely identifiable as the antecedent of "it") skirts nervously into oblivion beyond the frame:

> It darts, it stretches out along the dry hard ground,
> it cannot find the end, it darts, it stretches out—
> (70)

Although "Immobilism" is relatively open-ended, it repeats with variations a theme and technique that Graham had used to good advantage in *Erosion*, her "art" book, filled with homages to painters and the processes of visualization. In "Scirocco" (*Erosion*, 8–9), she takes what might be the occasion for an ordinary touristic poem and converts it into a religious exploration of the way what we look at looks back at us. The title wind blows over Keats's apartment in the Piazza di Spagna, but it evades description itself, working itself through us:

> . . . Who is
>         the nervous spirit
> of this world
>         that must go over and over
> what it already knows,
>         what is it
>
> so hot and dry
>         that's looking through us,
> by us,
>         for its answer?

This personified wind, "working the invisible" (i.e., both for it and through it), fingers the dry leaves around the plaza, touching even the grapes that have begun to grow on the terrace arbor. Soon, these will soften and "enter"

> our world, translating
>         helplessly
> from the beautiful
>         to the true. . . .

Whatever the spirit,
    the thickening grapes

are part of its looking.
(9)

Looking at us, the world wants us to receive it, mend it, and calm it. Seldom does Graham pay such explicit homage to a traditional trope, even when converting the wind-as-spirit into a dry desert plague, and in her later poetry she will turn away from such neat conclusions as she creates here, but even early on our transactions with the world—our looking at it—are met by its looking at and through us. On the lookout ourselves, we are always observed.

"Is there a new way of looking?" Graham asks ("Notes on the Reality of the Self," *Materialism*, 3), placing the question significantly at the start of her most literary book. But this is the essential question she has asked implicitly all along. The poem begins with a descriptive phrase ("Watching the river, each handful of it closing over the next, / brown and swollen") whose very personification brings nature into close companionship with its onlooker. But right after the query Graham reverts to the language or at least the imagery of *Hybrids*: "Is there a new way of looking— / valences and little hooks—inevitabilities, proba- / bilities?" Everywhere she wants mechanical as well as organic connections or the promise of them. When she quotes a phrase from Jeffrey Hamilton on George Oppen in "Steering Wheel," we know she is borrowing in order to affirm one of her central tenets: "we have to regain the moral pleasure / of experiencing the distance between subject and object" (5). Everywhere Graham wants to engage with the physical world, the world of her perception, but at the same time she wants to experience the moral pleasure of keeping it at arm's length.

Framing allows her to relish both sides of her temperament, the sensuous and the puritanical. When she observes "the day unfolding its stern materialism" ("In the Hotel," *Materialism*, 7) it is her own sternness that is at issue. She can neither fully evade nor fully enjoy the sensuous world. Hence, in "Steering Wheel" (*Materialism*, 5–6) we have a unique twist on her own tropes of framing, revising as well the parable of Plato's Cave: she watches the world in reverse, as she looks into her car's rearview mirror as she backs out of the driveway. The frame of the mirror exists only to frustrate, not to contain, as what is witnessed is swirling leaves, suctioned into an updraft along with someone's hat from down the block. The poet moves out of the driveway watching a framed or reflected scene, which, far from stationing or capturing the things of this world, obeys its own laws of movement as well as gravity:

—me now slowly backing up
the dusty driveway into the law
composed of updraft, downdraft, weight of these dried
           mid-winter leaves,
light figured-in too, I'm sure, the weight of light,
and angle of vision, dust, gravity, solitude,
and the part of the law which is the world's waiting,
and the part of the law which is my waiting,
and then the part which is my impatience—now; *now?*—

though there are, there really are,
things in the world, you must believe me.

This is a kind of desperate, daring updating of the trope of the fallen leaves
that is scattered from Homer to Howard Nemerov.[19] It also demonstrates
Graham's unwillingness ever fully to let go of the things of this world,
trapped as she seems to be in a paradoxical Limbo always in motion.

    In 1987, Graham observed in an interview, "In my physical experience
of reality, I feel the presence of another world, whether we think of it as *the
world in the instant before we perceive it*, or *the dead*, or *the invisible.* There are
different terms for it: where the angels are. I feel most alive in the particular
enterprise which involves sensing the translation of the invisible world into
the visible."[20] Thomas Gardner quotes this quasi-religious, quasi-Steven-
sian claim, which looks forward to Graham's use of angels in *The Errancy*
(1997); he then remarks, especially of the poems in *The End of Beauty*, that
they try to locate themselves "actively in what Graham calls the 'slippage' of
language which renders unstable the delicate, wisteria-scented surfaces we
call beauty."[21] This instability has proved a leitmotif throughout her career.
When she says (in the long poem "Manifest Destiny," *Materialism*, 97) that
"What's real slides through," she means both that it appears and disappears
from sight. Framing is an inevitable tool for any shaper, especially one with
an eye for art; it also offers the chance to test the waters, to hold nectar in a
sieve, to capture or name the ephemeral, the invisible, the unnameable. It is
for this reason (among others) that Graham chooses to begin some poems
inductively, with observation, and others deductively, working from abstraction to individuation. "Young Maples in Wind" (*Materialism*, 136), quoted
above, begins as a "descriptive poem," nervous fragments, quicksilver detail:

Green netting set forth;
spectrum of greens a bird arcs through; low and
           perfect
postponement.

> The wind moves the new leaves aside—as if there were
> > an inventory
> taken—till they each wink the bit of light
> they're raised into.

Such attention to the visible shows that the Wordsworthian eye still lives in the contemporary scene. Alternatively, we have the beginning of the adjacent poem, "Opulence," whose title is exemplified by the plant that is semi-described throughout. "The self-brewing of the amaryllis rising before me" (134): here the fragment initiates less observation of the trumpet-plant than an occasion for self-reflexiveness and a meditation *on* self-reflexiveness.

This looking—at the world and at the self—has dangerous consequences, which Graham often wants to avoid. In "The Surface" (*Materialism*, 143), she begins with simple observation in an equally simple grammar: "It has a hole in it." "It" is a river surface, but not until the poem's penultimate line do we get a complete sentence rather than a fragment. Instead, Graham articulates a world of breakage, a river "ribbonning, twisting up" and an internal river "of my attention laying itself down" upon the river, which becomes at last an article of permanence and a constant flux, with its "slowed-down drifting performances / of the cold / bed." At the end, "I say *iridescent* and I look down. / The leaves very still as they are carried" (143). The severe focus on the leaves amounts to little, because they continue to evade her mental or physical grasp. Permanence is possible only in the finality of death and in the grammatical presence of the final (verbless) phrase. The poet's pronouncement: Do we take it as command, observation, or wish? This she will not say, but the final line exemplifies the cost exacted of such a vision. The shining the poet observes glints from the dead leaves, which are borne away. Nothing stays. Framing fails in the same way that verbs fail: the containments of language cannot do justice to the temporal processes of observation.

Although *Materialism* and *Region of Unlikeness* were identified as breaking with many of Graham's earlier patterns of composition and her themes, in fact the same tenacious holding onto and somewhat reluctant letting go of the world, a looking at and a looking away from it, inform even the poems in *Erosion*, which is nominally her "art" book. Such breaking away—breaking of a frame, erosion, and blurring—explains why "San Sepolcro" (2–3) stands first in the volume. Piero's Madonna del Parto, that exquisite painting depicting the pregnant Virgin, housed until recently at a little temple in Monterchi, perfectly centers the poet's interest in process of many sorts. The poem locates the painting within the poet's life (its first half describes her house and landscape) before effecting a transition that cuts between stanzas, levels of diction, and theme:

There's milk on the air,
    ice on the oily
lemonskins. How clean
    the mind is,

holy grave. It is this girl
    by Piero
della Francesca, unbuttoning
    her blue dress,
her mantle of weather,
    to go into

labor. Come, we can go in.
    It is before
the birth of god. No-one
    has risen yet
to the museums, to the assembly
    line—bodies

and wings—to the open air
    market. This is
what the living do: go in.
    It's a long way.
And the dress keeps opening
    from eternity

to privacy, quickening.

The mind, that holy grave, a repository of images and thoughts alive as well as dead, contains or recollects all it has seen and witnessed. It becomes the living maid about to go into labor, recalled by the poet as an invitation to the person she is addressing. The Virgin is about to give birth; Christ is about to come out of his mother's body, just as the tourists are about to enter the small chapel. The living are always going in, somewhere, somehow, to a chapel like an eternal grave that is also an eternal womb. As the "dress keeps opening," so does the moment of Mary's lamentation. The poem ends:

Inside, at the heart,
    is tragedy, the present moment
        forever stillborn,
    but going in, each breath
        is a button

coming undone, something terribly
    nimble-fingered
finding all of the stops.
(3)

A viewer of the painting realizes that birth is a moment and part of a process; we bear witness to its just-about-to-happen, its already-having-begun, its always-already-having-happened. Although I earlier referred to Graham as a poet of space rather than of time, clearly in these early poems she tries to explore and to blur the boundaries within and between these two primary categories.[22]

Boundary becomes the great subject of this volume. The catastrophic floods of 1966 that ruined the art treasures of Florence gave the teenage Graham a firsthand look at overflowing and erosion of several sorts (she participated in the relief efforts) and also offered her a retrospective understanding of how the self "is an act of / rescue / where the flesh has risen, / the spirit / loosened" ("In What Manner the Body Is United with the Soul," 14). From the start Graham looked carefully at the world, and at art, but noticed the ways things fell apart, melted, or abraded through the visible. Her attraction to the liminality of Elizabeth Bishop appears early, in a poem called "Wanting a Child," whose setting is a tidal estuary, "the living echo . . . of some great storm far out at sea, too far / to be recalled by us / but transferred / whole onto this shore by waves, so that erosion / is its very face" (29). Crossing the bar laterally, as she does here, or vertically, as she does in "The Age of Reason" (*Erosion*, 19–20), Graham can never get enough of exploring:

How far is true
    enough?
How far into the
    earth
can vision go and
    still be

love?
. . . . .
    There is
no deep

enough. For what we want
    to take
inside of us, whole orchard,
    color,

name, scent, symbol, raw
    pale

blossoms, wet black
    arms there is
no deep enough.

Graham here alludes to but then goes beyond the delicate imagist petals on a wet black bough that Pound made famous as a meager dose of "the thing itself." Her greed for possession forces her to look and to gather; her sense of the inadequacy of all efforts at capture or recollection inhibits and frustrates. In a poem called "Tragedy," in which the poet from her window watches her neighbor across the yard in *her* window frame, she observes: "Then she and I, / each at our gap, / sustain the visible" (28).

Sustaining the visible means, in part, being sustained by it (just as looking, as I have suggested, often complements being looked at), but it also means that visible objects are "beautiful interruptions" of consciousness, jagged lines of light coming into one's sight ("Still Life with Window and Fish," 32). While Graham often positions herself inside looking out, or about to enter an interior space like the chapel at Monterchi, the outside world often seems to want to come inside and to penetrate the inner space of a domestic scene or the poet's own consciousness. She loves "it in here where it blurs, and nothing starts or / ends, but all is / waving, and colorless, / and voiceless" (32). Likewise, in "For John Keats" on the occasion of visiting his grave in the Protestant Cemetery in Rome, Graham repeats her preference: "We live up here // by blurring boundaries, calling it *love, the present moment*, or / *the beautiful*" (50–51).

Graham may share with both Bishop and Stevens a double allegiance to landscapes: raised in Italy and trained to love the richness of its countryside and its art, she responds as a connoisseur of lushness to its warmth and color. ("We are too restless / to inherit / this earth," she announced in "Still Life with Window and Fish" [33]). That is her "south," her Key West. Her "north," the Iowa landscape she inhabited for more than a decade until she moved to Cambridge in the later 1990s, offers a cleaner, barer image of reality. Like that native Iowan Amy Clampitt, Graham respects the empty spaces of the prairie. The title poem of this volume praises dissolution—things falling apart or down—rather than growth. In "For John Keats" she could not find the dividing lines between the plots in the cemetery: "we break every / enframement, being / entirely // transitive" (50). Erosion is a version of more sudden breakings: a slow dissolution or blurring rather than a rapid one. The title poem prepares us for the "The Sense of an Ending," not only an appropriate conclusion to *this* volume but also a preparation for *The End of Beauty* in its themes and methods.

"The Sense of an Ending" has (mostly) an American setting and opens, like many of Graham's poems, with an entire section of phrasal, almost verbless units, describing and setting a scene in northern California. She tests the limits of the visible; it always disappoints her. Neither does it grant access to things themselves, nor does it deliver access to the realm of the invisible. The poem contains what will become Graham's signature methods: an anecdote or two, a fugal intertwining of various elements, a reminisence (a memory of going to a Roman eye clinic to correct blurred vision), meditation on an abstraction. The leitmotif is enclosure, whether of a plant, a walled garden, or a caged wolf, and how the promises of enclosure are undone: "Because the body must open / for its world // so that we know there is a wall / beyond which we can't go" (*Erosion*, 79). As with paradise, a walled garden, so with the caged wolf: there is a thin line between containment and imprisonment.

Graham's style features fragments and ellipses as indexes of boundaries and the slippages between them. Thus, the title essentially gives onto the opening line and demands that we fill in an essential element, as: "The sense of an ending . . . [is best heard] . . . There in the sound of a chainsaw winding down" (78). The last section begins in the same way: "Or [you might find the sense of an ending] where the draft is from an unseen / gap" (82). The conclusion, redolent of Platonic/Virgilian myths of birth and rebirth, suggests that unborn human souls are greedy "to be born," that even the smallest amount of time here is "better than any / freedom, any wholeness" (83). Nothing, in other words, surpasses the demand for life, which necessarily means definition, enclosure, surrounding, and termination. The poem itself concludes with a revelation. It is almost as if the poet is surprised that she could come down so assertively on the side of lived life. The sense of an ending ensures the sense of a beginning. Rather than freedom and expansive wholeness, the poet comes to prefer

. . . this heaviness, this stilled

quickness, this skin, this line
all the way round and sealed into the jagged island

form, the delicate
ending, better, even for an instant, even if never brought

further than term
into this broken mewing, this dust of lilacs, cawing

ravens, door just slamming, someone
suddenly home in this lie we call blue light.
(83)

What M. H. Abrams long ago defined as the Romantic nature lyric, a poem
meandering from a specific beginning in time and place, through meditation
and recollection back to its origin as its terminus, here gives shape to Graham's own poem, winding at its close to the details with which it began.[23]
To end a discussion of Graham with this poem is unfair, of course: seldom
afterward does termination come as easily to her. Her own jitteriness, her
wariness when it comes to determining limits, gets the better of her, as I
have shown. But the new way of looking forces itself continually on and
through this poet, whose subject matter—the relation of body to soul, the
visible to the invisible—ought to place her among the poets of sexual and
religious bliss instead of those whose skepticism undercuts happiness, poetic
closure, and even the satisfactions of "just looking" (as Charles Tomlinson
put it) and rendering what one has seen. Because "what's *real* slides through"
("Manifest Destiny, *Materialism*, 97), any sense of an ending is tentative,
hopeful, and delusory at best.

# NOTES ✑

NOTES TO CHAPTER 1

1. "Poetry is getting something right in language." Howard Nemerov, "Poetry and Meaning," in *A Howard Nemerov Reader* (Columbia: University of Missouri Press, 1991), 281.

2. Willard Spiegelman, *The Didactic Muse: Scenes of Instruction in Contemporary American Poetry* (Princeton: Princeton University Press, 1989).

3. Willard Spiegelman, *Majestic Indolence: English Romantic Poetry and the Work of Art* (New York: Oxford University Press, 1995). Lisa M. Steinman, *Masters of Repetition: Poetry, Culture, and Work in Thomson, Wordsworth, Shelley, and Emerson* (New York: St. Martin's Press, 1998) treats description in the poetry of the Romantic tradition. Steinman's four central poets had to juggle the rival demands of aestheticism (and accompanying charges of indolence and uselessness) and the useful or programmatic "work" of poetry. She quotes several reviews of Wordsworth's two volumes of 1793 (*An Evening Walk* and *Descriptive Sketches*) that suggest the roots of contemporary impatience with mere description: the reviewer for *The Monthly Review* complained of more "descriptive poetry . . . Have we not yet enough?" See William Wordsworth, *Descriptive Sketches*, ed. Eric Birdsall (Ithaca: Cornell University Press, 1984), 299–301, for contemporary reviews. In addition, the remarkable, quirky book of Angus Fletcher, *A New Theory for American Poetry* (Cambridge, Mass.: Harvard University Press, 2004) came to my attention as I was finishing this work. Fletcher emphasizes an American pragmatism (although with a focus on the poetry of John Clare) at odds with visionary (British) Romanticism, and on our tendency to focus on the familiar. For him, "Description is the

expressive mode that works *in time*" (30). See, especially, the provocative chapters "The Argument of Form" (23–42) and "Description" (43–56).

4. Marjorie H. Nicolson, *The Art of Description* (New York: F. S. Crofts, 1925), v. What may have seemed unarguable eighty years ago ("The greatest art has always had a sensuous appeal" [128]), may seem to a more politically and socially aware contemporary audience to be mere bourgeois obfuscation. Whereas "description" per se used to constitute one entire unit in college expository writing classes, it is seldom even mentioned in today's classes in rhetoric and argument. See also Cleanth Brooks and Robert Penn Warren, *Modern Rhetoric* (New York: Harcourt Brace, 1949), 218–261, for a later attempt to categorize and distill types of description and to evaluate its place in imaginative prose composition, but not poetry. Brooks and Warren's use of terms such as "pattern" and "texture," often confusing or ambiguous, may strike a contemporary reader as quaint or, because of their relative absence from the critical scene, novel and helpful.

5. Within the past decade, a renewed interest in aesthetics and formalism suggests that the tide has turned. See, for example, George Levine, ed., *Aesthetics and Ideology* (New Brunswick, N.J.: Rutgers University Press, 1994); Elaine Scarry, *On Beauty and Being Just* (Princeton: Princeton University Press, 1999); James Soderholm, *Beauty and the Critic: Aesthetics in an Age of Cultural Studies* (Tuscaloosa: University of Alabama Press, 1997); Wendy Steiner, *The Scandal of Pleasure: Art in an Age of Fundamentalism* (Chicago: University of Chicago Press, 1996).

6. Ludwig Wittgenstein, *Philosophical Investigations*, trans. G. E. M. Anscombe (Oxford: Blackwell, 1967), sec. 133, sec. 109; Maurice Merleau-Ponty, *The Phenomenology of Perception*, trans. C. Smith (New York: Humanities Press, 1962), viii.

7. *Roland Barthes par Roland Barthes* (Paris: Editions du Seuil, 1975), 72.

8. Michael Riffaterre, "Descriptive Imagery," *Yale French Studies* 61 (1981): 125. This entire special issue, *Toward a Theory of Description*, contains valuable essays.

9. From Valéry, *Oeuvres* (Paris: Gallimard, Pléiade, 1960), 2, 1219–1220; also quoted in *Yale French Studies* 10 (1981).

10. Gotthold Ephraim Lessing, *Laocoön: An Essay on the Limits of Painting and Poetry*, trans. Edward Allen McCormack (New York: Bobbs-Merrill, 1962), especially pp. 78–97.

11. C. S. Baldwin, *Medieval Rhetoric and Poetic* (New York: Macmillan, 1928), 19. What he calls an "Alexandrian dilation of description" in his earlier book, *Ancient Rhetoric and Poetic* (New York: Macmillan, 1924), 218, Baldwin extends to anything—in oratory or poetry—that "instead of following Aristotelian counsels of specific concrete imagery . . . habitually generalized and rapidly became conventional" (19). Because he equates ekphrasis with all kinds of separable descriptions instead of limiting it to descriptions of works of art, Baldwin is able to label as decadent even more tastefully handled passages in De Quincey, Pater, and Sterne. He betrays his own late-Victorian sensibilities; he also too easily equates ancient or medieval rules concerning oratory and rhetoric with rules about writing and poetry.

12. Horace, *Ars Poetica*, ll. 1–23. Warburton (in Lessing, 214) quotes Pope on "The Epistle to Dr. Arbuthnot," ll. 340–341 and 148–149 ("who could take offence, / When pure Description took the place of Sense?"). Lessing, in turn (89–90), refers to Pope's dismissal of descriptive poetry.

13. Baldwin (189) refers to "the rhetoric of dilation," involving disease, excess, and femininity. See also W. J. T. Mitchell, *Iconology: Image, Text, Ideology* (Chicago: University of Chicago Press, 1986), 109, who calls "the laws of gender . . . the most fundamental ideological basis for [Lessing's] laws of genre" even though Lessing makes no such overt statement; and his chapter, "Ekphrasis and the Other," in *Picture Theory: Essays in Verbal and Visual Representation* (Chicago: University of Chicago Press, 1994), 151–183. The distaste for unnecessary, wandering descriptions can be found even in etiquette guides. For example: "It was all pleasant conversation. There were no long and tedious descriptions of scenery; no dull narration of a movie or a book; no slander; no gossip; no vulgar jokes." Sophie C. Hadida, *Manners for Millions* (New York: Sun Dial Press, 1932), 216.

14. A. R. Ammons, *Garbage* (New York: Norton, 1993), 108.

15. *The Oxford Book of Modern Verse, 1892–1935* (New York: Oxford University Press, 1936), ix.

16. Stanley Cavell has been the primary investigator of this phenomenon. See *In Quest of the Ordinary: Lines of Skepticism and Romanticism* (Chicago: University of Chicago Press, 1988).

17. Dave Smith, "In the Nansemond River," in *Fate's Kite* (Baton Rouge: Louisiana University Press, 1995), 14.

18. Elizabeth Bishop, *The Complete Poems, 1927–1979* (New York: Farrar, Straus and Giroux, 1979), 91: "embroidered nature . . . tapestried landscape"; Thomas Bolt, "Meditation in Loudon County," in *Out of the Woods* (New Haven: Yale University Press, 1989), 13; Wallace Stevens, *Opus Posthumous*, rev. and ed. Milton Bates (New York: Knopf, 1989), 205 (hereafter *OP*).

19. Robert Pinsky, *The Situation of Poetry: Contemporary Poetry and Its Tradition* (Princeton: Princeton University Press, 1976), 97. Pinsky associates description with "wonder" as well as "derangement" in his chapter "Convention of Wonder," 97–133.

20. John Haines, "The Writer as Alaskan: Beginnings and Reflections," in *Living Off the Country: Essays on Poetry and Place* (Ann Arbor: University of Michigan Press, 1981), 19.

21. Ralph Waldo Emerson, *Collected Poems and Translations*, ed. Harold Bloom and Paul Kane (New York: Library of America, 1994), 190; Thomas H. Johnson, ed., *The Poems of Emily Dickinson* (Cambridge, Mass.: Belknap Press of Harvard University Press, 1955), 2: 482; Harold Bloom, *The Western Canon: The Books and Schools of the Ages* (New York: Harcourt Brace, 1994), 307.

22. The sense of being observed appears again in an unlikely place, Paul Rudnick's popular novel *I'll Take It* (New York: Random House, 1989): 131: "Everyone was dressed to see the leaves change; they wanted to look nice, in case the leaves looked back."

23. Jorie Graham, *Hybrids of Plants and of Ghosts* (Princeton: Princeton University Press, 1980), 46; "Act III, Scene 2," in *Region of Unlikeness* (Hopewell, N.J.: Ecco Press, 1999), 66.

24. Henry G. Bugbee Jr., *The Inward Morning* (1958; New York: Harper and Row, 1976), 167–168, 168–169. Bugbee alludes to Wordsworth's famous phrase in the preface to *Lyrical Ballads* pertaining to "the grand elementary principle of pleasure, in which we live, and move, and have our being." See also Nathan A. Scott, Jr., *Visions of Presence in Modern American Poetry* (Baltimore: Johns Hopkins University Press, 1993), and Elissa New, *The Line's Eye: Poetic Experience, American Sight* (Cambridge, Mass.: Harvard University Press, 1998) for a recent discussion of seeing, vision, and American landscape and poetry.

25. Howard Nemerov, "A Spell Before Winter," in *Collected Poems* (Chicago: University of Chicago Press, 1977), 246.

26. Anthony Hecht, *Venetian Vespers* (New York: Atheneum, 1980), 65; Langdon Hammer, "An Interview with Anthony Hecht," *Sewanee Review* 104, no. 1 (1996): 101.

27. Ralph Waldo Emerson, *Complete Works*, ed. Edw. Waldo Emerson, 12 vols. (Boston: Houghton-Mifflin, 1903–1904), 5: 288.

28. W. H Auden, *The Dyer's Hand* (New York: Random House, 1962), 359.

29. In both England and the United States, the 1990s witnessed the development of so-called ecocriticism (or green criticism): see, for example, Jonathan Bate, *Romantic Ecology: Wordsworth and the Environmental Tradition* (London: Routledge, 1991); Lawrence Buell, *The Environmental Imagination: Thoreau, Nature Writing and the Formation of American Culture* (Cambridge, Mass.: Harvard University Press, 1995); and Karl Kroeber, *Ecological Literary Criticism: Romantic Imagining and the Biology of Mind* (New York: Columbia University Press, 1995).

30. Wordsworth, *The Prelude* (1850 edition), 13, l. 376.

31. The citations from Emerson come from Ralph Waldo Emerson, *Essays and Lectures*, ed. Joel Porte (New York: Library of America, 1983), 11, 75, 473, 545. A new interest in landscape is borne out not just by books about gardening, or Michael Pollan's genial collection *Second Nature: A Gardener's Education* (New York: Atlantic Monthly Press, 1991), but also by an anthology such as Robert Pack and Jay Parini, eds., *Poems for a Small Planet: Contemporary American Nature Poetry* (Hanover, N.H.: Middlebury College Press/University Press of New England, 1993), which begins predictably with a citation from Emerson (1836, *Nature*): "Nature is the symbol of the spirit" (xiv), and continues by noting that the poems in the anthology "are all, implicitly more than explicitly, responses to the ecological crisis. . . . Nature is now a pressing political question, the question of survival" (xv). In his afterword, Pack calls for "the need for balance between the wildness of untamed nature and the human cultivation of nature" (273), and cites Leo Marx, *The Machine in the Garden: Technology and the Pastoral Ideal in America* (New York: Oxford University Press, 1964) and Roderick Nash, *Wilderness and the American Mind* (New Haven: Yale University Press, 1967); his larger point is that virtually all poems are nature poems.

32. F. Scott Fitzgerald, *The Great Gatsby*, ed. Matthew Bruccoli (Cambridge, UK: Cambridge University Press, 1991), 140.

33. See Tony Tanner, *The Reign of Wonder* (Cambridge, UK: Cambridge University Press, 1965) for a discussion of the general commitment in American literature to the primacy of perception with a naïve, reverent eye. He seems, however, to ignore the origin of such reverence in Wordsworth and Coleridge.

34. Wallace Stevens, *The Collected Poems of Wallace Stevens* (New York: Knopf, 1954), 339–346 (Hereafter, *CP*).

35. See Helen Vendler, *On Extended Wings: Wallace Stevens' Longer Poems* (Cambridge, Mass.: Harvard University Press, 1969), 217–230, especially 228 on transitive and intransitive verbs. James Longenbach reminds us of the political conditions in the "real" world that Stevens was trying to evade in this poem: he calls it "a resolutely Paterian poem in which a metaphor's power to shape experience is championed with little sense of a how a place like wartime Germany might resist even the most powerful description of it." See Longenbach, *Wallace Stevens: The Plain Sense of Things* (New York: Oxford University Press, 1991), 282–283.

36. Wallace Stevens, *Letters*, ed. Holly Stevens (New York: Knopf, 1966), 494.

37. Irving Feldman, "Antonio, *Botones*," in *Leaping Clear* (New York: Viking, 1976), 37.

38. Wordsworth, *The Prelude* (1850), 12, ll. 128–129.

39. Helen Vendler, *Soul Says: On Recent American Poetry* (Cambridge, Mass.: Belknap Press of Harvard University Press, 1995), 117–129. There are parallels, of course, in the work of A R Ammons, for example, his claim that "it is not so much to know the self / as to know it as it is known / by galaxy and cedar cone" ("Gravelly Run").

40. Bonnie Costello, "'What to Make of a Diminished Thing': Modern Nature and Poetic Response," *American Literary History* 10 (1998): 586–587. Costello's entire essay covers much of the territory I am interested in here, although her focus is "nature" as both observed and constructed, rather than description as a rhetorical tool. Her recent book, *Shifting Ground: Reinventing Landscape in Modern American Poetry* (Cambridge, Mass.: Harvard University Press, 2003), deals with many of the same issues and poets that I treat in the following chapters.

41. Stephen Owen, "A Monologue of the Senses," *Yale French Studies* 61 (1981): 244–260, reminds Western readers helpfully that "description" is a term that Chinese poets neither have nor use. The major poetic genres (these extend to Japan) are the *fu*, a concern with categories or ontology, in order to consider how a thing (e.g., a tree, the snow) *is*; and the *shih*, a reconstitution of scenes, the "articulation of that which the mind is intensely fixed on." Mutatis mutandis, "Description . . . would be that art of noticing pattern incarnate in the sensible world: pattern is neither the excessive lush totality of a scene nor disembodied abstraction: it is a medial form in which the general case and the particular case are one" (257). In other words, the equivalent of Western phenomenology as articulated by Henry Bugbee, above.

42. Gary Snyder, *No Nature* (New York: Pantheon, 1992), iii. All references are to this edition.

43. Quoted by Mark Ford, "Reality Bites" [review of Robert Hass, ed., *The Essential Haiku* (New York: Ecco Press, 1994)], *The New Republic* 211, no. 18 (Oct. 31, 1994): 50.

44. The matter of metaphor, of figuration in general, is a vexed one, especially given the differences between Eastern and Western aesthetics. See Patrick D. Murphy, ed., *Critical Essays on Gary Snyder* (Boston: G. K. Hall, 1991) for a variety of responses. Thomas Parkinson, "The Poetry of Gary Snyder," 21–34, is an especially good introduction. One essay that takes exception to the predominant view, endorsed by Parkinson, that Snyder lacks metaphor, is Julia Martin, "The Pattern Which Connects: Metaphor in Gary Snyder's Later Poetry," 188–210. Chinese poetry is nonmetaphorical because vehicle and tenor are always joined. Whether Snyder's—like Pound's—emulation of Chinese and Japanese forms is successful or legitimate in English is another matter. The T'ang Dynasty *shih* uses nouns that are invariably concrete (Chinese lacks inflections; nouns lack gender and number); consequently, they must denote unindividualized objects. Abstractions are linguistic impossibilities. See also Jody Norton, "The Importance of Nothing: Absence and Its Origins in the Poetry of Gary Snyder," 166–188.

45. Tim Dean, *Gary Snyder and the American Unconscious* (New York: St. Martin's Press, 1991), 90. Charles Altieri, "Gary Snyder's Lyric Poetry: Dialectics as Ecology," in Murphy, 48–58, tries to make the same point as Dean and Vendler (that Snyder "forgoes any explicit references to himself as subject" [51]) and that the use of paratactic syntax, spatial organization, participles and gerunds instead of normal verbs ensures the sense of a still point that is "immanent and in flux, not transcendent and permanent" (54). My larger point throughout my commentary is that Snyder can never avoid human subjectivity for very long.

46. In a 1977 interview, Snyder distinguishes between poets "who have fed on a certain kind of destructiveness for their creative flow," and those like himself, Wendell Berry, and Robert Duncan, "who have composed themselves and turned part of themselves back in on themselves to become richer and stronger." Quoted in Jack Hicks, "Poetic Composting: Gary Snyder's *Left Out in the Rain*," in Murphy, 247.

47. Nemerov, *A Howard Nemerov Reader*, 236.

48. Ibid., 223.

49. The relevant poems are "I Wandered Lonely as a Cloud," "The Fish," and "The Venetian Vespers."

NOTES TO CHAPTER 2

1. Charles Tomlinson, "Response to Hopkins," in *The Door in the Wall* (Oxford: Oxford University Press, 1992), 45. Unless otherwise noted, all references are to

*Collected Poems* (New York: Oxford University Press, 1985), which contains selections from *The Necklace, Seeing Is Believing, A Peopled Landscape, American Scenes and Other Poems, The Way of a World, Written on Water, The Way In and Other Poems, The Shaft,* and *The Flood.* Additional references are to the following volumes: *Seeing Is Believing* (New York: Oxford University Press, 1960), *Annunciations* (New York: Oxford University Press, 1989), *The Return* (New York: Oxford University Press, 1987), and *Jubilation* (New York: Oxford University Press, 1995).

2. In *Some Americans: A Personal Record* (Berkeley: University of California Press, 1981), Tomlinson has collected essays concerning his visits to the States and his relationships with Moore, Williams, O'Keeffe, et al.

3. Calvin Bedient, *Eight Contemporary Poets* (London: Oxford University Press, 1974), 8.

4. Two helpful, recent full-length studies of Tomlinson that treat his surface "objectivity" are Richard Swigg, *Charles Tomlinson and the Objectivist Tradition* (Lewisburg, Penna: Bucknell University Press, 1994) and Michael Kirkham, *Passionate Intellect: The Poetry of Charles Tomlinson* (Liverpool: Liverpool University Press, 1999).

5. John Ruskin, "Of Truth of Space," in *Modern Painters*, vol. 1, pt. 2, sec. 2, chap. 5, reprinted in *The Genius of John Ruskin: Selections from His Writings*, ed. John D. Rosenberg (Charlottesville: University of Virginia Press, 1991), 28.

6. Charles Tomlinson, "Poet as Painter," in *Charles Tomlinson: Man and Artist*, ed. Kathleen O'Gorman (Columbia: University of Missouri Press, 1988), 209. This entire volume contains valuable essays.

7. Humphrey House and Graham Storey, eds., *The Journals and Papers of Gerard Manley Hopkins* (London: Oxford University Press, 1959), 204.

8. A comparable poem by the young American poet Thomas Bolt, "Thomas Eakins: Max Schmitt in a Single Scull," in *Out of the Woods* (New Haven: Yale University Press, 1989), 20, uses Eakins's painting of this name as a starting point for considering the artist's looking outward at the vivid scene before him. The poem, in other words, works backward from a painting to its imagined origins in a natural scene. As one might expect, a Nabokovian "description of nature" can come at second- or even thirdhand.

9. Octavio Paz, "The Graphics of Charles Tomlinson," in O'Gorman, 194.

10. Ibid., 193.

11. John Hollander, *Rhyme's Reason*, 3rd ed. (New Haven: Yale University Press, 2001).

12. Richard Howard, *Like Most Revelations* (New York: Pantheon, 1994), 49.


NOTES TO CHAPTER 3

1. The quotations come from Charles Berger, "Poetry Chronicle," *Raritan* 10 (1991): 123; Mary Karr, "Against Decoration," *Parnassus* 16, no. 2 (1991): 277; and

Robert McDowell, "The Wilderness Surrounds the Word," *Hudson Review* 43 (1991): 673.

2. Amy Clampitt, *The Collected Poems of Amy Clampitt* (New York: Knopf, 1997). All page numbers are cited from this edition; throughout, I refer parenthetically to the volumes in which the poems originally appeared, thus: *The Kingfisher* (*K*); *What the Light Was Like* (*WTLWL*); *Archaic Figure* (*AF*); *Westward* (*W*); and *A Silence Opens* (*ASO*).

3. Karr, 277.

4. Ralph Waldo Emerson, "Nature" [*Essays*, 1st series], in *Essays and Lectures*, ed. Joel Porte (New York: Library of America, 1983), 545.

5. See Bonnie Costello, "Amy Clampitt: Nomad Exquisite," in *Shifting Ground: Reinventing Landscape in Modern American Poetry* (Cambridge, Mass.: Harvard University Press, 2003), 117–142, originally published in *Verse* 10, no. 3 (winter 1993): 34–36 (an issue devoted to Clampitt), for a discussion of Clampitt's sense of "belonging" or not belonging to a specific place and of her connections to Elizabeth Bishop (another nomad) and Marianne Moore.

6. See especially Mark Doty, *Atlantis* (New York: Harper/Perennial, 1995). The opening poem, "Description," asks pointedly: "What is description, after all, / but encoded desire?" Language grants access to, even temporary control over, the external world that we try to contain.

7. Someone like W. S. Merwin, who has written whole volumes without punctuation, hardly fits into the same category as Clampitt, nor do the L-A-N-G-U-A-G-E poets, although comparisons between them and Clampitt might prove instructive.

8. I except, of course, critics whose training was primarily New Critical: John Hollander, Christopher Ricks, Helen Vendler, and even Stanley Fish. Richard Howard turns an appropriate phrase when he writes of Clampitt: "The poem is wreathed around its grammar, often being one very long sentence, submissive to the voice, observant of the local inflections, but governing the weight of the lines on the page, *down* the page. . . . [Clampitt's lineage may be traced to] the incremental redundancies of Robert Browning, whose music is syntactical, not a matter of chiming." "The Hazardous Definition of Structures," *Parnassus* 11, no. 1 (1983): 271–272.

9. Calvin Bedient, "Sentencing Eros," *Salmagundi*, no. 97 (winter 1993): 179.

10. Elizabeth Bishop, *The Complete Poems 1927–1979* (New York: Farrar, Straus and Giroux, 1979), 173.

11. The issue of the colon in this volume is a vexed one: the majority are conventionally printed, and the others have either been printed unconventionally for a specific effect or else by error. In addition, there are discrepancies between the appearance of some poems in *The Collected Poems* and their earlier appearances in journals or single volumes. Either Clampitt or her editors made changes or failed to proofread carefully. Among other poets, Muriel Rukeyser was the most eccentric in her use of colons: virtually all of them are separated by several spaces on either side from what precedes and follows them. Poets conventional in other ways

often have punctuational idiosyncracies: I think of Yusef Komunyaaka's insistence on "&" for "and."

12. An analogue to this phenomenon, in Whitman, is "Song of Myself," section 33. The third paragraph, beginning "By the city's quadrangular houses—log huts, camping with the lumberman," moves through thirty-nine anaphora-laden lines to a simple finale: "I tread day and night such roads." A more complicated example is "Scented herbage of my breast" (*Calamus*), which has a fuller, more varied anaphora than my previous example, and moves, with no full pauses (except some question marks and exclamations, which nevertheless do not signify closure), through thirty-seven lines from one vocative ("Scented herbage") to another (addressed to Death): "That may-be you are what it is all for, but it does not last so very long, / But you will last very long." No line in the poem is as short as its conclusion.

13. Stephen Cushman, *Fictions of Form in American Poetry* (Princeton: Princeton University Press, 1993). Cushman follows the lead of John Hollander in understanding that, in poetry, "scheme" can become "trope," that shape and form produce, as well as convey, meaning; see the exemplary chapters in Hollander's *Melodious Guile: Fictive Pattern in Poetic Language* (New Haven: Yale University Press, 1988), and *Vision and Resonance: Two Senses of Poetic Form* (New York: Oxford University Press, 1975).

14. Ernest Hartley Coleridge, ed., *The Letters of Samuel Taylor Coleridge* (Boston: Houghton Mifflin, 1895), 2: 558–559, to Thomas Poole, January 28, 1810: "Of parentheses I may be too fond, and will be on my guard against them. But I am certain that no work of impassioned and eloquent reasoning ever did or could subsist without them. They are the *drama* of reason, and present the thought growing, instead of a mere *Hortus siccus*. The aversion to them is one of the numberless symptoms of a feeble Frenchified public."

15. M. H. Abrams, "Structure and Style in the Greater Romantic Lyric," in Frederick W. Hilles and Harold Bloom, eds., *From Sensibility to Romanticism* (New York: Oxford University Press, 1965), 527–560. In their roundedness, many of Clampitt's meditative poems owe a considerable debt to the construction of poems such as "Tintern Abbey" and "Frost at Midnight."

NOTES TO CHAPTER 4

1. Wallace Stevens, *The Collected Poems of Wallace Stevens* (New York: Knopf, 1954), 382, hereafter *CP.*

2. For recent scholarly assessments and evaluations of Wright's work, see Tom Andrews, ed., *The Point Where All Things Meet: Essays on Charles Wright* (Oberlin, Ohio: Oberlin College Press, 1995), which contains essays and reviews by Calvin Bedient, Mutlu Konuk Blasing, Bonnie Costello, Stephen Cushman, Mark Jarman, David Kalstone, J. D. McClatchy, and Helen Vendler, inter alia.

3. See, inter alia, Wright's interview with Matthew Cooperman, in *Quarter Notes: Improvisations and Interviews* (Ann Arbor: University of Michigan Press, 1998), 167, or the interview with Sherrod Santos, in *Halflife: Improvisations and Interviews, 1977–87* (Ann Arbor: University of Michigan Press, 1991), 109–110.

4. Interview with J. D. McClatchy, *Quarter Notes*, 120.

5. Santos, 28, 34.

6. Charles Wright, *The World of the Ten Thousand Things: Poems 1980–1990* (New York: Farrar, Straus and Giroux, 1990), 11, hereafter *World*. All references to Wright's poetry are from either this volume, which includes poems from *The Southern Cross*, *The Other Side of the River*, *Zone Journals*, and *Xionia*, or from *Country Music: Selected Early Poems* (Middletown, Conn.: Wesleyan University Press, 1982); the most recent volumes are *Chickamauga*, *Black Zodiac*, and *Appalachia* (all New York: Farrar, Straus and Giroux, 1995, 1997, 1998, respectively), subsequently gathered together in *Negative Blue: Selected Later Poems* (New York: Farrar, Straus and Giroux, 2002). The phrase from the title to this chapter ("the metaphysics of the quotidian") appears in the commonplace book whose name gives the title to *Halflife*, 22.

7. J. D. McClatchy, *Quarter Notes*, 107.

8. Howard Nemerov, "Strange Metamorphosis of Poets," in *The Collected Poems of Howard Nemerov* (Chicago: University of Chicago Press, 1977), 451.

9. Samuel Taylor Coleridge, *Table Talk*, in *Collected Works*, ed. Carl Woodring (Princeton Bollingen Series), 14, no. 1 (1990): 444–445.

10. Wright has described his breaking of the line as different from similar efforts by Pound, Williams, O'Hara, and Olson: he wants "to keep the line from breaking under its own weight. . . . It is always one line, not two, and broken in a particular place to keep the integrity of the single line musically" (McClatchy, *Quarter Notes*, 79–80). Although he maintains that his primary goal is the conversational musicality of his line, Wright would not be unsympathetic, I suspect, to the more individual "readings" of specific effects I have proposed here.

11. Ammons is only one of several poets who make us compare the shape of poetry on the page to its effect on the mind and in the ear. Ezra Pound, Marianne Moore, Allen Ginsberg, and e. e. cummings make comparable demands, and the triads of William Carlos Williams, which even a conservative poet like Charles Tomlinson has adopted, make for a synaesthetic experience. In Wright's case, lineation becomes a visually mimetic homage to observed and depicted landscapes.

NOTES TO CHAPTER 5

1. Of the vast amount of scholarly work on ekphrasis, I have found the following most useful: Michael Davidson, "*Ekphrasis* and the Postmodern Painter Poem," *Journal of Aesthetics and Art Criticism* 42, no. 1 (fall 1983): 69–79; E. H. Gombrich, "*Icones Symbolicae*: Philosophies of Symbolism and Their Bearing on Art," in *Symbolic Images: Studies in the Art of the Renaissance* (London: Phaidon,

1972), 123–195; Jean H. Hagstrum, *The Sister Arts: The Tradition of Literary Pictorialism and English Poetry from Dryden to Gray* (Chicago: University of Chicago Press, 1958); James Heffernan, *Museum of Words: The Poetics of Ekphrasis from Homer to Ashbery* (Chicago: University of Chicago Press, 1993); John Hollander, *The Gazer's Spirit: Poems Speaking to Silent Works of Art* (Chicago: University of Chicago Press, 1995); Murray Krieger, *Ekphrasis: The Illusion of the Natural Sign* (Baltimore: Johns Hopkins University Press, 1992); W. J. T Mitchell, *Iconology: Image, Text, Ideology* (Chicago: University of Chicago Press, 1986); Grant Scott, *The Sculpted Word: Keats, Ekphrasis, and the Visual Arts* (Hanover, N.H.: University Press of New England, 1994); Wendy Steiner, *The Colors of Rhetoric: Problems in the Relation between Modern Literature and Painting* (Chicago: University of Chicago Press, 1982), and *Pictures of Romance: Form against Context in Painting and Literature* (Chicago: University of Chicago Press, 1988). See also Beverly Whitaker Long and Timothy Scott Cage, "Contemporary American Ekphrastic Poetry: A Selected Bibliography," *Text and Performance Quarterly* 9 (1989): 286–297.

2. Theodore Weiss, *Recoveries* (New York: Macmillan, 1982), 54; all references are to this edition.

3. Heffernan, 3.

4. See especially Maurice Merleau-Ponty, *The Prose of the World*, ed. Claude Lefort, trans. John O'Neill (London: Heinemann, 1974), 124–125; and, more generally, *Phenomenology of Perception*, trans. Colin Smith (New York: Humanities Press, 1962).

5. Paris Leary and Robert Kelly, *A Controversy of Poets: An Anthology of Contemporary American Poetry* (Garden City, N.Y.: Anchor, 1953), 553.

6. Irving Feldman, *All of Us Here* (New York: Viking Penguin, 1986), 19. Subsequent references are cited by page number in the text.

7. Richard Howard, "Touching Extremities," in Harold Schweizer, ed., *The Poetry of Irving Feldman* (Lewisburg, Penna.: Bucknell University Press, 1992), 56.

8. John Hollander, in his review of Feldman's volume, *The New Republic* 195 (July 14, 1986), 28–30, lambastes the sculpture as much as he praises the poems they have inspired.

9. Kenneth Gross, *The Dream of the Moving Statue* (Ithaca: Cornell University Press, 1992), 25, 27.

10. Svetlana Alpers, *The Art of Describing: Dutch Art in the Seventeenth Century* (Chicago: University of Chicago Press, 1983), xxi. Alpers's larger thesis is that Dutch painting is descriptive rather than imitative of significant human action.

11. Quoted in Andrew Graham-Dixon, *Howard Hodgkin* (New York: Harry N. Abrams, 1994), 7.

12. Susan Sontag, "About Hodgkin," in Michael Auping, John Elderfield, and Suan Sontag, *Howard Hodgkin Paintings* (New York: Harry N. Abrams, in association with the Modern Art Museum of Fort Worth, 1995), 107.

13. See Paul Fry, "The Torturer's Horse: What Poems See in Pictures," in *A Defense of Poetry: Reflections on the Occasion of Writing* (Stanford: Stanford Univer-

sity Press, 1995), 70–87. Fry overemphasizes the necessity of envy in ekphrasis and plays down the possibilities for genuine and grateful homage that one art pays to its sister. If painting is free not to signify, then "poems confronted with an image can't stop asking questions" (83). But a nonrepresentational form, rather than a genuine iconic image, seems to fluster rather than to inspire human questioning.

14. Terrence Diggory, "Ekphrasis and Abstraction in the Work of Frank O'Hara," unpublished essay.

15. "Nostalgia for presence" is a phrase from the compelling essay by Bonnie Costello, "Effects of an Analogy: Wallace Stevens and Painting," in Albert Gelpi, ed., *Wallace Stevens: The Poetics of Modernism* (Cambridge, UK: Cambridge University Press, 1985), 65.

16. Frank O'Hara, *Art Chronicles, 1954–1966* (New York: George Braziller, 1975), 30.

17. It is perhaps significant that O'Hara's various poems to Willem De Kooning, Helen Frankenthaler, Grace Hartigan, Franz Kline, and even his famous "On Seeing Larry Rivers' *Washington Crossing the Delaware* at the Museum of Modern Art" (a poem with representational content) include relatively insufficient descriptive detail.

18. John Hollander, "The Speaking Pictures," *Canto* 20 (1981): III.

19. Kenneth Koch, "The Artist," in *Selected Poems 1950–1982* (New York: Random House, 1985), 28–36.

20. Edward Hirsch, *Transforming Vision: Writers on Art* (Boston: Little Brown, 1994); the Johns-Yau selection appears on 74–75. See also John Hollander and Joanna Weber, eds., *Words for Images: A Gallery of Poems* (New Haven: Yale University Art Gallery, 2001), containing poems about works of art in the Yale art museums. There are works inspired by Joseph Stella, Kurt Schwitter, Pollock, Rothko, Agnes Martin, and, most interestingly, Stephen Burt, "FRANZ KLINE: Ravenna" (84), which mingles "objective" description of the canvas with a meditation on the view from the poet's window in upper Manhattan.

21. Richard Howard, *Like Most Revelations* (New York: Pantheon Books, 1994), 3.

22. One might cite, as well, the pair of poems "Two for Franz Kline" ("The Gunner" and "The Dark Hallway") by Gilbert Sorrentino, in *Black and White* (New York: Totem Books, 1964), n.p., which take the fact of Kline's dramatic black-and-white pictures as the occasion to contemplate a world solely in black and white. Both poems are digressions inspired by Kline. In the same volume, "The Abstraction" deals with the same painter without naming him, but from the standpoint of the artist's psychology, which translates an impulse into a gesture and into a single color. None of these is, strictly speaking, ekphrastic or descriptive. Later in the volume, Sorrentino inquires in a poem for Philip Guston ("What Shapes Hide"): "What Shapes Hide . . . [the title elides into the first line] . . . there, behind the harsh / colors?" The first half of the poem tries to identify images in a picture; the second half applies the attempt to understanding the anonymous shapes and bodies in the rooms that make up a city.

23. Douglas Crase, "Blue Poles," in *The Revisionist* (Boston: Little Brown, 1981), 69.

24. Charles Wright, *Chickamauga* (New York: Farrar, Straus and Giroux, 1995), reprinted in *Negative Blue: Selected Later Poems* (New York: Farrar, Straus and Giroux, 2000), 61.

25. Frank Kermode, *Romantic Image* (New York: Macmillan, 1957).

26. Wordsworth, *The Prelude*, 2, ll. 315–318.

27. See William H. Galperin, *The Return of the Visible in British Romanticism* (Baltimore: Johns Hopkins University Press, 1993) for a discussion of these concerns in English Romantic poetry and art. The thesis on which he expatiates is that "a visible world—accessible to the material, bodily condition of sight and thus prior to idealization—is manifest in certain texts, including verbal texts," of the period (19). In the case of a poet's response to a visible but nonrepresentational artifact, however, both bodily sight *and* a certain degree of idealization (or understanding at secondhand) would be required for response, explanation, and comprehension.

28. Randall Jarrell, "Against Abstract Expressionism," in J. D. McClatchy, ed., *Poets on Painters* (Berkeley: University of California Press, 1988), 192.

NOTES TO CHAPTER 6

1. Among the many critics who have written on Ashbery, I have found the following most helpful: Harold Bloom, ed., *John Ashbery: Modern Critical Views* (New York: Chelsea House, 1985); Bonnie Costello, *Shifting Ground: Reinventing Landscape in Modern American Poerty* (Cambridge, Mass.: Harvard University Press, 2003); Angus Fletcher, *A New Theory for American Poetry: Democracy, the Environment, and the Future of Imagination* (Cambridge, Mass.: Harvard University Press, 2004); David Lehman, ed., *Beyond Amazement: New Essays on John Ashbery* (Ithaca: Cornell University Press, 1980); Susan Schultz, ed., *The Tribe of John: Ashbery and Contemporary Poetry* (Tuscaloosa: University of Alabama Press, 1995); David Shapiro, *John Ashbery: An Introduction to the Poetry* (New York: Columbia University Press, 1979); John Shoptaw, *On the Outside Looking Out: John Ashbery's Poetry* (Cambridge, Mass.: Harvard University Press, 1994); Vernon Shetley, *After the Death of Poetry: Poet and Audience in Contemporary America* (Durham, N.C.: Duke University Press, 1993). In addition, many critics have remarked, in obiter dicta or more extensively, Ashbery's interest in landscape, e.g., Andrew Ross, "Taking the Tennis Court Oath": "and Ashbery is nothing if not a landscape poet" (in Schultz, 197). The relation between Ashbery's lack of a sense of self, his interest in place, and his whirling style is clear in a remark to David Lehman: "I must have a sort of cuckoo instinct that makes me enjoy making my home in somebody else's nest" (Lehman, 111).

2. John Ashbery, *Selected Poems* (New York: Viking, 1985), 262. Unless otherwise noted, all references are to this edition and are cited by page number alone. References to poems not in this edition are from *The Double Dream of Spring*, hereaf-

ter *DD* (New York: Dutton, 1970), *Hotel Lautréamont*, hereafter *HL* (New York: Knopf, 1992), *Flow Chart*, hereafter *FC* (New York: Knopf, 1991), and *A Wave* (New York: Viking, 1984).

3. Shoptaw, 275–285. Wallace Stevens, "Auroras of Autumn," in *Collected Poems* (New York: Knopf, 1954), 413. Ashbery has always identified Stevens as his favorite poet. See Charles Berger, *Forms of Farewell: The Late Poetry of Wallace Stevens* (Madison: University of Wisconsin Press, 1985), 187–188 on Stevens's legacy to Ashbery, especially with regard to "the occlusion of random facts" in both poets.

4. Johann Wolfgang von Goethe, *West-Östlicher Divan* (Frankfurt: Deutscher Klassiker Verlag, 1994), 1: 197.

5. Ralph Waldo Emerson, *Essays and Lectures*, ed. Joel Porte (New York: Library of America, 1983), 585, 1111. Subsequent references are to this edition.

6. Gaston Bachelard, *The Poetics of Reverie*, trans. Daniel Russell (Boston: Beacon Press, 1971), 5. See also 152, in which Bachelard describes the illusion, brought by or in reverie, of being more than one is: "Upon his less-than-being (*moins-être*) which is the relaxed state where the reverie takes form, there emerges an outline in relief—a relief which the poet will know how to swell into a more-than-being." Several critics have preceded me in using Bachelard as an entry into Ashbery, notably James McCorkle, "Nimbus of Sensations: Eros and Reverie in the Poetry of John Ashbery and Ann Lauterbach," in Schultz, 101–125.

7. Denis Donoghue, *Walter Pater* (New York: Knopf, 1995) defines reverie as "the faculty of mind that escapes mere intelligence" (128): "In reverie the mind goes into itself, resorts to desires thwarted in the world, charms itself to make a space for further charms. It evades the wear and tear of its worldly existence or the force of habit by diving under them or musing beyond them: making a rival world of forms elsewhere" (129).

8. Ibid., 131, 133.

9. T. M. Raysor, ed., *Coleridge's Shakespearian Criticism* (Cambridge, Mass.: Harvard University Press, 1930), 2: 65.

10. See John Koethe, "The Metaphysical Subject of John Ashbery's Poetry," in Lehman (87–100), for a discussion of Ashbery's move away from a conception of the "psychological subject" to a more abstract model.

11. Emerson, "Beauty," in *Nature*, 18–19.

12. Frederic Jameson, *Postmodernism, or, The Cultural Logic of Late Capitalism* (Durham, N.C.: Duke University Press, 1991), ix.

13. Emerson, "Circles," 414.

14. See Stanley Cavell, "Thinking of Emerson," in *The Senses of Walden* (San Francisco: North Point Press, 1981), 123–138.

15. Julie Ellison, *Emerson's Romantic Style* (Princeton: Princeton University Press, 1984), 76.

16. A. R. Ammons, *Sphere: The Form of a Motion* (New York: Norton, 1972), 72.

17. "I grasped at a wall or tree to recall myself from this abyss of idealism to reality." William Wordsworth, *Poems in Two Volumes, and Other Poems, 1800–1807*, ed. Jared Curtis (Ithaca: Cornell University Press, 1983), 428.

18. Wordsworth, *The Prelude*, 1850 version, 13, ll. 375–376.

19. Shoptaw, 205.

20. Barbara Packer, *Emerson's Fall: A New Interpretation of the Major Essays* (New York: Continuum, 1982), 26. See her entire first chapter, "The Lapses of Uriel: Emerson's Rhetoric," 1–21 for a full discussion of his stylistic peculiarities.

21. Quoted in ibid., 1.

22. Emerson, "The Poet," 454.

23. See Warren D. Goldfarb, "I Want You to Bring Me a Slab: Remarks on the Opening Sections of the *Philosophical Investigations*," *Syntase* 56 (1983): 265–282, on Wittgenstein's "intentional naivete" (269) in preferring description to explanation.

24. Shoptaw, 208–209.

25. Stevens, *Collected Poems*, 67.

26. Charles Altieri, "Ashbery as Love Poet," in Schultz, 34.

27. Wordsworth, *The Prelude*, 1805 version, 2, ll. 401–402.

28. For the relationship between skepticism (and its various threats) and poetry, see Stanley Cavell, *The Claim of Skepticism: Wittgenstein, Skepticism, Morality, and Tragedy* (New York: Oxford University Press, 1979) and, especially, *In Quest of the Ordinary: Lines of Skepticism and Romanticism* (Chicago: University of Chicago Press, 1988).

29. The classic study of endings remains Barbara Herrnstein Smith, *Poetic Closure: A Study of How Poems End* (Chicago: University of Chicago Press, 1968).

30. David Kalstone, *Five Temperaments: Elizabeth Bishop, Robert Lowell, James Merrill, Adrienne Rich, John Ashbery* (New York: Oxford University Press, 1977), 176–177, gives a cogent reading of the poem's opening lines; his entire chapter (170–199) is a valuable treatment of the first half of Ashbery's career.

NOTES TO CHAPTER 7

1. Wallace Stevens, *Opus Posthumous*, rev. and ed. Milton Bates (New York: Knopf, 1989), 193, 196.

2. Ernest Hartley Coleridge, ed., *The Letters of Samuel Taylor Coleridge* (Boston: Houghton Mifflin, 1895), 2: 558–559.

3. Jorie Graham, "Young Maples in Wind," in *Materialism* (New York: Ecco Press, 1993), 137. All references to Graham's work are cited in the text. The other volumes included in this discussion are *Hybrids of Plants and of Ghosts* (Princeton: Princeton University Press, 1980), *Erosion* (Princeton: Princeton University Press, 1983), *The End of Beauty* (New York: Ecco Press, 1987), and *Region of Unlikeness* (New York: Ecco Press, 1991). Graham's books of the past decade, which I do not discuss in this chapter, are *The Errancy* (New York: Ecco Press, 1997), *Swarm* (New York: Ecco Press, 2000), and *Never* (New York: Ecco Press, 2003).

4. Howard Nemerov, "Writing" and "The Blue Swallows," in *The Collected Poems of Howard Nemerov* (Chicago: University of Chicago Press, 1977), 203, 397.

5. In a forthcoming essay, "Jorie Graham Listening," I discuss the changes in Graham's ongoing engagements with birds, their flight, and their songs. See Thomas Gardner, ed., *New Essays on Jorie Graham* (Madison: University of Wisconsin Press, 2005).

6. Mark Doty, *Atlantis* (New York: HarperPerennial, 1995), 5, 90.

7. See Thomas J. Otten, "Jorie Graham's _____s," *PMLA* 118 (2003): 239–253 for the fullest discussion of Graham's lacunae, which Otten calls "a material idiom of mediation, a repertoire of images and substances that shape and reflect back to us our understanding of social bonds, and affective ties, of what is between us" (250).

8. Thomas Gardner, *Regions of Unlikeness: Explaining Contemporary Poetry* (Lincoln: University of Nebraska Press, 1999), 216–217. Gardner includes both an interview with Graham (214–237) and a critical essay about her ("Jorie Graham's Incandescence," 168–213).

9. In "Repetition and Singularity," *Kenyon Review* 25, no. 2 (2003): 149–168, I discuss Graham's debt to Bishop in her latest volume, *Never*.

10. Gardner, *Regions of Unlikeness*, 230.

11. Ibid.

12. Ibid., 233, 235.

13. From almost the start, Graham has found a champion in Helen Vendler. See Vendler's *Soul Says: On Recent Poetry* (Cambridge, Mass.: Belknap Press of Harvard University Press, 1995), 212–256; *The Breaking of Style: Hopkins, Heaney, Graham* (Cambridge, Mass.: Harvard University Press, 1995), 71–95; and *The Given and the Made: Strategies of Poetic Redefinition* (Cambridge, Mass.: Harvard University Press, 1995), 84–130.

14. James Merrill, *Collected Poems* (New York: Knopf, 2001), 185.

15. John Ashbery, *Selected Poems* (New York: Viking, 1985), 200.

16. Elaine Scarry, "Counting at Dusk (Why Poetry Matters When the Century Ends)," in Elaine Scarry, ed., *Fins de Siècle: English Poetry in 1590, 1690, 1790, 1890, 1990* (Baltimore: Johns Hopkins University Press, 1995), 25.

17. See Adrienne Rich's 1966 poem, "Necessities of Life," in *Collected Early Poems* (New York: Norton, 1993), 205, for another example of the relation between oozing or melting in painting and fluctuations in personal identity; for Rich, all boundaries are—or were at that point in her work—permeable. I have already discussed interruption as a structural, formal, and thematic device in the work of James Merrill. See "Breaking the Mirror: Interruption in the Trilogy," in David Lehman and Charles Berger, eds., *James Merrill: Essays in Criticism* (Ithaca: Cornell University Press, 1982), 186–210. What D. H. Lawrence long ago referred to as the breakdown of the old stable ego has produced some of the most interesting poetic experiments of the past four decades.

18. Ashbery, 195.

19. See Nemerov, "For Robert Frost, in the Autumn, in Vermont," 405, on the trope of the fallen leaves.

20. Thomas Gardner, "Accurate Failures: The Work of Jorie Graham," *The Hollins Critic* 24, no. 4 (October 1987): 2.

21. Ibid., 6.

22. See Bonnie Costello, "Jorie Graham: Art and *Erosion,*" *Contemporary Literature* 33 (1992): 373–395, for a discussion of the way the poems in *Erosion* enact a modernist concern with aesthetic wholeness.

23. M. H. Abrams, "Structure and Style in the Greater Romantic Lyric," in Frederick W. Hilles and Harold Bloom, eds., *From Sensibility to Romanticism* (New York: Oxford University Press, 1965), 527–560.

# INDEX &